THE
FAILURE
FACTORY

Also by Bill Gertz

BETRAYAL
How the Clinton Administration Undermined American Security

THE CHINA THREAT
How the People's Republic Targets America

BREAKDOWN
How America's Intelligence Failures Led to September 11

TREACHERY
How America's Friends and Foes Are Secretly Arming Our Enemies

ENEMIES
How America's Foes Steal Our Vital Secrets—and How We Let It Happen

THE

FAILURE FACTORY

How Unelected Bureaucrats,

Liberal Democrats, and

Big-Government Republicans Are

Undermining America's Security

and Leading Us to War

BILL GERTZ

CROWN
FORUM
NEW YORK

Copyright © 2008 by Bill Gertz

Published in the United States by Crown Forum,
an imprint of the Crown Publishing Group,
a division of Random House, Inc., New York.
www.crownpublishing.com

CROWN FORUM with colophon is a registered
trademark of Random House, Inc.

Library of Congress Cataloging-in-Publication Data
Gertz, Bill.
     The failure factory / Bill Gertz.—1st ed.
          p. cm.
     Includes index.
  1. United States—Politics and government—2001–
  2. United States—Foreign relations—2001–
  3. Intelligence service—United States—Evaluation.
  4. Political corruption—United States. I. Title.
JK275.G47   2008
973.931—dc22   2008027692

ISBN 978-0-307-33807-5

Printed in the United States of America

10 9 8 7 6 5 4 3 2 1

First Edition

FOR DEREK

Contents

We are a nation that has a government—not the other way around. And this makes us special among the nations of the Earth. Our government has no power except that granted it by the people. It is time to check and reverse the growth of government, which shows signs of having grown beyond the consent of the governed.

—RONALD REAGAN, Inaugural Address, January 20, 1981

THE FAILURE FACTORY

On June 12, 1987, President Ronald Reagan stood on the podium in front of the Brandenburg Gate near the hated Berlin Wall, which divided Communist East from free West. He declared: "General Secretary Gorbachev, if you seek peace, if you seek prosperity for the Soviet Union and Eastern Europe, if you seek liberalization: Come here to this gate! Mr. Gorbachev, open this gate! Mr. Gorbachev, tear down this wall!" It was one of the most memorable speeches by a U.S. president, and amazingly, only two years later the Berlin Wall did come down. The sight of Germans knocking down that wall with sledgehammers is one of the most significant of the Cold War.

Yet this memorable line from the Reagan speech was almost never delivered. On three different occasions leading up to the speech, State Department bureaucrats, worried about offending the Communists in Russia, pressed the president and his aides as hard as possible within the councils of government to remove the quote from the speech. Reagan refused. The rest is history.

The U.S. government today is in crisis. The power of bureaucrats— unelected government officials—has grown wildly out of control. Although the United States has been governed by an ostensibly conservative administration for the past eight years, it is in fact dominated

1

by left-liberal political activists and government bureaucrats with their own agenda. The officials, entrenched throughout the government, are supposed to follow the policies set by the administration the American people elected, but in fact they actively subvert those policies and programs. These unelected bureaucrats have undermined representative government.

Sadly, among the culprits are not just liberal Democrats but some so-called Republicans as well. They are all part of what the late Jeane Kirkpatrick called the "Blame America First crowd." They view the United States, not America's enemies, as the source of the world's evils.

The crisis is leading to weakness, a lack of national purpose, and ultimately to war—not merely regional conflicts in Iraq and Afghanistan that are the outgrowth of the war against Islamist extremism, but even a global conflict against the emerging power of the nuclear-armed Communist dictatorship in China and the many autocratic states and tyrannies that support it. Many strategists compare the current era to the 1930s, when Adolf Hitler was rising and leaders in the West failed to see and respond to the danger. Winston Churchill noted that World War II was the most unnecessary war in history. If only the leaders in the West at the time had had the will, foresight, and courage to take a firm stand, Hitler would have been stopped and the deaths of more than 72 million people could have been averted.

Today, a comparable threat is posed by Communist China, whose leaders have adopted a secret strategy to defeat the United States—with arms or without. And as in the 1930s, U.S. and allied leaders for several decades have sent all the wrong signals to a regime that is to blame for the deaths of at least 60 million of its own people.

Other dangers include a resurgent authoritarian Russia, still armed with nuclear weapons and bent on recovering the status of the lost Soviet empire. Then there is the radical clerical regime in Iran, which is intent on building nuclear weapons and the long-range missiles to deliver them, and is led by an Islamist zealot who has vowed to wipe Israel off the face of the earth. The rogue state of North Korea, with its 2006 demonstration of nuclear weapons and an arsenal of long-range missiles, poses a direct threat to the United States, and years of feckless negotiations promoted by government bureaucrats did little to promote disarmament but instead provided the failed totalitarian state with time and ultimately international legitimacy that it did not deserve.

The bureaucrats and careerists, officials at the upper and middle levels of government agencies, have adopted policies and programs set by liberal elites who view the United States, not America's enemies, as the source of world evil. They are driven by their anti-American liberalism into constraining the United States from taking necessary action, whether it's an exercise in hard power (military force) or in soft power (political or ideological influence).

The crisis of government bureaucracy is accelerating. At no other time has the need to reform the subversive nature of the system been more critical than now. The presidential election of 2008 will be a referendum on the excesses of government bureaucracy. On one side is the Democratic vision of Senator Barack Hussein Obama, a charismatic but misguided liberal with little experience who will allow his fellow liberal bureaucrats not only to preserve but actually to enhance their unelected power. On the other side is the moderate Republican senator John McCain, a combat veteran of Vietnam who understands the multiple crises facing the nation. He has shown that he does not fully understand the nature of the problem of government bureaucracy, though at least he knows that government red tape is holding back the country.

But the problems run much deeper. The vast network of bureaucrats and their enablers in the political class have had a devastating effect on American national security. The anti-American forces have:

- subverted get-tough policies toward our enemies Iran,
  North Korea, and Russia (ignoring Moscow's creep back to
  totalitarianism and its growing anti-Americanism)

- undercut the U.S. position in the war on terrorism, preventing aggressive military, intelligence, and law-enforcement operations against Islamist extremist groups by undermining the national consensus that emerged after the 9/11 attacks for waging a global war against terrorism—instead shifting back to the ineffective law-enforcement–dominated approach of the Clinton administration
- overrun the power departments of the U.S. government, including the State Department, the Pentagon, the Justice Department, and the White House National Security Council
- populated the upper ranks of military with holdovers and sympathizers from the Clinton administration, including a generation of "Clinton generals" who have been schooled in political correctness and who vehemently oppose the administration's conservative policies and programs
- blocked vitally needed reforms for U.S. intelligence agencies in the aftermath of intelligence failures related to September 11 and Iraq's weapons of mass destruction programs—proving so resistant to reform that Congressman Pete Hoekstra, vice chairman of the House Permanent Select Committee on Intelligence, felt compelled to write, "I have been long concerned that a strong and well-positioned group within the [CIA] intentionally undermined the administration and its policies"
- politicized the FBI and other law-enforcement agencies, instituting politically correct policies and hamstringing prosecutions and investigations
- prevented much-needed domestic security programs through a misguided outreach program to Muslim groups that are covertly linked to the global Sunni extremist organization the Muslim Brotherhood
- prompted the rise of a new antiwar leftist movement that

Democrats have exploited for political gain, with little or no regard for the potentially devastating consequences of a U.S.-led surrender in Iraq

- gutted American know-how through misguided business and trade policies, blocking aggressive security policies against states like China and Russia, which have stepped up efforts to steal or otherwise illicitly acquire U.S. technology and trade secrets

- appeased Communist China by controlling key positions related to Asian affairs within the U.S. government, including the State Department, the intelligence community, the Pentagon, the Justice Department, and the White House National Security Council; by some estimates, the U.S. national security community—military, diplomatic, and intelligence—have lost at least a decade in responding to counter the growing threat from China.

Blame America First

In order to accomplish the work of government, cadres of professional people are needed. The problem in the U.S. government is that misguided bureaucrats have come to dominate the entire system. Instead of following the policies and programs espoused by the elected president and vice president and their approximately 3,000 political appointee representatives, bureaucrats hold these elected and appointed officials in contempt. The bureaucrats believe they are the ones who should direct government and often take steps contrary to U.S national interests. These are the gray men and women who toil in obscurity but who mainly oppose conservatives, from Ronald Reagan to George W. Bush, and seek to quietly thwart their policies. They are the keepers of rice bowls—protecting their bureaucratic areas in mindless turf wars. Their modus operandi is to oppose all moves to action.

But most of all they are frightened and vehemently oppose going on the offensive.

The main reason bureaucrats have accrued so much power is that they are civil servants who can't be fired, unless arrested and jailed for major crimes. Their uppermost ranks can make upwards of $170,000 per year, plus annual all-but-guaranteed bonuses of $15,000 to $20,000. The top ranks become "senior executive service" or "senior intelligence service" officials.

They fear action, because it entails producing tangible and measurable results that could expose their failings and shortcomings. They fear risk, for risk can cause them trouble. They especially fear criticism, since criticism will force them to be held accountable for their work.

And most important, bureaucrats are resistant to change. "That's not how we do things" is the bureaucrat's frequent rejoinder to those directing their activities.

Aside from the bureaucrats there is also the political establishment class. Like the bureaucracy, the political class is infested with true believers of the political Left who show sympathy for nearly every anti-American group—Islamofascist terrorists, the Chinese Communists, the Cubans, the Iranians, and the North Koreans, among others. These are the elites who will not say a word against the rise of a leftist tyrant like Venezuela's Hugo Chávez. They are the demoralizers, the accommodationists who favor appeasing all the rogues states and enemies of the United States. They are the defeatists—like those opposing the Iraq War.

In recent years this political class has become known primarily for expressing utter hatred for President George W. Bush, who was ill-served by those supposedly working for his administration. The political establishment has gone after not just Bush but also those appointees who dared to try to institute strong conservative policies that put American national security first, such as former United Nations ambassador John Bolton, who while in office spoke truth loudly in denouncing America's enemies, from Fidel Castro to China's Communist leaders. For his efforts, he was vilified by the liberals and bureaucrats and forced from office.

These attitudes and pathologies are not merely a nuisance to the function of government. They are dangerous. The defeatist, anti-American postures of these domestic opponents of the United States undercut all the tools of statecraft. They have limited the United States primarily to using the "kinetic" option of military power and prevented the use of the much-talked-about soft power. Bureaucrats and their allies in the political class favor feckless diplomacy—talking with enemies just to talk—that is undermining real diplomacy. The six-party talks with North Korea are a case in point. Six years of pressing the idea that it is better to talk than to apply real pressure has actually encouraged North Korea's rogue regime to engage in worse behavior.

Liberals and bureaucrats in recent years have adopted the "MTV attitude" toward the use of public diplomacy. That is, they favor showing the world videos about American values rather that what is really needed: an offensive strategy and tactics designed to counter and ultimately defeat Islamist ideology. A real war of ideas, ultimately, represents the best hope for prevailing against the Islamist extremists, but the United States has utterly failed to adopt a policy to that end. Contributing to this failure are the Big Government Republicans who oppose aggressive information operations against terrorist enemies. The result of these policies is that seven years into the global war on terrorism, there is no comprehensive effort to use ideas against Islamist extremists, a fatal flaw that unless reversed will lead to defeat.

The Intelligence Mess

The Failure Factory is also responsible for the persistent shortcomings of the U.S. intelligence community. Despite annual spending of nearly $44 billion, the intelligence system remains broken because it is led by bureaucrats who oppose urgently needed reforms that would transform U.S. intelligence into an effective tool of state-craft. Despite numerous commissions and studies identifying needed changes, government leaders from the president to middle-level appointees still are denied the capacity to understand real threats facing the country. If we cannot even understand those threats, we cannot expect to stand up to them properly.

As the newly installed CIA director in 2004, Porter Goss tried to set rules for intelligence bureaucrats that would counter the outrageous anti-Republican, anticonservative positions that had come to pervade the agency. "As agency employees," Goss stated, "we do not identify with, support or champion opposition to the administration or its policies." The mere fact that Goss had to send such a note highlights the seriousness of the problem. Unfortunately, the bureaucracy turned on Goss, and eighteen months later, he resigned. The opponents of intelligence reform, the bureaucrats, were back in power at the CIA.

It was after the Goss purge that Congressman Hoekstra sounded the alarm about the "strong and well-positioned group within the agency" that was intentionally undermining the administration's policies. He made his warnings in a letter to the president dated May 18, 2006. Hoekstra added, "This argument is supported by the Ambassador [Joseph] Wilson/Valerie Plame events, as well as by the string of unauthorized disclosures from an organization that prides itself with being able to keep secrets."

The president apparently never took Hoekstra's message to heart, because he named as Goss's replacement a career intelligence bureaucrat, former National Security Agency director Michael V. Hayden. In the Valerie Plame matter, a career government prosecutor was allowed to operate freely in going after senior political appointees despite being notified early on in his investigation that the source of a leak of Plame's CIA covert status had come from a liberal Republican in the number-two post at the State Department, Richard Armitage, and not from conservatives in the White House. Yet I. Lewis "Scooter" Libby,

Vice President Dick Cheney's conservative national security adviser, became the target and victim of federal prosecutor Patrick Fitzgerald.

The Real Power

The liberal bureaucrats in the national security policymaking agencies and intelligence community have made America dangerously vulnerable to enemies like China, Russia, Iran, North Korea, Cuba, and Venezuela, as well as al Qaeda and its Islamist extremist allies. These enemies have identified the main U.S. strategic weakness: an inability to use nonmilitary elements of power makes the United States vulnerable to aggressive denial and deception. Thus, to counterbalance U.S. power, the main enemies of America are engaged in aggressive denial and deception activities—using lies and half-truths to deny their dangerous activities, whether it be Iran's nuclear program, North Korea's nuclear program, or China's anti-U.S. military buildup.

The Failure Factory simply does not understand the need to take an aggressive, offensive posture against these programs, and therefore has gutted the country's ability to use the tools of so-called soft power. Soft power is still power, and a strategic campaign to use this vital tool represents the greatest hope for advancing U.S. objectives in the world and countering our enemies' efforts.

But now, thanks to the liberals and bureaucrats whose power continues to grow, the United States is sending dangerously wrong signals to both its friends and enemies. The message being conveyed is of U.S. weakness, indecision, and lack of will. That is discouraging friends abroad and, worse, encouraging enemies into possibly making a disastrous miscalculation in dealing with the United States. The danger that a global nuclear conflict will break out as the result of perceived U.S. weakness is real and growing, and must be reversed.

The loss of U.S. soft power is not the only danger. Our hard power as well is under assault. Liberal bureaucrats' policies are severely eroding U.S. military capabilities, to the point that in the near future the United States may not be able to prevail in a conventional war. Misguided bureaucrats and their liberal supporters have engaged in drastic cuts in both forces and weapons systems with little or no regard for the negative effect they have on overall U.S. military power. In Iraq, politically correct policies imposed by lawyers have forced soldiers to use vague rules of engagement that leave troops questioning whether they can fire back when terrorists or insurgents shoot at them.

"The United States is facing the greatest crisis in the preservation of government of the people, by the people and for the people since the decades of the 1850s and 1860s," said former House speaker Newt Gingrich in a speech in May 2008. "We find ourselves crippled by political correctness and incapable of having honest conversations about meeting the threats around the world."

That crippling political correctness plagued President Bush's administration. Many of the 3,000 political appointees the president chose for his administration were either Democrats left over from the Clinton administration or liberal Republicans who shared many of the Democrats' views. By picking or keeping the wrong people, the president got the wrong policies. And American national security was severely undermined.

A new president will sweep into office at the beginning of 2009, and that leader will make thousands of political appointments that will profoundly shape America's future course. But the real power—a power that until now has gone largely unnoticed—will remain within the Failure Factory.

THREE BLIND MICE

THE UNTOLD STORY OF BUREAUCRATIC

BETRAYAL ON IRAN

On December 3, 2007, a remarkable event took place that changed the power structure in Washington in fundamental and very damaging ways. At a nondescript office building on K Street in Northwest Washington, reporters were called to take part in a background briefing where senior U.S. intelligence officials planned to announce the results of a new National Intelligence Estimate, or NIE.

NIEs are the U.S. intelligence analytical community's most prized product. They are supposed to represent the consensus views of hundreds if not thousands of intelligence analysts and collectors. These personnel are spread out among the sixteen U.S. intelligence agencies, which in 2007 had a combined annual budget of $43.5 billion—more money than most countries spend on their entire national defense budgets.

Of course, by 2007, NIEs were no longer considered incontrovertible. First, a dysfunctional U.S. intelligence system had missed the threat and ultimate attacks of September 11, 2001. Then, to compensate for its failure in 2001, it falsely assumed that Iraq under Saddam Hussein had stockpiled weapons of mass destruction, without ever sending any agents of its own to check firsthand. The flawed 2002 NIE on Iraq's WMD was used as one of the bases for the invasion of

Iraq. Five years later, the credibility of the intelligence community lay in tatters.

But this lack of credibility was not much of an obstacle to the intelligence analysts responsible for the report presented at this background briefing. It was an opportunity, in fact.

As the intelligence officials outlined it for reporters on December 3, the NIE dramatically reversed a 2005 estimate that had concluded Iran was secretly building nuclear arms through its development of uranium enrichment capabilities, obtained from the Pakistani nuclear supplier network headed by Abdul Qadeer Khan, the father of Pakistan's nuclear arms program. Directly contradicting that earlier report, the new estimate said that "we"—meaning all U.S. intelligence analysts—"judge with high confidence that in fall 2003, Tehran halted its nuclear weapons program."

This conclusion was the lead item on the unclassified sheet of "key judgments" that the intelligence officials passed out at the briefing. Since it did not identify the sources of information used in reaching the judgments, the unclassified summary produced more questions than answers. But the report emphasized that NIEs are the most authoritative written judgments on national security issues, "designed to help U.S. civilian and military leaders develop policies to protect U.S. national security interests."

It also took pains to distance the intelligence community from the flawed 2002 Iraq estimate—and, notably, from the 2005 NIE on Iran. The unclassified overview stated that a number of steps had been taken over the previous year and a half to improve the NIE process under the newly created Office of the Director of National Intelligence. The new and improved NIE process supposedly was designed to better check "source reporting and technical judgments" and to apply "more rigorous standards."

But these claims were false.

The real story of the 2007 NIE on Iran has not been told. A close investigation reveals that while NIEs are supposed to reflect the views of the entire intelligence community, this 140-plus-page classified report was essentially the work of three liberal bureaucrats at the top of the intelligence food chain. And far from reflecting "more rigorous standards," their report was an overtly politicized policy document. The tenets of intelligence analysis prohibit such policymaking.

These three liberal officials, all from the State Department bureaucracy, used the 2007 NIE to try to block what they regarded as an out-of-control president from threatening to use military force against the Iranian regime over its refusal to give up an illegal uranium-enrichment program. After claiming with "high confidence" that Iran had halted its nuclear weapons program in 2003, their report made a telling admission: "This NIE does *not* assume that Iran intends to acquire nuclear weapons." Instead they said they had taken "full account of Iran's dual-use uranium fuel cycle and those nuclear activities that are at least partly civil in nature."

In other words, these biased analysts accepted at face value the claims of a radical Islamist regime and state sponsor of terrorism. Their goal was to spin the intelligence to cast doubt on Iran's nuclear weapons development and promote the view of the liberal bureaucrats who argued Iran's nuclear program was "civil" and not military in nature.

In pursuing their own policy agenda, this cabal of liberal intelligence officials undermined months and even years of international efforts to apply political and diplomatic pressure on the Iranian regime to give up an illegal nuclear weapons program. The analysts did so despite the fact that a nuclear-armed Iran would fundamentally change the balance of power in the Middle East and pose a major threat to the United States and its allies.

In the end, the December 3 meeting capped off one of the boldest power plays by unelected bureaucrats in American history. The analysts had sought to prevent an elected president from conducting the foreign policy of the United States. In the past that would have been considered treason.

And yet these three officials were never taken to task for their policy crimes. Indeed, they remained in their important posts, free to influence U.S. government policy.

Subversion

I t would be fair to ask just how unelected bureaucrats gained enough power to be able to subvert the official policy of the United States. Sadly, this kind of subversion has been going on for years.

The term "bureaucrat" usually conjures the image of a bland paper pusher. There are certainly plenty of those within the federal government, which now has 1.7 million employees (and this figure doesn't even include the 5 million federal contractors, many of whom are former government bureaucrats, and 1.4 million military personnel). But a relatively small number of activist bureaucrats, perhaps several hundred to several thousand, have real power, despite toiling in relative obscurity. They pose a serious threat to the United States and the world at large.

The biggest danger involves the professional bureaucrats within the national security and foreign policy establishment—especially in such key agencies as the State Department, the Defense Department, and the Justice Department, and on the White House executive staff. Many of them have their own agenda, one that is overwhelmingly dominated by the long-discredited left-liberal policies that came to dominate the worst of the Democratic Party in the 1960s and 1970s. Political polling data is not available, but experts estimate that the federal bureaucracy is overwhelmingly Democrat—perhaps as much as 90–95 percent Democrat.

Take the example of one newly hired U.S. intelligence analyst, a young woman in her twenties who was asked to describe the Venezuelan movement known as Bolivarism, whose leader is President Hugo Chávez. The analyst responded by saying simply that it was a "social justice movement." Of course, Chávez is well known for his outspoken anti-Americanism, and his leftist Bolivarism has nothing to do with real social justice and everything to do with advancing Communist subversion throughout the Western Hemisphere. Chávez in 2007 praised the Colombian terrorist group FARC and called for them to be delisted as international terrorists. All this was apparently lost on the analyst. "She was simply repeating what she had learned in school," an astonished senior U.S. intelligence official said.

The democratic system is set up to support duly elected officials who are trying to implement policies according to the wishes of the American people, but unelected figures burrowing into the bureaucratic structure have upended this system. "That's not how we do things" is the bureaucrats' standard response when ordered to implement a policy by a "political," as political appointees are called.

As a result, these bureaucrats have blocked or subverted many conservative policies that restored America to greatness during the administration of Ronald Reagan. Their very goal is to thwart these policies, in fact. The Hatch Act, passed it 1939, limits federal employees from engaging in partisan political activities, but the federal bureaucracy has nonetheless become incredibly politicized.

The subversive nature of the modern national security bureaucracy took root in the Kennedy administration. As defense secretary, former Ford automotive chairman Robert S. McNamara put in place much of the modern policy analysis and planning system used today by bureaucrats. His use of systems analysis was a quasiscientific approach to making decisions on such elements as force requirements, weapons systems, and other policy issues. The process used mainly civilians instead of military personnel, to avoid what McNamara feared was a bias of the military. Systems analysis basically meant considering every decision as broadly as possible while reducing complex problems to their component parts to make them easier to understand. But far from making objective decisions, McNamara's aides, who became known as the "whiz kids," used system analysis to support McNamara's predetermined and misguided liberal policy goals.

McNamara used his corporate approach to systematize the bureaucracy and to cut off the generally conservative military from major policy analysis and decisions. For example, he developed the complex, long-term budgeting process that is still in use today, including the Five-Year Defense Plan. He also used draft presidential memorandums and other management reports to shape the president's final decisions, which limited the ability of military leaders to communicate directly with the commander in chief.

The result today is a national security bureaucracy that remains steeped in the left-liberal political mindset when it comes to both formulating policy and planning it. Even those who sought to tame the bureaucracy, such as Richard Nixon and Ronald Reagan, were unable to do so. Reagan's conservative revolution brought down the Soviet Union and ended the Cold War, but the entrenched bureaucracy remained largely untouched by Reagan's brand of conservatism.

The problem with George W. Bush's administration was that it did little to counter the subversion. It was plagued by a combination of bad political appointees and the president's unwillingness to press officials to support his policies, especially after the 2003 Iraq War and the failures of intelligence related to the September 11 attacks and the weapons of mass destruction in Iraq.

Those failures have proved costly—not only to Bush's political fortunes but, more important, to U.S. national security.

The "Game Preserve"

The backstage story of the 2007 NIE on Iran reflects the extraordinary power unelected bureaucrats have grabbed for themselves, and the Bush administration's inability (or refusal) to address the problem.

According to current and former intelligence and policy officials I spoke with, the three senior bureaucrats responsible for the estimate were Vann Van Diepen, a former State Department arms official who in 2006 became the National Intelligence Officer for Weapons of Mass Destruction; Thomas Fingar, who served in the Office of the Director of National Intelligence as deputy director of national intelligence for analysis and as chairman of the National Intelligence Council; and Kenneth Brill, another liberal State Department bureaucrat who was removed from his post as U.S. ambassador to the International Atomic Energy Agency (IAEA) but landed in the plum post of head of the newly formed National Counterproliferation Center, an interagency center.

The officials told me that the principal Iran NIE author was Van Diepen, who had last worked in an intelligence role in the 1980s, when he served in the State Department's Bureau of Intelligence and Research (INR). Van Diepen had repeatedly tried to block conservative efforts within the U.S. government to get tough on international arms proliferators like China and Russia, despite the fact that he was director of the State Department's Office of Chemical, Biological, and Missile Nonproliferation for fourteen years.

In short, he resisted opportunities to prevent illegal weapons proliferation *even though such prevention was his primary responsibility for a decade and a half.*

Van Diepen was, like many others in the national security bureaucracy, devoted to toothless arms-control policies like the 1972 U.S.-Soviet Anti-Ballistic Missile Treaty. This put him at odds with the Bush administration's national security policies. The administration rejected the ABM Treaty because it hindered the development of needed defenses against missile attack (and also because one of the two parties to the treaty, the Soviet Union, was now defunct). Thus Van Diepen clashed with hard-headed conservative realists, who believed that action was needed to prevent the spread of dangerous weapons.

Van Diepen's perspective was not particularly surprising, given that he earned a master's degree from the Massachusetts Institute of Technology Defense and Arms Control Studies Program in 1983. The

MIT program is known in conservative policy circles as a bastion of muddleheaded liberalism for the arms-control advocates who almost venerate the 1972 ABM Treaty.

Once ensconced in the State Department Nonproliferation Bureau, Van Diepen became the champion of what State arms-control bureaucrats called the "Game Preserve" approach to international arms control. Through his office he controlled sanctions against those who violated U.S. laws in spreading dangerous arms and technologies to rogue states. But he pointedly chose not to employ this vital tool for dealing with weapons proliferators.

Instead, the word went out that nations considered key strategic states were not to be punished under any circumstances. "We don't hunt on the game preserve," he told a coworker.

Those on Van Diepen's "game preserve" included Russia and China, the most egregious violators of arms-proliferation norms. These countries would sell just about any weapon to anybody. Beijing, for example, supplied an endless stream of technology to Pakistan throughout the 1980s that ended up creating a new and highly unstable nuclear state. Van Diepen repeatedly let the Chinese off the hook for their arms sales to such rogue states as Iran, Syria, and North Korea by claiming that the Beijing government could not control the main exporters in China. But the fact is that the vast majority of all Chinese businesses are state-run and that the Communist system still in place has extensive controls on all arms and arms-related technology.

Russia, meanwhile, supplied large amounts of nuclear technology to Iran. But according to Van Diepen, Iran's nuclear program was peaceful. This was not a conclusion he reached only after studying all the evidence in assembling the 2007 NIE. For years Van Diepen was a leading proponent of the false and misleading view that Iran's nuclear effort was not aimed at building weapons, despite extensive evidence to the contrary.

According to officials who worked with them at State, Van Diepen and his boss—Assistant Secretary of State John Wolf, another entrenched liberal bureaucrat who worshiped at the altar of arms-control treaties—vigorously subverted U.S. counterproliferation law. The law required the State Department to implement legal sanctions on states and companies caught engaging in transfers of WMD and missiles, but "their preference was to continue the Clinton-era policies where the State Department dragged its feet and looked the other way on WMD sanctions cases," one official told me.

One of the most flagrant examples of Van Diepen's sabotage nearly got him removed from his post within the State Department's Nonproliferation Bureau. It occurred early in Bush's first term, as he defied an order from John Bolton, at the time undersecretary of state for arms control and international security.

One of Bolton's main responsibilities was making sure the State Department followed U.S. nonproliferation laws that required sanctions to be imposed on rogue states like Iran and Syria for arms-proliferation activities. The liberal State Department bureaucrats hated these sanctions because they upset diplomacy and negotiations.

During a meeting with Van Diepen, Bolton ordered him to send a cable to U.S. ambassadors requiring them to inform host governments about the sanctions. Bolton was unusual for a senior official in that he personally read all the cables his nonproliferation office received and sent. The morning after the meeting he noticed that the cable he had ordered Van Diepen to send had been modified; the requirements put on the American ambassadors had been softened.

Bolton was furious and called Van Diepen into his office. "What are you doing?" he demanded to know. Van Diepen replied that he thought the order from Bolton was somehow "illegal," which was why he modified it. A shouting match followed, and Van Diepen was dressed down and told never to make another unauthorized change to a cable. Aides to Bolton wanted Van Diepen fired, but firing was not Bolton's style. The aides appealed to Bolton to at least file a formal letter admonishing Van Diepen, but the undersecretary also rejected that idea. Thus an opportunity to limit future damage caused by Van Diepen was missed.

The bureaucrats' opposition to U.S. policy was so intense that Bolton was ultimately compelled to hire a lawyer from outside the department in order to force them to implement sanctions laws. In 2003, he brought on Stephen A. Elliott, a tough, no-nonsense lawyer for the Navy Department, as a legal adviser. Elliott worked with Bolton to counter the foot-dragging and outright opposition to enforcing U.S. sanctions laws within the division.

Something has gone very wrong when a high-level official appointed by the president of the United States and confirmed by the U.S. Senate must bring in an attorney to make intransigent subordinates carry out the official policy of the United States. But that is the mindset of the liberal bureaucrats entrenched in the federal government: though it is their responsibility to carry out U.S. policy, they will not only refuse to do so but will actually undercut that policy.

John Wolf, one of the most partisan opponents of the Bush administration's foreign policy, captured this mindset when he defended Van Diepen by saying that he "wasn't anti–President Bush, he was anti–John Bolton." But again, Bolton was the man appointed by the president to carry out his policies; Wolf's distinction was absurd, and telling.

Ultimately, a reorganization stripped Van Diepen of most of his office's authority over missile proliferation. With his office gutted, he appealed to his longtime friend and fellow State Department intelligence analyst, Thomas Fingar, the government's most senior intelligence analyst, who appointed Van Diepen to be the National Intelligence Officer for Weapons of Mass Destruction and Proliferation in February 2006.

Sleight of Hand

Like Vann Van Diepen, Fingar was a major proponent of the soft view on Iran. He rose to power in the intelligence structure as a China specialist. While at Stanford University he wrote his doctoral thesis on why the United States should provide high technology to

China, a position opposed by almost all national security officials, since Beijing is relentlessly buying and stealing American know-how for its military buildup—a buildup that could eventually be used in a conflict with the United States. Fingar worked at Stanford from 1975 to 1986, as a senior research associate at the university's Center for International Security and Cooperation and director of its U.S.-China relations program, both bastions of liberal policy advocacy.

Fingar's perfidy was in evidence when he took part in a U.S.-government–approved conference in China in September 2006 that included representatives of Beijing's Ministry of State Security, which American counterintelligence officials say is stealing vast amounts of government and private-sector secrets. Fingar's pro-China sentiments have clouded his view of the threat posed by Beijing. In 2005, Chinese General Zhu Chenghu threatened to use nuclear weapons against the United States. When asked about General Zhu's inflammatory comment, Fingar dismissed concerns by saying, "They have their crazy generals too." Thus he equated U.S. generals to China's Communist military.

Fingar rose to prominence by a bit of sleight of hand related to the failed 2002 NIE on Iraq, which critics have falsely claimed was the entire basis for launching the Iraq War. The NIE stated that Iraq had stockpiles of chemical and biological weapons and was working to develop nuclear weapons. Fingar, as the State INR director, offered a "dissent" that he was later to ride to the top position for analysis within the Office of the Director of National Intelligence. Fingar wrote a State/INR "Alternative View of Iraq's Nuclear Program" that appeared in a box in the 2002 estimate. It said that the assistant secretary of state for INR, namely Fingar, believed Saddam Hussein "is pursuing at least a limited effort to maintain and acquire nuclear weapons–related capabilities," but argued that the activities detected did not add up to a compelling case that Iraq was currently pursuing "an integrated and comprehensive approach to acquire nuclear weapons."

After the invasion of Iraq failed to turn up WMD, Fingar made it seem that he had challenged the entire prewar estimate. He carefully exploited this image as the lone dissenter on the Iraq NIE to catapult himself to his senior ODNI position.

But in fact Fingar did not offer a sweeping dissent to the 2002 estimate. His dispute with the report was limited to the issue of special metal tubes that Iraq had purchased. The U.S. Energy Department believed that these tubes were intended for centrifuge rotors, which would be used to make highly enriched uranium for bombs. Fingar, in contrast, believed the tubes, which were purchased without great secrecy, were probably for artillery rockets. That was the only basis for his skepticism on the Iraq WMD intelligence. He did not dissent from the estimate's other assumptions related to Iraq's chemical and biological weapons.

In any case, we have since learned that Saddam *did* intend to pursue "an integrated and comprehensive" WMD program. In January 2008, CBS's *60 Minutes* ran an interview with Saddam's FBI interrogator, George Piro, who spent seven months with the former Iraqi dictator before his execution. Saddam told Piro that while the Iraqis had gotten rid of most of their weapons of mass destruction under United Nations pressure, he fully intended to produce WMD again someday. "The folks that he needed to reconstitute his program are still there," Piro said. "He wanted to pursue all of WMD. So he wanted to reconstitute his entire WMD program," including chemical, biological, and nuclear weapons.

By the time that news came out, however, Fingar had long since taken over as chairman of the National Intelligence Council, which produces the NIEs. That is how the 2007 Iran estimate came to be written in conformity to the liberal, pacifist, pro–arms-control views of Fingar, Van Diepen, and the third key player, Kenneth Brill.

Going Native

While Fingar and Van Diepen became widely known for their role in the Iran NIE, another key drafter was Brill, a liberal arms-control proponent who distinguished himself for undermining American policies while serving as ambassador to the International Atomic Energy Agency (IAEA). Officials who worked with Brill told me that he worked against the Bush administration at the Vienna posting and essentially "went native," seeking to adopt the international organization's feckless policies as those of the United States. He was a proponent of toothless concessions to the international organization that were tantamount to appeasement.

In 2004, when the Bush administration was trying to step up pressure on Iran through the international community, Brill was posted to the IAEA and refused to support Bolton's efforts to place trusted U.S. representatives within the international organization. At one point, Bolton sent an aide to Vienna and Brill tried to block him from coming into the country. The situation reached a peak at a meeting at the State Department when Bolton confronted Brill over his actions and his failure to support the policy on Iran. In front of a group of State Department officials, Bolton told Brill that he was "playing too much tennis" and not doing the work that was needed. It was an extraordinary dressing-down of a senior diplomat.

Brill, like Fingar and Van Diepen, believed passionately that only international arms agreements, and never military or intelligence action, should be used to stop the spread of arms. He opposed Bolton's Proliferation Security Initiative, the bold international grouping that sought to use international pressure in the form of maritime interdictions and other military pressure to stop the spread of deadly arms. Brill tried to block authorized high-seas interceptions, claiming falsely that the intelligence wasn't good enough to support the action. And on Iran he was the softest of the bureaucrats' soft-liners.

Brill's performance at the IAEA was so bad that even liberal Republicans like Secretary of State Colin Powell and Deputy Secretary of State Richard Armitage refused to allow Brill to take up another ambassadorial posting. He was rescued by a former Foreign Service colleague, John Negroponte, who picked him to head the newly formed National Counterproliferation Center, the base from which he helped subvert U.S. policy on Iran's nuclear program.

Officially, Fingar and Van Diepen claimed that Brill was not a major influence on the NIE on Iran. But other intelligence officials close to the process said Brill, as the head of the National Counterproliferation Center, played a major role in the estimate and made sure that the estimate reflected the soft-line views on the Iranian nuclear program that he shared with Fingar and Van Diepen.

When Negroponte appointed Brill to the National Counterproliferation Center, former Pentagon official Frank Gaffney wrote, "The last thing the United States needs at the pinnacle of the intelligence apparatus assigned to countering what is widely agreed to be the most dangerous threat of our time—the scourge and spread of weapons of mass destruction in the hands of terrorists and their state-sponsors—is someone whose past track record suggests that he misperceives the threat, opposes the use of effective techniques to counter it, and is constitutionally disposed to accommodate rather than defeat the proliferators."

But that is what the United States got. And the 2007 NIE on Iran was the predictable consequence.

Defining Away the Iranian Threat

The Iran NIE left the bureaucrats with a major victory after years of battling conservative and liberal Republican political appointees who had set out to implement the president's policies. The victory was even sweeter in light of the fact that the liberal bureaucrats had opposed the policy decision to go to war with Iraq; they never favored using military forces to achieve political objectives. By pushing through their NIE asserting that Iran was not producing nuclear weapons, they erected a massive obstacle to any U.S. efforts to put pressure on the Islamist regime.

David Wurmser, a State Department official and a former aide to Vice President Dick Cheney, said that the NIE "smells of policy validation.

"These guys were State Department bureaucrats," Wurmser said. "It is hardly surprising that they now use their new positions to try to prove they were right. One has to look at the agendas of the primary movers of this report, to judge how much it can really be banked on."

The reaction of U.S. allies, especially in Europe, was one of anger. The governments of Britain, France, and Germany, which had been working their own diplomatic effort to pressure Tehran into halting uranium enrichment, were livid. They took out their frustrations on Eric Edelman, the U.S. undersecretary of defense for policy, who traveled to Europe to meet with the Europeans in mid-December 2007.

Criticism was fierce in the United States as well, especially in Congress and among former officials. John Bolton went public with his disgust, penning an op-ed in the *Washington Post* in which he declared that the NIE showed that "too much of the intelligence community is engaging in policy formulation rather than 'intelligence' analysis."

Bolton pointed out that the NIE's "key judgments" were misleading, and intentionally so. They were presented in such a way as to ensure that the conclusion would be that Iran was not building nuclear weapons, when in fact, Bolton said, "there is little substantive difference between the conclusions of the 2005 NIE on Iran's nuclear capabilities and the 2007 NIE." The intelligence itself may not have changed substantially, but these bureaucrats, intent on making policy rather than merely analyzing the intelligence, wanted to guarantee that their soft line on Iran prevailed.

In the words of Norman Podhoretz, the veteran journalist and commentator on international affairs, "By leading with the sensational news that Iran had suspended its nuclear-weapons program in 2003, [the NIE's] authors ensured that their entire document would be interpreted as meaning that there was no longer anything to worry about."

But as Podhoretz noted, the bureaucrats responsible for the NIE "took care to protect themselves" with what's known as two-handed analysis (*on the one hand, on the other hand*). Immediately after the headline grabber that Iran had halted its nuclear arms program in 2003, the NIE stated that the intelligence community assessed with "moderate-to-high confidence" that Iran might still build nuclear arms. It was, as Podhoretz put it, a "self-protective caveat"—one of several in the NIE to which "scarcely anyone paid attention," as the authors surely expected would be the case.

Other assessments that drew little attention were actually crucial to understanding the 2007 NIE. Most notably, the estimate's authors were forced to acknowledge that they could state with only "moderate" confidence that Iran had not secretly restarted the nuclear weapons program.

Perhaps, then, the mullahs *had* started building nuclear arms again. U.S. intelligence couldn't say for sure. Why the difficulty addressing this fundamental question? Because, the NIE admitted, there were significant "gaps" in U.S. intelligence on Iran.

As Bolton observed, "This alone should give us considerable pause."

Former CIA director James Schlesinger also took aim at the Iran NIE. In an opinion article in the *Wall Street Journal* that bore the headline "Stupid Intelligence on Iran," he wrote, "Clearly, the key judgments in the NIE were overstated. And that, in turn, may reflect the very late decision to declassify the key judgments, written in a kind of shorthand, and thus incautiously phrased."

Schlesinger punctured the heart of the NIE: "The crucial decision, hidden in a footnote, was to define the 'nuclear weapons program' which had been halted to mean only 'Iran's weapon design and weaponization work and covert . . . uranium enrichment-related work.'

Thus it excludes Iran's overt enrichment program monitored by the International Atomic Energy Agency."

Schlesinger correctly noted why that exclusion was so flawed: "We have long understood that the production of fissile material, whether overt or covert, remains 'the long pole in the tent' in the development of a nuclear capability. Thus the NIE defines away what has been the main element stirring international alarm regarding Iran's nuclear activity."

Or as John Bolton phrased it, the NIE's "distinction between 'military' and 'civilian' programs is highly artificial, since the enrichment of uranium, which all agree Iran is continuing, is critical to civilian and military uses. Indeed, it has always been Iran's 'civilian' program that posed the main risk of a nuclear 'breakout.'"

Both Bolton and Podhoretz recognized another flawed conclusion in the NIE: that international pressure had persuaded Iran to halt the program in 2003. In fact, no such pressure had been applied. Bolton wrote that the NIE "implies that Iran is susceptible to diplomatic persuasion and pressure, yet the only event in 2003 that might have affected Iran was our invasion of Iraq and the overthrow of Saddam Hussein, not exactly a diplomatic pas de deux. As undersecretary of state for arms control in 2003, I know we were nowhere near exerting any significant diplomatic pressure on Iran. Nowhere does the NIE explain its logic on this critical point."

Podhoretz, for his part, noted that the NIE ignored the real motivators of Iran's nuclear weapons drive, including Islamist and nationalist passions.

The NIE even drew the ire of former secretary of state Henry Kissinger. He wrote an op-ed in which he stated, "I have often defended the dedicated members of the intelligence community. This is why I am extremely concerned about the tendency of the intelligence community to turn itself into a kind of check on, instead of a part of, the executive branch. When intelligence personnel expect their work to become the subject of public debate, they are tempted into the roles of surrogate policymakers and advocates."

Spin Cycle

As criticism of the flawed NIE mounted, the bureaucrats struck back, telling the *Wall Street Journal* that the estimate was good. Fingar said, "The idea that this thing was written by a bunch of non-professional renegades or refugees is just silly." Again he played up his image as the brave dissenter on the 2002 Iraq NIE, this time to try to cut off criticism of the 2007 NIE. The spin was that "hundreds" of officials took part and that thousands of documents were used in producing the report. Fingar claimed that since taking over as head of the National Intelligence Council, he had introduced more rigorous vetting and analysis methodology into the national-estimate process to prevent further intelligence disasters like the one in 2002.

But Fingar's claim was dismissed as "nonsense" by one senior U.S. intelligence analyst. "This is theater contrived by Fingar to play up his contention that prewar intelligence was politicized," the official said. "There was no political pressure on previous NIEs—as we know from the 9/11 Commission, the 2005 WMD Commission, and the 2004 Senate Select Committee on Intelligence Iraq Report. George Tenet would not have tolerated it, nor would any other career CIA officer."

The bogus German intelligence defector from Iraq codenamed Curveball (real name: Rafid Ahmed Alwan) is often cited as the reason for the new analytical process, but intelligence officials reveal that Curveball's fabrications were overstated in influencing the 2002 Iraq NIE. "This source only influenced the biological weapons section, not the nuclear, chemical, or missiles section of the NIE," the analyst said. "This was an exceptional situation that happened because analysts and collectors did not follow the rules." Political pressure played no role in the faulty estimate, despite what liberal critics of the Bush administration contend.

Contrary to Fingar's claims that his supposedly more rigorous review process brought in hundreds of analysts, his system further sealed off the analytical process from oversight by policymakers. Since Fingar became the official in charge of intelligence production at the Office of the Director of National Intelligence, there has been actually less dissent in intelligence products than before. This is supposedly because of the new process Fingar imposed to "work out" differences in advance. In reality, "this amounts to pressure on analysts at an early stage to accept a politically correct corporate bottom line," the senior analyst said.

In the *Wall Street Journal* story that aired the bureaucrats' spin, Bolton was quoted calling for the entire estimate to be released, not just the key findings. But the intelligence agencies have refused to release the report. "You couldn't read the key judgments [of the report] and not assume that this was intended to change policy," Bolton said. "It shredded the Bush administration policy."

Won't Get Fooled Again

The reason for the shredding is simple: The report was not really the work of "hundreds" of analysts. It was Van Diepen who wrote the NIE on Iran, under the close supervision of Fingar. And so the Iran estimate was, in the words of a veteran U.S. intelligence analyst, "poorly drafted and badly sourced."

This official said that the estimate is getting high-level attention among Republicans on Capitol Hill, but that Democrats sympathetic to the liberal views of the authors will not formally challenge it, or hold hearings.

The NIE should be exposed for what it is: a politically motivated document predicated on biased assumptions and filled with major mistakes.

The most glaring problem, the fatal flaw in a document riddled with flaws, was fundamental: *The NIE was based on bogus Iranian intelligence.*

Yes, U.S. intelligence agencies—or at least the analysts who hijacked the NIE process—got fooled again.

This is the real story behind the 2007 NIE on Iran: U.S. intelligence had discovered a secret Iranian communication channel and begun intercepting messages there. But the channel had been compromised in 2004 when Iraqi exile leader Ahmed Chalabi was arrested for allegedly supplying information to Iran. An investigation cleared Chalabi of the charge but revealed that a U.S. intelligence contractor, in a drunken lapse, had disclosed to an Iranian agent that the U.S. National Security Agency (NSA) had broken the codes used by the Ministry of Intelligence and Security, the main Iranian spy agency. Amazingly, even after the press disclosures, the NSA continued to monitor and report intelligence from the compromised channel without ever suspecting that Iran was feeding disinformation through it.

This is where analysts picked up the supposedly new information that Iran had halted its nuclear arms program in 2003. That information was the basis for Fingar's analysts changing the Iran nuclear estimate.

And it was completely false.

The Consequences of the Subversion

The liberal arms controllers within the intelligence process got what they wanted. A January 2008 report by the DNI Open Source Center, an intelligence unit set up to examine and analyze foreign materials obtained from the Internet and from published sources, stated that the release of the NIE on Iran's nuclear program had eased the pressure on Tehran. "After the 3 December release of the US National Intelligence Estimate (NIE) on Iran's nuclear program, the conduct of several prominent Iranian political figures—including the Supreme Leader—suggested that their anxiety about a potential military conflict with the United States may have abated," the report said.

Thus years of efforts to press the Iranians into abandoning a dangerous nuclear program had been severely undermined and U.S. national security suffered greatly as a result of this betrayal.

In his 2002 State of the Union speech, President Bush vowed that the United States "will not permit the world's most dangerous regimes to threaten us with the world's most destructive weapons," and added later that waiting for threats to fully materialize would be waiting too long. And yet his administration did little in response to the betrayal of the 2007 NIE. Bush's weak national security adviser, Stephen J. Hadley, did not denounce the politicized NIE or the bureaucrats who wrote it. Instead, Hadley said the new estimate provided "grounds for hope" that the Iranian nuclear threat could be solved diplomatically and without resorting to military or other types of force, such as covert-action intelligence operations.

The NIE also undermined the new French government under incoming president Nicolas Sarkozy, whose aides had made clear in the weeks before the NIE was released that the use of military force must not be ruled out.

Other European leaders, including British prime minister Gordon Brown and German chancellor Angela Merkel, were blocked in by the left-liberal political forces in their own countries and forced to abandon the "stick" of international pressure that was the last hope for forcing Iran to give up its illegal uranium-enrichment program. This is exactly what the liberal bureaucrats wanted, of course. It all but ensured that Tehran's mullahs would be in possession of the nuclear weapons infrastructure in short order.

But by the spring of 2008, even the most senior U.S. intelligence officials could no longer publicly defend the flawed Iran NIE. Both CIA Director Michael V. Hayden and Director of National Intelligence J. Michael McConnell backpedaled from the NIE's conclusions and tried to blame the press for misrepresenting the estimate.

CIA Director Hayden said during a meeting with the *Washington Times* on March 11 that there are three key elements of a nuclear

weapons program: fissile material, weaponization, and delivery systems. "What came out in a lot of coverage [of the NIE] was 'Iran stops
nuclear program,'" Hayden said. "The only thing we claimed had
been halted in '03 was the weaponization. The development of fissile
material and the development of delivery systems continued. And one
can make the case the development of delivery systems make no sense
with just conventional warheads on top of them." In truth, the declassified NIE key judgments made no mention of delivery systems and
focused extensively on the halted program, so it can't be said that the
press focused too much on the 2003 halt.

McConnell, meanwhile, told a Senate hearing that the NIE was
confusing because it was too rapidly declassified and poorly focused.
"If I had it to do over again, I would be very specific in how I described what was cancelled and what continued," McConnell said. Of
course, the very first sentence of the declassified estimate was very em-
phatic and not confusing at all when it declared, "We judge with high
confidence that in fall 2003, Tehran halted its nuclear weapons program." This was the impression the liberal bureaucrats wanted to con-
vey. Now the intelligence leaders were trying to distance themselves
from this dramatic conclusion by asserting that the sentence only referred to work on a nuclear warhead.

To critics of the flawed NIE, the final straw came from the IAEA
itself. On February 25, 2008, the agency's deputy director general,
Olli Heinonen of Finland, addressed a closed-door meeting of the
IAEA in Vienna, revealing that Iran had worked on a nuclear device
beyond 2003—which of course flies in the face of the NIE's central
thesis.

Heinonen reported that the agency's investigation of Iran's nuclear
program had turned up many documents that provided new details
on three Iranian nuclear-related projects with weapons applications.
They included the conversion of uranium dioxide, which was labeled
the Green Salt project; research into ultrahigh explosives that can be
used to trigger a nuclear blast; and the development of a missile re-

entry vehicle, or warhead. Some of the Iranian documents, Heinonen said, showed plans, photographs, contract sheets, and film relating to manufacture of nuclear weapons, including a missile reentry vehicle dubbed Project P111. That project, according to Heinonen, was carried out from July 9, 2003, through January 14, 2004—beyond the alleged halt touted in the NIE. The warhead documents discussed a reentry vehicle for a Shahab-3, Iran's most powerful ballistic missile, and an airburst detonation at an altitude of 1,800 feet—a height suitable for a nuclear blast and not for a conventional bomb.

Heinonen's closed-door presentation was disclosed to the French newspaper *Le Monde* and confirmed as accurate by U.S. intelligence officials as a smoking gun.

The liberal bureaucrats' betrayal with the 2007 NIE could have dire consequences for the United States and its allies. Iran's militaristic regime has made its intentions perfectly clear. In April 2008, Iranian leader Mahmoud Ahmadinejad declared Iran to be "the most powerful and independent nation in the world" and then offered this menacing statement: "None of the current world powers are capable of, and have the courage to, threaten the Iranian nation and its interests and security." This is the same leader who had threatened to wipe Israel off the face of the earth.

And that was not an isolated threat. A day before Ahmadinejad made his chest-thumping statement about the power of Iran, a senior commander in the Iranian army, deputy commander in chief Mohammad Reza Ashtiani, warned, "If Israel wants to take any action against the Islamic Republic, we will eliminate Israel from the scene of the universe."

Combine Iran's nuclear program with its missile development, which includes the building of space launchers that are the perfect cover for long-range missile development, and one can see that the bureaucrats within the U.S. government have vastly increased the danger that Iran one day will fire a missile with a nuclear warhead at an American city or a vital U.S. ally.

This danger is very real, as Tehran's radical Islamist regime made clear within just a few months of the release of the NIE.

First, in February 2008, the Iranians test-launched a new long-range missile. Tehran claimed that the test was part of its satellite-launch program. But the authoritative British magazine *Jane's Intelligence Review* revealed why that was again simply cover for missile development. *Jane's* analyzed commercial satellite photographs and Iranian TV footage of the launch and found that, contrary to Iranian government claims, the new missile was a single-stage version of Iran's Shahab-3.

A U.S. defense official I spoke to about the Iranian test confirmed that the missile identified by *Jane's* seemed to resemble the Shahab-3, a medium-range ballistic missile. It thus appeared that Iran was following the example of North Korea in cobbling together a long-range missile. The North Korean Taepodong-2 uses a first stage that is similar to Iran's liquid-fueled Shahab-3, a second stage similar to the Scud, and a solid-fueled third stage.

Then, in April, Ahmadinejad proclaimed that the Iranians had tested and begun installing 6,000 new centrifuges for their uranium-enrichment program. The declaration, coming fast on the heels of the NIE, made a mockery of the soft approach to Iran. It called to mind John Bolton's prophetic warning that "civilian" uranium enrichment posed a grave risk.

By announcing this advance in uranium enrichment, the mullahs were thumbing their noses at international efforts to halt Iran's nuclear program, especially United Nations efforts. The UN Security Council had already imposed three separate rounds of sanctions against Tehran to try to force the Iranians to stop their uranium enrichment.

So much for the wonders of diplomacy.

A Firing Offense?

But diplomacy remained the obsession of the Failure Factory, even after the Iranian mullahs had telegraphed—once again—their true aims.

Most notably, Democratic presidential candidate Barack Obama championed diplomacy as the magic solution to dealing with Iran. Even after the Iranian missile test and its centrifuge production, Obama did not back off from the position he had set out in a Democratic debate when he affirmed that he would meet with leaders of Iran (and other rogue regimes) "without precondition"—a reckless, and indeed dangerous, approach to dealing with the radical clerical regime. Since then he has repeatedly reiterated that he wouldn't set preconditions. For example, he has said, "When you say preconditions, what you're really saying is, 'I'm not going to talk to you until you agree to do exactly what I want you to do.' Well, that's not how negotiations take place." And he told the *New York Times* in November 2007 that as president he would "engage in aggressive personal diplomacy" with Iran.

Even in May 2008, when the pressure led Obama to equivocate somewhat (he said, for instance, that he wasn't sure "Ahmadinejad is the right person to meet with right now"), the candidate's "Plan to Secure America and Restore Our Standing"—featured prominently on the Obama campaign's website—proudly and unambiguously declared, "Obama is the only major candidate who supports tough, direct presidential diplomacy with Iran *without preconditions*" (emphasis added).

But that same month Obama received support from a seemingly unlikely source: President Bush's defense secretary, Robert M. Gates. On May 14, Gates told a reporter that he favored the conciliatory approach to Iran espoused by liberal *New York Times* columnist Thomas Friedman—an approach that happened to run counter to the administration's stated position. "We need to figure out a way to develop some leverage with respect to the Iranians and then sit down and talk with them," Gates said. The defense secretary explicitly proposed making concessions to Ahmadinejad's radical regime: "If there's going to be a discussion, then they need something too."

The timing of these comments was astounding. It was bad enough that Gates made these remarks in the wake of Iran's missile test and Ahmadinejad's boasting about the 6,000 centrifuges. But as defense secretary he should have been acutely aware that at that moment Americans were being killed in Iraq by EFPs—explosively formed penetrators—that Iran had covertly supplied to the Iraqi insurgents; these deadly weapons were designed to pierce the armored-plated Humvees used by patrolling U.S. and allied troops.

Even more shocking, Gates expressed his willingness to make concessions to Iran's radical Islamist regime just one day before President Bush gave a speech to Israel's Knesset warning that to hold talks with terrorists and radicals like those in Iran was nothing short of "appeasement." The remarks were reportedly directed at Obama. But they just as easily could have been aimed at his own defense secretary.

Gates's remarks prompted justifiable outrage from conservatives. "Tehran's leaders need to pay the price for their terrorism, not be rewarded," said retired army major general Paul E. Vallely. "It is appalling for anyone to suggest that the Ahmadinejad regime whose EFPs are the number-one killer of American troops in Iraq would be offered concessions."

Gates had committed what in any normal presidential administration would have been a firing offense: publicly defying the administration's stated policy on one of the most pressing national security issues.

But nothing happened. Pentagon press secretary Geoff Morrell was sent out to try to spin the defense secretary's comments, insisting against the clear evidence that there was no difference between the secretary's and the president's views.

It was a telling incident. The president of the United States had se-lected someone for the position of top defense aide who publicly de-fied his policies—who had, in fact, lined up behind a view that the president himself made a point of ridiculing in an international speech. Such is the power of the Failure Factory.

Reaching Out to

Terrorists

Two men sat facing each other in a nondescript E-Ring office on the Pentagon's upper floor, where the offices of both the secretary of defense and deputy secretary of defense are located. One man was an Egyptian-born senior aide to the deputy defense secretary, and the other was a reserve Army major and lawyer who served as an analyst with the Joint Staff, the U.S. military's highest-ranking staff organization within the Pentagon.

It was November 2007, and the Joint Staff analyst, Stephen Coughlin, had been brought into the E-Ring because he had ruffled the politically correct feathers of the Pentagon brass, and of many others in the U.S. government.

This meeting was nothing less than a showdown.

On the one hand there was the senior Pentagon aide, Hesham Islam, who was in charge of the Pentagon's major public relations effort to "reach out" to Muslim groups and diplomats in the United States. He was one of the leading proponents of the argument, so prevalent within the U.S. government, that by engaging Muslim organizations in a dialogue, the United States would mitigate the threat of Islamist extremism.

On the other hand there was Coughlin, the Pentagon's leading authority on Islamist law doctrine, who had dared to blow the whistle on the disastrous consequences of the U.S. government's insistence on taking such a soft view on radical Islam.

The fundamental disagreement between the two men lies at the heart of the debate over how the United States should address the most significant threat to Americans and our allies overseas—the threat of international terrorists.

Only one official emerged unscathed from the showdown. Unfortunately for American national security, the victor was not Stephen Coughlin.

Hijacked?

In a speech six days after the September 11 attacks, President George W. Bush took pains to declare that the war on terrorism would not be an ideological struggle. "The face of terror is not the true faith of Islam," the president declared. "That's not what Islam is all about. Islam is peace. These terrorists don't represent peace. They represent evil and war."

This speech set the tone for the U.S. government's efforts in the war against terrorism, as the president's view became widespread throughout the Pentagon, which is waging the military war, as well as the Justice Department and the FBI, which are carrying out the law-enforcement element. Under the Bush administration, the U.S. government began focusing on reaching out to Muslim groups.

The Muslim outreach program quickly spun out of control. It was led by liberal bureaucrats, many of them lawyers, left over from President Bill Clinton's administration. The Clinton-era multicultural and diversity programs continued on autopilot during the Bush administration. Instead of promoting a clearheaded program of identifying the warfighting strategy, tactics, and motivation, or ideology, of Muslim extremists, liberal bureaucrats pushed the notion that Muslims were misunderstood and as a result were in danger of being persecuted.

By the second Bush term, Hesham Islam had become the point person for the Pentagon's Muslim outreach. The program was part of Hesham Islam's portfolio as a top aide to Gordon England, who in 2005 was appointed deputy defense secretary—the number-two man in the whole Pentagon.

Islam explained his philosophy in a news story that was posted on the Pentagon's website on October 15, 2007. "I am a strong believer that there are no relationships between countries," he told the American Forces Press Service. "Relationships are between people, and those relationships are what bring countries together." The news story referred specifically to Hesham Islam's outreach to the Muslim community. It quoted him as saying, "This war can't be won by just Americans. It's a war that has to be fought by Muslims. Islam has been hijacked, and it is time to take it back."

But the Muslim outreach that Hesham Islam spearheaded was based on misguided notions and has had disastrous results. It has lent credibility to Muslim extremist sympathizers. Worse, it has helped foster a covert terrorist support network in the United States.

It was Stephen Coughlin who led the way in uncovering the truth about the U.S. government's failures to tackle the Islamic threat.

Ignoring Extremism

The Joint Staff sits at the pinnacle of U.S. military policy. Stephen Coughlin provided advice and analysis for the staff's chairman and vice chairman, military service chiefs, and their aides in his area of expertise: the relationship between Islamist law and terrorism.

Coughlin, working as a contract employee, was being paid to help wage a war of ideas against Islamist extremists, a war of ideas being the most deficient aspect of the U.S.-led global war on terrorism. He was among a handful of government and military specialists who argued that Islam was not simply a religion of peace "hijacked" by extremists.

Rather, he identified it as a religion whose legal tenets encourage and support terrorism—jihad—in pursuit of Islam's ultimate objectives, the establishment of an Islamist Caliphate and the elimination worldwide of all non-Muslim ideas. Having closely studied Islam and Muslim preachings on jihad, he recognized that basic Islamic law, and not simply the Koran, was crucial to understanding the motivations and warfighting strategy of Muslim terrorists.

Coughlin's master's thesis, which he completed in the summer of 2007 at the National Defense Intelligence College, directly contradicted the position of Hesham Islam and others within the U.S. government. In the paper, entitled "To Our Great Detriment: Ignoring What Extremists Say About Jihad," he stated, "It is the conclusion of this thesis that Islamic law forms the doctrinal basis for the *jihadi* threat that can only be understood through an unconstrained review of the Islamic law of *jihad.*"

In other words, it may sound comforting to declare that Islam is a religion of peace, but the vast majority of Muslims do not agree with that notion.

According to Coughlin, Americans have naïvely misunderstood the threat from Islamic extremism. It had been more than five years since the United States launched the war on terrorism, he wrote, and "we still don't understand the nature of the enemy," a failure that represented "a devastating indictment of the Intelligence Community's inability to define the *jihadi* threat."

Coughlin worked diligently on the Joint Staff to strengthen U.S. efforts in the all-important war of ideas, but he did not attract much public attention until he wrote a memorandum reporting on the significant evidence introduced at a federal terrorism trial involving a Islamic charity group called the Holy Land Foundation for Relief and Development.

The federal government listed the group as a Specially Designated Global Terrorist because of its international connections to extremist groups. In July 2004 the Holy Land Foundation was indicted in federal court, accused of conspiracy, providing material support to a foreign terrorist organization, tax evasion, and money laundering. From 1995 to 2001, the indictment showed, the group provided some $12.4 million to the Palestinian terrorist organization Hamas, of which a Holy Land Foundation founder was a member.

The case went to trial in Dallas in 2007, but the jurors could not reach a verdict and a mistrial was declared. A news report by the Investigative Project on Terrorism at the time said one of the jurors intimidated other jurors into opposing a guilty conviction.

The outcome was a major setback for federal counterterrorism law-enforcement efforts. But a wealth of documents the prosecutors uncovered in the case highlighted the security threats posed by terrorist front groups within the United States. Coughlin was one of the first to recognize the significance of this material. He wrote his memo on September 7, 2007, even before the mistrial had been declared.

Coughlin's September 7 memorandum, a copy of which I obtained, explicitly criticized a number of groups that the U.S. Justice Department had targeted as part of its Muslim outreach program. He identified them as front groups for the Muslim Brotherhood, the Egyptian-based jihadist organization that is considered one of the world's deadliest terrorist groups. The Muslim Brotherhood seeks to mask its extremism by claiming to oppose violence, but in reality it provides tactical, material, and political support to Sunni extremists and thus has been a crucial part of the Islamist war against the West. For example, Ayman al-Zawahiri, the number-two figure in al Qaeda and its most important operational leader, came from the Muslim Brotherhood.

Coughlin stated in his memo that documents on the Muslim Brotherhood from the Holy Land trial identified twenty-nine different U.S. Muslim groups that were part of a subversion plan against the United States. "These documents are beginning to define the structure and outline of domestic jihad threat entities, associated nongovernmental organizations and potential terrorist or insurgent support systems," Coughlin stated.

One document in particular, a 1991 memorandum from the Muslim Brotherhood, offered a plan for organizing Muslims in North America. The memo "describes aspects of the global jihad's strategic information warfare campaign and indications of its structure, reach and activities," Coughlin wrote. He quoted the 1991 memo as saying that all Muslim Brotherhood members "must understand their work in America is a kind of grand jihad in eliminating and destroying the Western civilization from within, and 'sabotaging' its miserable house by their hands and the hands of believers so that it is eliminated and God's religion is made victorious over all other religions."

As a result, Coughlin warned that "outreach strategies must be adjusted in the face of credible information that seeming Islamic humanitarian or professional nongovernmental organizations may be part of the global jihad with potential for being part of the terrorist or insurgent support system."

A recent Justice Department "outreach" effort involved one of the very groups revealed in the 1991 document to be part of the Muslim Brotherhood: the Islamic Society of North America (ISNA), one of more than three hundred unindicted coconspirators in the Holy Land Foundation trial. Just days before Coughlin released his memo, the U.S. Justice Department had participated in an ISNA-sponsored conference in Chicago, even after two members of Congress wrote to Attorney General Alberto R. Gonzales to protest the participation. Representatives Pete Hoekstra, Michigan Republican, and Sue Myrick, North Carolina Republican, wrote that the Justice Department's involvement in the ISNA conference was a "grave mistake" because it would legitimize a group with "extremist origins."

The Justice Department dismissed the lawmakers' concern even though Hoekstra was the vice chairman of the House Permanent Select Committee on Intelligence and knew what he was talking about. Justice responded in a letter saying that there was no threat of legitimizing terrorist supporters, and that attending the Labor Day weekend conference was an important community-relations effort. The letter described Justice's participation in the ISNA meeting as part of "outreach efforts . . . to educate the public about how the department works to protect religious freedom, voting rights, economic opportunity, and many other rights." It was an example of the bureaucracy at its worst.

Coughlin was clear: Such outreach efforts "can cause those responsible for its success to so narrowly focus on the outreach relationship that they miss the surrounding events and lose perspective. This could undermine unity of effort in homeland security, lead to potential for embarrassment for the [U.S. government] and legitimize threat organizations by providing them domestic sanctuary."

After I reported on Coughlin's memo in the *Washington Times,* the liberal Republicans on the White House National Security Council staff and the bureaucrats at Justice complained loudly to Coughlin's bosses at the Joint Staff. He was called on the carpet by the J-2, as the intelligence director within the Joint Staff is known, and told in no uncertain terms that he could no longer write any memos for public consumption. Henceforth, Coughlin would limit all memorandums and reports to the classified channels within the Pentagon.

Political Correctness Trumps National Security

Coughlin, working as a contract employee, was being paid to help wage a war of ideas against Islamist extremists. The swift effort to silence him after he wrote his memo helps explain why the war of ideas has been the most ineffective portion of the war on terrorism. Even though it is obvious to even the most casual observer that the terrorists are motivated by Islamic law, political correctness within government bureaucracies has disabled ideological efforts against terrorism. Amazingly, almost a decade into the war on terrorism, the military had not produced a single comprehensive study on how Muslims wage war.

Few besides Coughlin understood the ideological extremist threat. One analyst who did properly gauge the danger was Army lieutenant colonel Joseph C. Myers, former analyst for the Defense Intelligence Agency (DIA). Myers had been chief of DIA's South America division and senior military analyst for Colombia. As Myers observed, the documents disclosed in the Holy Land trial evidence revealed that, according to the military's own definition, radical Islamist groups in the United States linked to the Muslim Brotherhood represent both a security and military threat to the country.

Myers said that the Muslim Brotherhood meets the U.S. Army counterinsurgency manual threshold of "an organized movement aimed at the overthrow of a constituted government through the use of subversion and armed conflict." Also, because the Muslim Brotherhood conducts military training for jihadists around the world, its U.S. front groups must be considered as having "latent military capabilities." The Muslim Brotherhood and its offshoots should be viewed as a single entity and it should be understood that its information warfare goal is to attack U.S. foundations and support global jihadists who are working to create a Caliphate, a goal supported by al Qaeda terrorists.

Myers added that the Muslim Brotherhood meets the threshold of a Pentagon directive that gives defense and military intelligence agencies the authority to spy on the group and its affiliates. "The Muslim Brotherhood in America is part of the radicalization infrastructure that supports the 'phases of radicalization' described in the recently published New York Police Department report 'Radicalization in the West: The Homegrown Threat,'" Myers stated.

Former intelligence analyst William Gawthrop was another specialist who understood the danger posed by Islamist ideology. In an unclassified briefing paper from 2007, he described the concept of "al Taqqiya," which essentially permits Muslims to hide the true nature of Islam from non-Muslims in order to spread the faith. "Islamic spokesmen repeat similar themes ranging from Islam is tolerant and peace loving to the claim that mandatory wearing of the veil offers women more freedom (therefore women in Muslim countries are 'freer' than women in western countries)," Gawthrop stated. "The effect of such defensive scripts and their sweeping generalities effectively precludes further critical examination of the underlying issue."

That underlying issue is what Coughlin and a handful of others in government fought valiantly to debate. Yet they were stifled and silenced. Political correctness trumped national security. Appearing to support Muslims became a pillar in the Bush administration's so-called compassionate conservatism, even though the groups being courted were enemies of the United States.

"A Christian Zealot with a Pen"

Stephen Coughlin's problems did not end with his scolding by the J-2. In fact, they were only beginning.

Hesham Islam, disturbed by Coughlin's September memorandum, called on the analyst to meet with him at the Pentagon. When they sat down in the E-Ring in November, the Pentagon aide challenged Coughlin's views on the nature of Islam. He argued that not all Muslims are extremists, and that Coughlin needed to stop trying to equate Islam with terrorism. He wanted the Joint Staff analyst to tone down his critique when briefing U.S. military leaders.

But Coughlin stood his ground in this showdown. Islamic law was the motivator not just for Muslim devotion but for terrorism as well, he insisted. The two could not be separated; in order to understand the nature of Islamist extremism, it was vital to know the links to Islamic law. It was an inconvenient truth.

The meeting ended, but later Hesham Islam wryly noted to a colleague that Coughlin was "a Christian zealot with a pen" who wouldn't listen to more moderate views on the nature of Islam.

It was at this point, according to Pentagon insiders, that Hesham Islam and Gordon England decided that Coughlin had to go. His hard-line views upset the liberal bureaucrats' program to reach out to Muslims, who were more and more frequent guests of England. The deputy defense secretary even hosted Pentagon "Iftars," as ceremonies marking the Muslim holy month of Ramadan are called.

Days after my December 28, 2007, *Washington Times* column exposed Islam's "zealot" comment against Coughlin, the pressure on Coughlin reached the breaking point. The J-2 called him into his office and said he had become "too hot." Considering first the September memorandum and now the disclosure about the meeting with Hesham Islam, the Joint Staff feared the wrath of Gordon England and his powerful aide. Coughlin was notified that his contract would not be renewed after March 2008.

He had been sacked. He thus became one of the casualties in the war of ideas against Islamist extremism. Only this time the enemy was not on Al Jazeera or jihadist websites. It was the liberal bureaucracy within the Pentagon, and other government agencies as well, abetted by liberal Republican political appointees. There would be no ideological challenge to Islamist extremism.

Sacked

When my item "Coughlin Sacked" appeared in the *Washington Times* on January 4, it was picked up and carried in the Pentagon's daily clipping service, called the "Early Bird." A coworker cut it out and came by Coughlin's desk to give it to him. Upon reading it, Coughlin said, "Yeah—who loves ya, baby!" The wry comment signaled that although Coughlin had many supporters at the senior levels, he had run afoul of the deputy secretary of defense and thus been a victim of Pentagon politics. It was obvious that others on the Joint Staff had their own doubts about Hesham Islam.

In fact, according to Pentagon sources, the Joint Staff official who fired Coughlin made it clear that he was not happy with the decision to let him go; the J-2 was just the messenger. "He went to bat for Steve often, and there is no reason to think he didn't do so this time," one defense official said. "The only conclusion is that England's office was involved."

Coughlin's support to the Joint Staff and the chiefs was invaluable, since only he could perform that complex ideological work. "There is no way in hell that they wanted to get rid of him and likely succumbed to pressure from above," the defense official said. "He did not intend to cancel his contract. He was making great headway within the [Joint Chiefs of Staff] and was excited about it, even though he had to start over every time personnel rotated out. He was particularly pleased to have the [Joint Staff intelligence directorate] stamp of approval on his briefings to war colleges and other groups." The official explained that Coughlin had not had that kind of support when he was working at Central Command, which surprisingly is even more politically correct and averse to waging ideological war against extremism than the Joint Staff.

Several current and former generals backed Coughlin, including Marine Corps major general Samuel Helland, commanding general of the First Marine Expeditionary Corps, who stated in a letter sent in November that Coughlin's briefing for Marines bound for Iraq "hit the mark in explaining how jihadists use the Koran to justify their actions."

"Your presentation has armed service men and women with more intellectual ammunition to take the fight to the enemy," Helland said.

Central Command counterterrorism analyst Neal Harper warned darkly in an e-mail to friends that if Coughlin was allowed to become a casualty in the war of ideas, "then I'm deeply concerned about the future course of the war on terrorism."

"Ignoring Steve Coughlin's honest assessments and terminating his contract sets a dangerous and disturbing precedent," Harper stated. "We struggled for many years to get our heads around radical Islam, and Steve has been a leader in the effort." Harper said Coughlin should be promoted, but instead "Hesham Islam is allowed to insult him publicly."

"How is it that he is allowed to call anyone a Christian zealot?" he asked. "This alone exposes his bias, his poor perception of Christians, and a complete lack of professionalism, at best. Should we instead be asking who is this guy and how did he get inside? Is he representative of those who are leading this Muslim outreach? Does Muslim outreach mean that we are not allowed to question or confront those we are trying to communicate with and the doctrine upon which they stand? When speaking the truth gets one fired, we all should be concerned and at the very least need to ask why."

The firing also sent shock waves through the U.S. intelligence community. Working-level spooks said it would hamper honest intelligence assessments. "The analyst now sees two threats to his work: the enemy and the uninformed policymaker," one analyst said. Officials noted that if the situation had been reversed and an analyst who supported politically correct Muslim outreach programs by the U.S. government were fired, the hue and cry would have been loud inside government and within the press. Instead, Coughlin, who questioned whether such outreach programs were legitimizing extremist front groups and their supporters, received little support from senior Bush administration policymakers, the Congress, or the liberal news media.

Pentagon public affairs bureaucrats did not stand by Coughlin at all. Supporting Gordon England and Hesham Islam, they responded with vitriol against reporters, like myself, who wrote about the story; they quietly suggested falsely that it was a campaign of "Muslim-bashing" by bigots.

Hesham Islam's "Outreach"

Coughlin was sent packing, but Hesham Islam was protected by his close relationship with the Pentagon's number-two official.

The October 2007 American Forces Press Service story that was posted on the Pentagon's website said that Islam's life had "all the makings of a Hollywood blockbuster." The piece claimed that he had endured bombings by Israeli jets in Egypt during the 1967 Six-Day War, had nearly been killed while working as a merchant seaman on an Iraqi freighter that was sunk in the Persian Gulf by an Iranian torpedo, and had worked in Iraq after his father set up a military academy there.

There was only one problem with this dramatic tale: Nothing could be found to verify these claims.

After investigative journalist Claudia Rosett raised serious questions about the veracity of Islam's stories, the Pentagon quietly removed the flattering biographical portrait from its website. But Islam refused to answer reporters' questions, and his spokesman, Kevin Wensing, only provided vague replies when asked about the discrepancies in Islam's bio.

The attention fueled speculation among U.S. intelligence and security officials about whether a Muslim Brotherhood sympathizer had penetrated the highest reaches of the Pentagon. It wasn't just doubts about Islam's bio, his role in the Muslim outreach program, or his confrontation with Stephen Coughlin. It also emerged that Islam was highly critical of Israel and the influence of American Jews on U.S. politics. In his master's thesis, written in 1992 at the Naval Postgraduate School, he put forth this argument, claiming that U.S. ties to Israel had harmed relations to other states in the Middle East.

Hesham Islam had become a trusted aide to Gordon England even before England became deputy defense secretary. While secretary of the Navy, England had picked up Islam as an assistant and used him for U.S. military engagement programs in the Middle East and elsewhere. "He's my interlocutor," England told the American Forces Press Service. "He represents me to the international community. He assists me in my own outreach efforts, and he's extraordinarily good at it." Islam also angered some White House officials when he began conducting his brand of personal diplomacy with Syria, a nation on the State Department list of state sponsors of terrorism.

One senior administration official said that he tried to question England's activities with Islam but was told, "Talk to Gates." It seemed Defense Secretary Robert Gates was protecting both England and Islam and the outreach program.

Pentagon spokesman Geoff Morrell said the department launched an investigation of Islam's comments about Coughlin, but by the spring of 2008, the Pentagon had quietly covered up the entire sordid affair. No real investigation was done by the Pentagon's inspector general or the Congress, despite the anti-Christian comments made by a senior aide to the number-two civilian official in the Pentagon. Morrell told me in April that "the deputy secretary's office has thoroughly reviewed the issues of concern raised by a few members of Congress and the media and has concluded there is no reason to question Commander Hesham Islam's credibility or his allegiance to his country."

According to the spokesman, England's investigators had determined that some things about the retired Navy commander's background remained "unknowable."

The deputy secretary's investigators also said that neither Islam nor England was behind the dismissal of Coughlin. Morrell said that Islam had assisted England for three years and was "a valuable adviser" who helped with England's contacts with foreign officials. England himself wrote to three members of Congress who had raised security concerns about Islam to state his support for the aide and the diplomatic outreach program he ran.

The final word came from Defense Secretary Robert Gates. After the secretary gave a speech at the Broadmoor Hotel in Colorado Springs, Claudia Rosett asked him about concerns raised by "Muslim groups with radical ties . . . sort of engaged heavily with the office of Deputy Secretary Gordon England." She also asked about "worrying signs" about Hesham Islam, "born in Cairo, schooled in Iraq, whose profile vanished from the Pentagon website when questions were raised about items in it which could not be substantiated." Rosett said to the defense secretary, "Has this crossed your radar at all? And if it has, could you explain to us why we should be confident this is all right?"

"I must say," Gates replied, "it has crossed my radar but it has been a very small blip. I don't believe I've met the gentleman in question [Islam]. But I have total confidence in Gordon England and in his ability to evaluate and judge quality people working for him."

Thus the bureaucracy continued on autopilot to undermine strategic efforts to wage ideological war against Islamist extremists.

STATE SUBVERSION

Days after the historic 1994 congressional elections that brought Republicans into the majority in both houses of Congress for the first time since 1946, Senator Jesse Helms, the new chairman of the Senate Foreign Relations Committee, wrote a letter to the secretary of state. Helms, the cigarette-smoking North Carolina Republican and pro-American conservative stalwart, made it clear to Warren Christopher that it would no longer be business as usual for liberal State Department appointees like Christopher and their acolytes in the Foreign Service.

The new Foreign Relations Committee chairman's convictions put him squarely at odds with the foreign policy establishment that dominated the State Department. He believed passionately that the United States needed moral foreign policies, that it must not appease dictators or go along with arms-control agreements that were not in America's best interests. But where Helms's goal was to serve America's national security and foreign policy interests, the unelected bureaucrats who controlled State, as the department is called, more often viewed the United States itself as the cause of the world's problems and a nation that needed to be shackled through international agreements.

The numerous "desks" in the State bureaucracy had long been known among conservatives for indirectly and sometimes directly promoting the interests of the states or regions they were in charge of producing policy for. Helms, who died in July 2008, argued that the State Department needed an "American Desk" to put U.S. interests back into the formulation and conduct of policy. "To the best of my ability," Helms wrote to Secretary of State Christopher, "the Foreign Relations Committee of the United States Senate will henceforth be that American desk for so long as I am chairman of the committee."

The problem Helms identified in 1994 has only grown worse. Under President George W. Bush, the State Department was overrun with liberal bureaucrats and foreign policy careerists who hijacked the pro-American policies Helms and others sought. Under Bush's first secretary of state, Colin Powell, a liberal, Nelson Rockefeller Republican, and his main assistant, former Pentagon official and Deputy Secretary of State Richard Armitage, the State Department spiraled out of control from a policy perspective. On vital strategic issues ranging from North Korea's nuclear weapons program, to the rise of Communist China, to the return of authoritarianism in Russia, to the failure to prevent the Syria-ization of Lebanon, to the rise of Cuban-style Communism in South America, U.S. power has been squandered and shackled.

Who is to blame? Ultimately, this was a failure of presidential leadership. The president never ensured that the people he appointed to key positions of power at the State Department promoted and carried out his policies. The subversion of those policies and the emergence of the State Department as the "Anti-America Department" is a story that has not been told.

Anticonservative Leadership

Colin Powell and Richard Armitage both spent long careers in the armed forces, something rarely seen among officials who have headed the generally antimilitary State Department. But if their background was different from that of many of their predecessors, they shared the same anticonservative outlook.

Powell worked numerous jobs in Washington before becoming secretary of state. He had had stints in Jimmy Carter's Pentagon, in Ronald Reagan's Pentagon, as Reagan's national security adviser, and as Bill Clinton's chairman of the Joint Chiefs of Staff, where he presided over the disastrous humanitarian intervention in Somalia. Powell was a Vietnam War veteran who became an antiwar advocate as a result. Under his theories on the use of force, which became known as the Powell Doctrine, military intervention could almost never be used. His theory was that overwhelming force is needed before undertaking any action, a strategy that partially worked in the 1991 Persian Gulf War but left Saddam Hussein in power.

Powell also supported arms-control treaties, even though they seemed always to produce the same outcome: the United States would scrupulously abide by their provisions while other signatories would ignore them with impunity. To devotees of arms control, results matter little. And these devotees have controlled the State Department's anti-American policies ever since the Clinton administration.

Armitage set the anticonservative tone in December 2000, shortly before his appointment to the State Department. He told the *Washington Post* that conservative critics of Powell's liberal political outlook, including former Reagan assistant defense secretary Frank Gaffney, were "pissants" because they did not have military service experience, a characteristic that was shared by Vice President Dick Cheney. "Frank Gaffney, Gary Bauer, these pissants who have never served in uniform—who would you rather have represent the nation, them or Colin Powell?" Armitage asked. Gaffney would later return the favor by identifying Armitage in a newspaper columnist as among the "disloyalists" within the Bush administration. Gaffney referred specifically to the fact that Armitage disclosed the identity of CIA operative Valerie Plame to a reporter but was never held accountable for it. Meanwhile an out-of-control prosecutor took it out on conservative Cheney aide I. Lewis "Scooter" Libby. Armitage faced no charges or even criticism for his role in the scandal and the dishonorable way he helped ruin Libby's career.

The appointment of Powell and Armitage, and the senior people they in turn put in place to help run the State Department, would do serious damage. As the top of the American diplomatic establishment, they oversaw the decline of U.S. diplomatic power throughout the world and did nothing to stop it. The mishandling of the North Korean nuclear crisis is the best example of how State turned U.S. foreign policy *against* America.

From a Hard Line to Appeasement

Early on in his administration, President Bush identified North Korea as part of an axis of evil in the world. But the people surrounding Powell and Armitage at the State Department made certain that the United States did not take a firm stance against this totalitarian state, where people are executed publicly for having a cellphone. By the end of Bush's administration, U.S. policy toward the Communist regime had become nothing less than appeasement. It seemed that no one at a senior State Department level was in charge.

Who was? It was career foreign service officer Christopher R. Hill, a liberal State Department apparatchik who was appointed assistant secretary of state for East Asian and Pacific Affairs in 2005. Prior to the appointment, Hill was U.S. ambassador to South Korea and previously to Poland, Serbia, and Albania. His liberal credentials were burnished while working on the staff of Congressman Stephen Solarz, New York Democrat, and in 1999 and 2000 he worked on President Clinton's National Security Council staff, as senior director for Southeast European Affairs. Hill's last official State Department biography carefully omitted the dates of his Clinton White House stint, but he played a role in negotiations on the Balkans that led to the Dayton Accords, and an ongoing U.S. commitment of troops to Bosnia.

Before being appointed to the assistant secretary position, Hill had been named the head of the U.S. government delegation to the six-party nuclear talks on North Korea. This position would overshadow his designated role as the key Asian affairs policymaker. It was in this role that Hill undermined conservatives within the Bush administration who sought to pressure North Korea into giving up its nuclear weapons.

Hill's North Korea policy was not the president's.

Not only did President Bush call North Korea one of three axis-of-evil states, he also was talking about Pyongyang when he promised in 2002 not to let the world's most dangerous regimes threaten the United States or its allies with weapons of mass destruction. By 2004, the president was adamant that North Korea must "completely, verifiably, and irreversibly dismantle its nuclear programs." He harshly criticized North Korean leader Kim Jong-il as a dictator who "starves" his people.

The administration backed up the rhetoric with tough policy. Under John Bolton, the conservative undersecretary of state for international security and arms control, and then his successor, Robert Joseph, the policy demanded that North Korea live up to its obligations in international nuclear treaties not to develop nuclear arms and also that it abide by the fraudulent 1994 Agreed Framework—the nuclear agreement negotiated with the Clinton administration—and dismantle its arms. As I disclosed in my 1999 book *Betrayal,* the Agreed Framework was designed to fail, since it had no verification procedures and gave the North Koreans ten years to dismantle their weapons program and five years to turn over their stockpile of plutonium. By early 1999, the Department of Energy intelligence office discovered what was to become a crisis within several years: solid intelligence revealing that the North Korean Daesong Yashin Trading Company was trying to buy "frequency converters" from a Japanese company in order to power gas centrifuges that would be linked together in a cascade. They would later get uranium enrichment help from the Pakistani supplier network led by A. Q. Khan, considered the father of Pakistan's nuclear arms program.

Vice President Dick Cheney ratcheted up the pressure on North Korea by saying in 2004 that "time is not on our side" in dealing with Pyongyang's refusal to give up its nuclear weapons.

But by 2005, the entire tone of the president's policy had changed for the worse. Pressure gave way to accommodation under the bureaucrats led by Hill. The new plan called for convincing North Korea to give up its nuclear programs using four other nations—China, South Korea, Japan, and Russia. But it was doomed to failure.

In calling for these six-party talks, the arms-control–oriented bureaucrats changed the rules. Bolton's policy of "CVID"—complete, verifiable, irreversible dismantlement—was jettisoned. In its place, the bureaucrats added a new term that was a concession: "disable." That is, the United States now merely called for the North Koreans to disable rather than completely dismantle their nuclear facilities.

The change came after Condoleezza Rice became secretary of state at the beginning of Bush's second term. According to officials close to the issue, the State Department bureaucrats were given total control over the North Korea talks. When Rice vacated the position of national security adviser, she was replaced by her second in command, Stephen Hadley. As national security adviser he continued functioning as if he was still her deputy rather than an independent adviser to the president. As a result Bush was not given the better policy options that he needed, leading to a policy that went horribly awry.

The shift in policy no doubt brought smiles to the faces of North Koreans. As in the past, they took the American accommodation and then demanded more.

The entire rationale for making the talks a six-nation forum was to avoid a repeat of the failed diplomacy of 1994 and the Agreed

Framework. But Hill turned around and completely undercut the six-party talks by meeting one-on-one with his North Korean counterpart, Kim Kye Gwan, in Berlin in January 2007, and then again in Singapore in April 2008.

The failed Chris Hill policy of endless negotiations and endless U.S. concessions emboldened North Korea not to completely dismantle in a verifiable way, or to fully disclose, its nuclear programs. Pyongyang missed three deadlines for providing a complete and full accounting of its nuclear programs, and still the United States ignored the violations. A State Department official went so far as to say that even though North Korea did not provide the required declaration of its nuclear programs, the United States was willing to take the Communist state off the list of state sponsors of international terrorism, a place it had earned when its agents began blowing up jetliners and South Korean cabinet officials in overseas attacks through the 1980s. Additionally, the U.S. Treasury Department bowed to the North Koreans' demand that it return money obtained by drug trafficking and other illegal activities that the United States had frozen. The U.S. government required North Korea to do nothing in return for getting the dirty money back.

North Korea showed its arrogance in October 2006, when it set off its first underground nuclear test. While the test was only partially successful, it placed North Korea in the exclusive group of nuclear powers.

Then in September 2007, an event took place that confirmed North Korean conniving and deception, though the State Department tried to ignore its enormous significance in order to protect the failing negotiations with the Pyongyang regime. Israeli warplanes conducted a secret aerial strike deep inside eastern Syria. Shortly after the raid, reports surfaced that the target was thought to be some kind of a nuclear facility, but State bureaucrats managed to keep the information secret, complying with Israeli wishes, for seven months. The Israelis feared that disclosing the information too soon would trigger a war with Syria; the State Department bureaucrats only wanted to protect their precious talks.

Finally, during a briefing for reporters, senior U.S. intelligence officials in April 2008 provided shocking details of the Israeli raid on a building along the Euphrates River at al Kibar. The building that was destroyed had been a joint Syrian–North Korean nuclear weapons facility modeled after the reactor at Yongbyon. So while North Korea had been negotiating the dismantlement of its nuclear weapons program, it was secretly helping a state sponsor of international terrorism to develop its own nuclear weapons. "The nuclear cooperation [in Syria] shows extremely bad faith on the part of the North Koreans," one congressional aide said about the Communist regime.

Jay Lefkowitz, the Bush administration's special envoy to North Korea on human rights, finally blew the whistle on the State Department appeasement. Lefkowitz, a New York lawyer who was not part of the bureaucracy, gave a speech in January 2008 in which he stated the obvious: "North Korea is not serious about disarming in a timely manner. . . . It is increasingly likely that North Korea will have the same nuclear status one year from now that it has today."

Secretary of State Condoleezza Rice sided with Hill and the bureaucrats and denounced Lefkowitz as not speaking for the administration. "He doesn't know what's going on in the six-party talks, and he certainly has no say on what American policy will be in the six-party talks," Rice declared.

But Lefkowitz knew full well what the six-party talks entailed, and the problems he saw prompted him to speak out publicly against the policy—a rare step for a senior administration official to take. The six-party talks, Lefkowitz noted, had deliberately excluded discussions of North Korea's human rights abuses. But Lefkowitz had, in his role as envoy, been steeped in the details of North Korea's gross violations of human rights. This savage totalitarian system kills its people for exercising even the most basic freedoms, such as listening to foreign radio broadcasts or communicating outside the country via cellular telephone. "The way the North Korean government treats its own people is inhumane and therefore deeply offensive to us," Lefkowitz said.

After months and months of delays, in June 2008 the North Korean regime finally presented its so-called declaration on its nuclear programs, supposedly providing a complete accounting. But the declaration omitted any information about North Korea's covert uranium enrichment program, the trigger for the entire nuclear crisis. It made no mention of Syria, either. And it lacked any kind of effective verification mechanism.

Nevertheless, the U.S. government encouraged North Korea's potentially deadly nuclear charade. Chris Hill defended the declaration's crucial omission of uranium by stating that the six-nation talks would continue to address uranium enrichment. And the Bush administration leaped to offer still more concessions to the totalitarian regime—most notably by following through on the idea of removing North Korea from the list of state sponsors of terrorism.

We had come a long way since the president's unapologetic proclamation that North Korea formed part of the "axis of evil."

North Korea's subsequent actions only mocked American weakness. According to U.S. officials familiar with the six-party talks that followed in Beijing in July, North Korean negotiator Kim Kye Gwan repeatedly insisted that North Korea had in fact become a nuclear-weapons power—a position Hill rejected. And as a further humiliation, Pyongyang refused to permit International Atomic Energy Agency inspectors back into the country to verify North Korea's claims to have disabled its nuclear program.

This is what the United States got for its concessions.

Turning Point: Iraq

With the U.S. invasion of Iraq in March 2003, the liberal State Department bureaucrats turned on President Bush and his administration with a vengeance. The Iraq War was a war the State Department opposed and fought against, through both Powell and

Armitage—not just when the administration was weighing the option of going to war but even after American soldiers were sent into harm's way and the war had become the official policy of the United States.

The bureaucrats' view was presented in the 2004 book by *Washington Post* reporter Bob Woodward, *Plan of Attack*. Woodward, whose typewriter keys moved in concert with Armitage's spin, put forward the thesis that Bush decided early on that he was going to war to remove Saddam Hussein and never even considered State's holy of holies, diplomacy. Powell, a soldier by training, opposed the plan for war and favored the endless diplomacy, or at the very least sending at least three times as many troops to Iraq as the 150,000 that were ultimately dispatched.

Powell is to blame for the failure due to picking the wrong people to support him at the State Department. His chief of staff, Lawrence Wilkerson, is the prime example. According to people who worked with Wilkerson at State, the retired Army colonel was an incompetent chief of staff who knew very little about diplomacy. Wilkerson's lack of experience contributed to the failure of the United States to use its diplomatic power to win support for the Iraq War—a major strategic blunder that undermined the entire military effort to oust Saddam Hussein.

In the months leading up to the conflict the Powell team—Powell, Armitage, and Wilkerson—did not make one trip to key European countries like France and Germany to muster diplomatic support for U.S. military action against Iraq.

Worse, the Powell team utterly failed to gain the support of Turkey for the military operation, again by not traveling to Turkey to meet with Turkish leaders. This failure blocked the plan to have the U.S. First Infantry Division enter Iraq from the north, across the Turkish border.

Powell, Armitage, and Wilkerson also were naïve to think that Iran would play a constructive role in Iraq, and they accepted uncritically an Iranian offer of such help shortly after the 2003 invasion. Others in the administration knew full well that Iran could never be

trusted, and they were proved correct, as Iranian intelligence continued to arm insurgents through 2008.

Wilkerson later became a liberal critic of the Bush administration
for its prosecution of the war in Iraq and for its detention of Islamic
terrorists in Guantánamo Bay, Cuba. In November 2005, months after
he left the State Department, he told the BBC that the postinvasion
planning for Iraq was "as inept and incompetent as perhaps any planning anyone has ever done." The main problem, he seemed to be saying,
was that he and Powell were not included in the planning. Wilkerson
pinned the blame on Vice President Dick Cheney and Defense Secretary Donald Rumsfeld, who, he said, led what he called an "alternative
decision-making process" that excluded the State Department.

But according to Defense officials involved in the planning, it was
the State Department and the U.S. Central Command leader, Army
general Tommy Franks, who were to blame for the postinvasion fi-
asco. Franks refused a direct order from Rumsfeld in the months leading up to the invasion to map out a "Phase 4" plan for Iraq, stating
that it was not his job and that the State Department would have to
do the postwar operations. Douglas Feith, the undersecretary of defense for policy, then sent a team of several hundred Pentagon and
military officials to the Pentagon's Joint Forces Command in Norfolk,
Virginia, to draw up a three-hundred-page postwar plan for Iraq. But
as Feith revealed in his 2008 book *War and Decision,* the plan was ignored, first by Franks, and then by the civilian head of the U.S.-led
occupation forces, L. Paul Bremer, a former State Department official.
The Pentagon plan called for putting Iraqi expatriates, or "externals,"
like Ahmed Chalabi into positions to run the new Iraq government.
Bremer, however, joined with State bureaucrats in opposing this plan,
instead getting rid of the entire official infrastructure and disbanding
the Iraqi military, with disastrous consequences.

Wilkerson's betrayal of the Bush administration bordered on the
pathological. Any anti-Bush outlet he could find would easily put him
on the air or print his quotes. Wilkerson claimed that the liberals in

the administration, led by Powell, wanted to do things much differently and that Cheney and Rumsfeld were criminals. "If what you say is correct, in your view, is Dick Cheney then guilty of a war crime?" the BBC interviewer asked Wilkerson.

"Well, that's an interesting question. . . . It was certainly a domestic crime to advocate terror and I would suspect that it is—for whatever it's worth—an international crime as well."

The real policy criminals are the likes of Wilkerson, who described himself as a Republican but who accused Congress of failing to provide oversight of the Bush administration. "I'm a Republican and that makes me mad," he said. "My party is not the party that I became a member of many years ago. The Congress as a whole should have been exercising its oversight." Wilkerson also proposed that Bush and Cheney be impeached for "high crimes and misdemeanors" while dismissing Bill Clinton's impeachment as little more than the result of his "peccadilloes."

His political coloration became clear in 2006, when he defected to the Democrats to endorse conservative turncoat Jim Webb for the Senate; Webb ran and won as a liberal Democrat after having served in the Reagan administration as Navy secretary.

For the State Department, Iraq was the beginning of an anti-Bush movement that continued to the end of his presidency. Anti-Bush posters began showing up inside State Department offices. No one at the political-appointee level would defend the president or even challenge the anti-Bush posters, which were only the outward manifestation of the policies that were aimed at defeating the president.

Taking Down Bolton

Powell and Armitage were outflanked at only one level of the department by a conservative. That was John Bolton, who would be influential in setting policy aimed at protecting U.S. national security. As the undersecretary for arms control and international security, he headed up the State Department bureau that was once the independent U.S. Arms Control and Disarmament Agency. Bolton got his job because of his credentials as a Reagan State Department appointee and protégé to Jeane Kirkpatrick when she served as U.S. ambassador to the United Nations. He would be the lone bright spot in an otherwise dark State Department.

As Bolton would later recount in his book *Surrender Is Not an Option*, the Bush administration in its early days achieved real results on curtailing North Korea's missile and nuclear tests by taking a hard line. "Strong diplomacy in the [United Nations] Security Council," he wrote, "produced two tough resolutions" against the North Koreans—resolutions that passed despite the initial objections of China and Russia.

But out-of-control bureaucrats gained the upper hand midway through the Bush presidency and weakened the North Korea policy. As Bolton observed, "Weak diplomacy in the six-party talks has allowed North Korea to consolidate and solidify its nuclear posture and taken the United States down the same road as the failed 1994 Agreed Framework." On February 13, 2007, the six parties issued a Joint Statement in Beijing. It stated that North Korea would shut down and seal the Yongbyon nuclear facility and would also provide a full and complete accounting of its plutonium- and uranium-enrichment programs by December 31, 2007, and in exchange, the five other nations would provide heavy fuel oil to North Korea. The deal was announced with great fanfare, but Bolton rightly called it "radically incomplete," since it did not deal properly with North Korea's existing nuclear weapons, much less its covert uranium-enrichment program. Sure enough, December 31 came and went—yet another deadline that North Korea missed to provide a full accounting of its enrichment programs. And the North Koreans skipped this deadline even after the U.S. Treasury Department released funds that had been frozen in a Macao bank as punishment for North Korean counterfeiting of U.S. currency.

John Bolton revealed that the bureaucrats were particularly strong in the State Department's East Asia–Pacific Bureau, known as EAP, where they are dubbed "EAPeasers" because of their penchant for appeasement over tough diplomacy and action. This was the bureau Assistant Secretary of State Christopher Hill oversaw.

Bolton understood well that America's enemies could not and should not be taken at their word. He recognized the importance of the fundamental principle of international affairs set by Ronald Reagan in dealing with the Soviet Union. Reagan would say to the world that while he was willing to talk, even negotiate arms reductions with Moscow, he believed in the Russian phrase *"Doveryay, no proveryay"*—"Trust, but verify." In this regard Bolton was just the kind of conservative the liberal arms-control devotees hated. Not surprisingly, then, he was reviled by bureaucrats within the State Department, especially Assistant Secretary of State John Wolf, who was known for viciously criticizing his subordinates.

Wolf would become a leading critic of Bolton in the spring of 2005, when Bolton was nominated to be the U.S. ambassador to the United Nations. This is when the bureaucrats sought revenge on Bolton for taking a hard conservative line on policy. They and their liberal Democrat collaborators mounted a full-scale smear campaign against him to try to scuttle his nomination.

While Wolf and other bureaucrats led the assault at State, the most significant figure on Capitol Hill battling to kill Bolton's nomination was a key aide to Senator Christopher Dodd of Connecticut. Senator Dodd was one of the public faces of the anti-Bolton campaign, but just as important was the work being done behind the scenes by his staffer Janice O'Connell, a left-wing, pro-Castro specialist who had been a fixture for decades on the Senate Foreign Relations Committee. O'Connell, according to administration officials, knew that Bolton was a key player in blocking liberal State Department policies and used her position to lobby Democratic senators against him.

To justify their vehement anti-Bolton campaign, Democrats accused him, falsely, of being brusque with subordinates and also of pressuring intelligence analysts over assessments of Cuba's biological weapons program. In fact, good intelligence indicated that Cuba was developing just such a program, but liberal State Department intelligence officials vigorously sought to play down or ignore all intelligence on Cuban weapons of mass destruction.

The liberals also accused Bolton of being too strident by calling North Korean leader Kim Jong-il a "tyrannical dictator" during a 2003 speech. State bureaucrats opposed the remark because it undermined the incredibly weak policy toward North Korea advocated by arms control advocates like Chris Hill.

But it was Wolf who tried the hardest to betray his former boss. Wolf had worked for Bolton as the assistant secretary of state for nonproliferation. He left the department to head a nonprofit group in Philadelphia, but he was among those who attacked Bolton for his manner with staffers. A copy of Wolf's April 28, 2005, testimony to the Senate Foreign Relations Committee staff revealed that he said Bolton "tended to have a fairly blunt manner expressing himself."

It was an odd charge coming from Wolf, who clashed frequently with Bolton's aides, trying to stop them from instituting tougher policies and sanctions against those who wanted to ignore dangerous arms transfers to rogue states. According to officials who worked with him, Wolf on several occasions lost his temper and screamed at coworkers over policy issues.

In one case, the officials told me, Wolf argued with a Pentagon official in 2001 over China's arms sales to rogue states. He said that China should not be sanctioned by the United States for illegal arms sales, but the Pentagon official told him in no uncertain terms that the Bush administration was no longer following the Clinton policy of ignoring Chinese arms proliferation.

During another meeting, Wolf was so abusive to another official, Assistant Secretary of State Paula DeSutter, that she feared for her safety, officials revealed. Like Bolton, DeSutter was a conservative— the worst of sins in the State Department.

According to the transcript of his testimony, Wolf was asked about these incidents. He admitted that they had occurred, though he did not acknowledge any broader temper issue. "It is true that at times I lost my temper in a couple of cases with people who were not at my level," Wolf said. "And I remember apologizing to both."

The ostensible complaints against Bolton were flimsy at best. The real reason so many liberal bureaucrats and politicians rallied to block his nomination was simply that he was a conservative who would not kowtow to their soft approach to international affairs. He dared to put U.S. national security first, and for that he would pay the price.

Senate Democrats filibustered in the summer of 2005, preventing a vote on his nomination, so President Bush made a recess appointment. Bolton served honorably and effectively at the United Nations in seeking to stem the flow of arms to rogue states and unstable regions, but the liberal campaign against him was unrelenting. Ultimately the combination of liberal Democrat Senate pressure and State Department bureaucratic perfidy proved to be too much. Bolton withdrew his nomination at the end of his recess appointment, in late 2006.

It was another scalp for the bureaucrats and their Democratic allies.

Diplomatic Revolt

As Bolton put it in his 2007 memoir, the serious cultural problems of the State Department need to be addressed on an urgent basis. "Succeeding secretaries of state have ignored reforming the department, leaving it essentially to run itself, which has only allowed the problem to fester and grow, to the point where our capacity to advocate American interests in foreign affairs is now severely impaired," Bolton stated.

The State Department's approach to the Iraq War is particularly shameful. Many diplomats have played an important role in providing assistance to Iraq by joining the State Department's provincial reconstruction teams. But the department has not been able to fill the several hundred positions in the U.S. embassy in Baghdad that was opened in 2004. The problem got so bad that in October 2007, State announced that because there were not enough Foreign Service volunteers for duty in Iraq, as many as fifty diplomats would be required to go to Baghdad. Although the department badly needed specialists to help stabilize Iraq, the diplomats simply did not want to go to the hardship post.

The diplomats' revolt was captured in the comments of Foreign Service officer Jack Crotty, who joined several hundred others during a town hall–style meeting at the State Department to criticize the forced assignment. "Incoming is coming in every day," Crotty said. "Rockets are hitting the Green Zone. So if you force-assign people, that is really shifting the terms of what we're all about. It's one thing if someone believes in what's going on over there and volunteers. But it's another thing to send someone over there on a forced assignment. And I'm sorry, but basically that's a potential death sentence, and you know it."

The clear implication was that the diplomats did not believe in the mission of Iraq: transforming an outpost of repression and terrorism into a center point for democratic and political reform in the heart of the Middle East.

A survey conducted by the American Foreign Service Association (AFSA), the diplomats' union, confirmed that the diplomatic corps' refusal to serve did not just involve concerns about personal safety but were largely about disagreement with the president's policies. The survey found that a majority of officers would not volunteer for Iraq missions because of "disagreement with policy."

So as diplomats it was their job to represent their country, but apparently they would now pick and choose when they felt comfortable serving their nation.

Congressman Duncan Hunter, a California Republican and ranking member of the House Armed Services Committee, was so incensed by the bureaucrats' refusal to serve in Iraq that he recommended firing all Foreign Service officers who declined to serve in Iraq. There was just one problem: Under federal employment rules it is almost impossible to fire federal workers, short of an employee engaging in illegal conduct.

Burns and the "Gutless Wonders"

A central figure in the State Department's failures during the Bush administration was Nicholas Burns, the undersecretary of state for political affairs, the number-three official in all of State. Burns was a liberal Democrat who had been the department's spokesman during the Clinton administration. Like other Clinton holdovers, Burns damaged U.S. national security policy during his years at the top of the foreign policy bureaucracy.

Any objective review of Burns's past role in the Clinton administration would have signaled that his loyalties were not with a Republican president. He got his political experience while working on the Clinton National Security Council staff, where he served as the top Eurasian affairs specialist from 1990 to 1995.

Burns, an ambassador to Greece and to the North Atlantic Treaty Organization (NATO) during George W. Bush's first term, carefully cultivated the new secretary of state in Bush's second term, Condoleezza Rice. Secretary Rice was a well-meaning liberal Republican who was loyal to Bush even though she did not agree politically with the president on many issues. Burns was among the most vociferous of the administration's liberal "conservative-haters," having spoken out against this writer and those in the State Department who sought to expose the policy crimes of the Clinton administration.

During a June 21, 1996, briefing, for example, Burns was asked to comment on my *Washington Times* report about North Korea shipping Scud missiles to Egypt. Burns expressed his anger that it involved "yet again another leaked document that made its way to the *Washington Times*." He added, "I think that the people who leaked the document are petty and they're gutless. Because once again, they have taken on a person in the State Department and they have tried to knife somebody in the State Department by leaking a document to the *Washington Times*. And if they had any ethics, they would fight this fairly. They're not doing it."

The veracity of the story seemed almost irrelevant to the State Department spokesman. Asked about the substance of the issue—that a nation, Egypt, that received $2 billion annually from the United States was buying missiles from a terrorist state like North Korea—Burns paid lip service to taking seriously such reports of arms transfers but said nothing to indicate that any real action would be taken to deal with the problem. He returned instead to complaining about the "gutless wonders" who were leaking documents "to fight interagency battles."

For Burns and the Foreign Service policy mafia, the most important objective was to prevent the United States from using military force again after the March 2003 invasion of Iraq. In other words, his was a policy of diplomacy no matter what. Burns interfered with efforts by conservatives in the administration, namely John Bolton and his successor Robert Joseph, to pressure both the Iranians and the North Koreans into abiding by the very arms-control agreements that liberal bureaucrats like Burns venerated.

Burns ensured that the United States would not be able to apply pressure on Iran over its nuclear program—specifically, *military* pressure. First, he made sure U.S. policy on Iran was subordinated to the joint policy of governments of Britain, France, and Germany. He thus prevented a real resolution of the Iranian nuclear crisis, which continues today. He also was a major force inside the Bush administration against using military force to stop the covert Iranian arms and explosives assistance to the Iraqi insurgency. Burns was among the policymakers in the State Department who accepted at face value Iranian government denials about the covert arms shipments. Those denials, however, continued to be exposed as false: Iranian-made weapons have regularly been discovered in Iraq, including extremely deadly, explosively formed projectiles that were specifically designed to kill American troops in their armored vehicles.

First and foremost, the bureaucrats needed to block the military, and they succeeded by forcing the resignation of Donald Rumsfeld as secretary of defense. Rumsfeld, while not a Reagan-style conservative, understood high-level politics and was a formidable interagency player in preventing the bureaucrats from having their way with national security policy. His ouster in 2006 (engineered, as will be shown later, by White House chief of staff Joshua Bolten, a Big Government Republican) began a policy slide that continued throughout the Bush administration's final days.

The liberal bureaucrats took a major step toward cutting the military option out of the U.S. foreign policy arsenal in early 2008. The State Department announced that it was doubling the number of diplomatic advisers to military commanders domestically and internationally. These State Department advisers—known as "polads," for political advisers—are loyal not to the U.S. military's Joint Chiefs of Staff or to the secretary of defense, or arguably even to the commander in chief. They instead answer to State.

Thus the department's agenda of appeasement and handcuffing U.S. power is being significantly strengthened. The number of polads has increased from about a dozen prior to the 9/11 attacks to thirty today. The State Department has exploited this growth as a way to take over efforts to use military power as a component of U.S. foreign policy. For example, it can now undermine the U.S. Pacific Command in dealing with China and North Korea, and the U.S. Central Command in waging war against Islamist extremism.

State has made so many inroads into the military that for the first time in modern U.S. history a Foreign Service officer was named to the rank of deputy commander of a U.S. military command. In September 2007, the newly formed U.S. Africa Command, based in Stuttgart, Germany, named senior diplomat Mary Carlin Yates deputy commander for civil-military activities. The fact that a diplomat could achieve such a high rank in the command showed that the U.S. Africa Command's mission was more diplomatic and humanitarian than military.

Prior to joining the U.S. Africa Command, Yates was the polad to the U.S. European Command and according to her bio "provided critical 'reach-back'" to the State Department. In other words, her main function was to make sure the command adopted the same appeasement-oriented and nonwarrior policies as the State Department.

Soft on Soft Power

Defense Secretary Robert Gates went along with the move to double the number of State Department polads, ostensibly to bolster America's use of so-called soft power—that is, ideological weaponry. But the truth is, the State Department long ago abandoned any attempt to use power, soft or hard, in the furtherance of American influence around the world.

Or as one senior U.S. intelligence official bluntly told me, "There is no soft power."

The campaign against terrorism is being fought on three levels: military; intelligence and law enforcement; and finally, the so-called war of ideas. On the first two, the U.S. government has done moderately well. But in the arena of ideas, it is losing; this is one of the bureaucrats' biggest failures. As Defense Secretary Gates put it, the United States is "miserable at communicating to the rest of the world what we are about as a society and a culture." Unless we can find the formula for waging ideological war, there will be no victory.

Historians will view February 19, 2002, as a dark day in the war on terrorism. On that day the *New York Times* reported on a program that was as important to the war on terrorism as the deployment of strategic nuclear forces was during the Cold War. The *Times* reported that the Pentagon's Office of Strategic Influence, created a month after the September 11 terrorist attacks, was the Pentagon's arm for waging "information warfare" and had plans to plant false news stories around the world.

The article prompted a backlash that continued nonstop for days. Defense Secretary Rumsfeld eventually caved in to liberal political pressure to kill the office, which had plans to spend up to $100 million to counter terrorist propaganda. An angry Rumsfeld told reporters on February 27, 2002, "The office is done. What do you want, blood?" The defense secretary understood that the office was a vital component in the war on terrorism and that ultimately victory would be achieved not through guns and bombs, or even secret snatch operations and covert action, but through ideas designed to defeat terrorists using their own perverted extremist Islamic ideology.

But the Pentagon agreed to disarm itself and could no longer take offensive action in the realm of ideas. That role had been shifted to the State Department, which since the end of the Cold War had been extremely ill-equipped to deal with what it called public diplomacy—the promulgation of ideas in support of American policies. After the Cold War the U.S. Information Agency, or USIA, had been folded into the State Department under a reorganization pushed, ironically, by Senator Jesse Helms, who unknowingly had undermined the promotion of American ideals despite recognizing the urgent need for an American desk at the department. The reorganization gutted the expertise and specialization that USIA had gained during the long twilight struggle, mainly ideological, against the Soviet Union and its empire.

In its place was left a less effective State Department undersecretariat for public diplomacy, headed by a succession of liberal nonprofessionals who left the United States essentially defenseless against its enemies, both true foes and so-called friends.

The first undersecretary was the Clinton administration deputy White House chief of staff Evelyn S. Lieberman, a public relations executive who in 2008 headed the presidential election campaign of Hillary Rodham Clinton.

Lieberman was followed by a Madison Avenue advertising executive, Charlotte Beers, who was appointed to the position in October 2001 and remained until 2003. As chairman of the advertising firm of Ogilvy & Mather, Beers was considered one of the most powerful women in America. But as America's public diplomat, she proved to be an utter failure. While she was in the position, she produced a series of slick video and media ads that were supposed to influence Muslim-majority nations, where anti-Americanism runs rampant and little is being done to counter it. Her main effort was a program called "Shared Values" that sought to portray American Muslims to other audiences around the world. Without an understanding of the true nature of the terrorist enemy, the campaign failed and Beers left office.

Following Beers was Margaret Tutwiler, who had been the State Department spokeswoman under Secretary of State James A. Baker, a typical country-club Republican liberal, during the Reagan and first Bush administration. She tried her hand at public diplomacy, with equally failed results. Tutwiler would quit shortly after prison photos were published showing U.S. Army abuse of prisoners at Iraq's Abu Ghraib.

President George W. Bush then turned to a trusted aide, liberal Republican Karen Hughes, to take on the difficult task of public diplomacy at State. Hughes's experience, however, was limited to political defense, in running Bush's Texas government and later his presidential campaigns. She had no understanding of the nature of the Islamist terrorist threat and thus spent most of her time traveling to the Middle East and going on Arabic television shows to try to tell audiences how much the United States liked the Middle East and Muslims.

Hughes approached public diplomacy like a U.S. political campaign, a model ill-suited for countering Islamist extremist ideology, which requires going on the offensive. She set up rapid-response units and sought to deploy regional public diplomacy "SWAT" teams. But the effort again was insufficient. Hughes was privately urged to wage ideological war on Islamist extremism by developing a critique-and-counterproposal approach to the problem—in essence, using the religion of Islam to prompt antiextremist Muslims to declare the terrorists "un-Islamic." But the idea was ignored. Hughes resigned in December 2007 and was replaced by American Enterprise Institute specialist James Glassman, who came into the position with only a few months left in the Bush administration's second term and a bureaucracy at the department that remained hostile to the administration and its political appointees.

Hughes signed on to the wrongheaded State Department view that the only solution to the war on terrorism was to punish Israel and make it succumb to its enemies. In an October 2007 Internet exchange in Washington, Hughes was asked about opposition to U.S. policies in the Middle East. Discussing the Israeli-Palestinian issue, she said that "President Bush made it the official policy of the U.S. that we support the creation of a Palestinian state, living side by side in peace with Israel," as if this would resolve the problem. As Natan Sharansky, the former Russian dissident who is now an Israeli political leader, put it in his book *The Case for Democracy,* the Palestinians' problem is that their leaders are corrupt and have ignored the plight of their own people for decades, preferring instead to wage terrorist war against Israel.

The standard liberal notion is that if only Israel were not such a close U.S. ally, Muslim extremists would go back to being moderates. The idea is totally false. The al Qaeda terrorists who carried out the 9/11 attacks had no interest in supporting the Palestinians until years after the attacks, when support for their extremist actions began to fade.

Intelligence Failure

by Design

By now the U.S. government should have radically reformed the way it gathers information and conducts secret operations around the world. The September 11 terrorist attacks and the U.S. intelligence community's failures related to Iraq, as well as a seemingly endless string of spy cases showing an inability to counter foreign espionage, have clearly demonstrated the need for fundamental changes. But even today the sixteen different intelligence agencies, which together cost nearly $44 billion annually, remain mired in bureaucracy, legalistic restrictions, political correctness, and a self-congratulatory culture that poses one of the most serious dangers to U.S. national security.

As threats to American security grow more dangerous, U.S. intelligence agencies are unprepared and ill-structured to meet the challenges. The problem is that the senior leadership of the institutions in charge of American national security has aggressively opposed urgently needed reforms, making the country more vulnerable and less prepared to meet the threats posed by terrorists, who are constantly evolving their techniques, and by enemy nations. U.S. intelligence agencies, by their refusal to reform, are actually endangering the country, rather than protecting it.

These deep-seated problems can be seen in both domestic and

overseas programs. Domestically, years after the country was attacked by Islamist extremists, the intelligence capability against radicals within this country remains virtually nonexistent. And internationally, FBI, Justice Department, and Pentagon efforts have focused less on tracking down terrorists and countering the threat of Islamist radicalism and more on politically correct policies to engage in "community outreach" programs with groups linked to international Muslim extremists, in a naïve and counterproductive effort to mitigate the threat.

Terrorist Groups Infiltrate U.S. Spy Agencies

The 9/11 and pre–Iraq War intelligence failures have been well documented, but shockingly, similar failures are occurring even today. One of the most disturbing cases involves U.S.-based spies for Hezbollah, the Iranian-backed international terrorist organization, who were able to gain access to the highest levels of the FBI and CIA. The Hezbollah penetration highlights the dangers these radical groups pose to America, as well as the fact that both agencies remain mired in bureaucratic problems that limit their ability to adequately protect the country.

On June 24, 1989, Nada Nadim Prouty, a nineteen-year-old Lebanese national, entered the United States posing as a student. A year later she paid a man in the Detroit area to pose as her husband, allowing her to obtain permanent residence status and, ultimately, U.S. citizenship. Ten years later, Prouty was sworn in as an FBI special agent.

In reality, U.S. counterintelligence officials say, she was a spy for Hezbollah.

During her years in the FBI and later in the CIA, she conducted one of the most damaging penetrations of U.S. intelligence in history, according to the counterintelligence officials. Her case is particularly shocking because of who she was spying for: one of the world's deadliest terrorist organizations. Foreign intelligence services have been trying to penetrate U.S. intelligence for many years—and have often succeeded. But this is the first major case showing that weak U.S. counterintelligence makes American spy agencies vulnerable to penetration not only by foreign intelligence but even by international terrorist organizations.

Prouty joined the FBI in 1999 during the Clinton administration, when politically correct diversity in the workforce was the order of the day and women and minorities were actively recruited. In Prouty's case, a Muslim woman was even more of a diversity coup for the Bureau and its liberal masters in the bureaucracy.

The problem persists. Instead of refashioning U.S. intelligence agencies to be the best at stealing secrets abroad from both foreign governments and terrorist groups, J. Michael McConnell, the director of National Intelligence, or DNI, has said "diversity" is a priority for all sixteen intelligence agencies. But the kind of diversity he is talking about is counterproductive to intelligence-gathering. Instead of hiring Asians and Arabic-language speakers, the agencies are simply trying to fill quotas for minorities and women. This politically correct diversity does not serve the goal of spying on America's enemies, and often inhibits it, as the Prouty case shows.

The FBI prided itself on conducting rigorous background checks of all applicants, but Prouty slipped through the cracks. The vaunted background check system failed utterly to identify her as a mole for Hezbollah, when even the most cursory of checks would have determined that her first marriage had been a sham. What makes the case even more devastating was that she was able to defeat not only the FBI's background system but also that of the CIA Directorate of Operations, considered the holy of holies for American intelligence gathering.

How could such a stunning security lapse happen? The answer can be found by examining the bureaucratic mindset on display in both the FBI and CIA recruiting efforts.

"Female Special Agents are critical members of the FBI team," one recruiting page on the FBI website says. "They contribute unique and important perspectives, experiences, and skills. In many cases, women possess different analytical skills, approach problems differently, and have different talents and abilities than do men. These different skills, approaches, and talents often spell the difference between success and failure on a case or investigation."

According to the FBI, investigative teams composed of a blend of female and male special agents "are much more effective at bringing complex investigations to a speedy and successful resolution." How this conclusion was reached is not explained. But the web page says some women are hesitant to apply to the Bureau because of certain "misperceptions," such as that law-enforcement or related experience is required or that "agents must be men."

"Nothing could be further from the truth," the website explains. "Women with a variety of different backgrounds play an influential role in the effective operation of the Federal Bureau of Investigation." It adds that the FBI recognizes "the tremendous value female Special Agents bring to the FBI."

After the Prouty spy case was publicly exposed, the FBI made no mention of her "tremendous value." Court papers in the case reveal that Prouty was nominated to be "female FBI agent of the year," and served on the advance team for a trip to the Middle East for FBI director Louis Freeh. The Bureau was too embarrassed to admit that its political correctness in seeking to add women to its workforce of special agents (some 2,000 of the 12,000 special agents are women) had resulted in a security disaster for the United States, which is currently engaged in a war against the same people Prouty was secretly linked to.

The FBI trumpets its supposedly rigorous background-check system in an explanation to new applicants. All candidates face a background investigation, because "the mission of the FBI is vital to the safety and security of our nation and its citizens." Because its work is often "very sensitive in nature," a Top Secret security clearance is required. To obtain the clearance, the FBI conducts an "intensive background investigation" that includes a polygraph (lie-detector) test, a test for illegal drugs, credit and records checks, and "extensive interviews with former and current colleagues, neighbors, friends, professors, etc." Disqualifiers for employment listed by the FBI include felony convictions, drug use, failure of a drug test, default on a student loan, and failure to register for the selective service.

"The polygraph will check the truthfulness of all of your responses on the FBI Background Investigation Forms," the website says. The thirteen-page national security questionnaire includes details of places where applicants have lived, schools attended, employment activity, a list of "people who know you well," spouses and former spouses, relatives and associates and their citizenship, and a listing of "your foreign activities." The form requests contacts or consultancies with foreign governments but not with foreign terrorist organizations, a loophole for Prouty and her connections to Hezbollah that would later complicate prosecutors' efforts to charge her with spying. The FBI form also requires listing foreign travel.

And last, the form asks applicants two key questions: "Have you ever been an officer or a member or made a contribution to an organization dedicated to the violent overthrow of the United States Government and which engages in illegal activities to that end, knowing that the organization engages in such activities with the specific intent to further such activities?" and "Have you ever knowingly engaged in any acts or activities designed to overthrow the United States Government by force?"

Prouty answered no to both questions and was granted her Top Secret clearance.

On June 29, 2003, Prouty left the FBI and went to work with the CIA, not simply as an analyst or Arabic linguist but as a member of the elite Directorate of Operations, which is in charge of both gathering intelligence and stealing secrets on foreign terrorist organizations. Now the CIA had a Hezbollah agent in its midst, someone recruited by the politically correct bureaucrats running the agency who saw in Prouty another "two-fer": a woman case officer and a Muslim minority—

exactly what the liberal bureaucrats wanted in order to show how fair they were to people of all races and religions.

The CIA's career page on its website is less pandering in its search for female employees than the FBI's is, but like the FBI, the agency outlines the long and supposedly rigorous application process and background check it puts candidates through. The website notes that the CIA examines, and then uses the polygraph to double-check, "your freedom from conflicting allegiances, potential to be coerced, and willingness and ability to abide by regulations governing the use, handling and the protection of sensitive information." Like the FBI, however, the CIA makes no specific prohibition against spies or terrorists applying for the job. Instead the website says that "to safeguard some of the nation's most sensitive information, CIA officers must be highly reliable and trustworthy" and must "adhere to the highest standards of integrity."

Of course, the CIA's scrutiny failed in the case of Prouty, just as the FBI's did. For all the talk about the thoroughness of their vetting process, FBI and CIA background checkers never even talked to Prouty's first "husband," who was paid several hundred dollars for the sham marriage. How can that happen? And did the CIA or FBI fire anyone for the lapse? No. Nothing happened.

Thus Prouty fooled both the FBI and the CIA into believing that she was a loyal Arabic-speaking special agent and case officer. Platitudes about trustworthiness and integrity were obviously ignored in allowing her to gain access to not just any information, but Top Secret data.

"This Was a Hezbollah Mole"

Prouty's scheme was finally discovered in December 2005, when the FBI learned that her brother-in-law, Talil Khalil Chahine, a Hezbollah fundraiser who ran several restaurants in the Detroit area, had discussed having a source of information inside the FBI who was providing him with information. Ultimately, though, she was not charged with the wartime crime of treason for her role in helping the terrorist enemy.

Instead, on November 13, 2007, the U.S. government announced that it had reached a deal with Prouty in which she pleaded guilty to lesser counts: conspiracy, immigration fraud, and illegally accessing computers.

Prosecutors were not happy with the outcome of the case. They wanted tougher charges against Prouty, for the obvious reason that the final deal, which carried a maximum jail sentence of only sixteen years, sent the wrong signal to other terrorist spies.

The plea deal released by the government said only that Prouty had gained access to the FBI's Automated Case Support computer system, which lists and includes details on ongoing FBI investigations. But according to officials familiar with the case, the deal was limited by what prosecutors could attempt to prove in court. One official with knowledge of the Prouty case took a strictly legalistic approach when asked about the lesser charges. "In this country," the official said, "prosecutors charge what they think they can prove. In this case, that was basically naturalization fraud and some unauthorized computer searches done at the FBI. At this point, that's all there is to it. If that ever changes, you'll hear about it."

But in defending the FBI and CIA, this official ignored the serious damage done by Prouty. Other U.S. intelligence and counterintelligence officials revealed that the Prouty case did far more harm than the plea deal acknowledged. One key reason is that, simply by working for the FBI and later in the CIA's Directorate of Operations, she gained access to extensive amounts of classified information.

"This was a Hezbollah mole, and all you have to do is look at her clearance to see how bad this is," one U.S. intelligence official said. Prouty as a Directorate of Operations officer held a Top Secret, Sensitive Compartmented Information clearance, giving her access to the most sensitive human-source intelligence, as well as electronic secrets.

Working in the area of counterterrorism, and by virtue of her Arabic-language skills, she probably had access to key source information from both the CIA and friendly intelligence services in the Middle East.

Intelligence officials explained another reason that prosecutors could not charge Prouty with espionage: there were legal concerns that espionage statutes might not fit the case because Hezbollah is not a foreign power. Clearly, if the United States is a nation at war with Islamist extremists, something should be done to change the law so that it applies to people who spy for terrorists. The problem will not go away and yet the U.S. government seems paralyzed and unable to upgrade its laws to prevent terrorists from infiltrating the repositories of its most important secrets.

Officials said that Prouty's case highlights other dangers as well. Based on a worst-case assessment of her treachery, they say, Prouty probably caused the loss of agents and electronic intelligence-gathering against one of the world's most dangerous terrorist groups. What's more, when global terrorist groups can gain access to U.S. intelligence secrets, they can neutralize efforts to counteract the terrorist threat—the single most important issue facing U.S. national security today. Additionally, there are worst-case fears that the compromise of U.S. secrets could undermine future military operations against the Iranian regime, because of the close links between Hezbollah and Iran.

The U.S. government did not publicly discuss any of these concerns in announcing the deal with Prouty. Intelligence agencies went into full damage-control mode to try to limit the negative publicity from the case. Word was circulated by public affairs officials that the case appeared mainly related to Hezbollah fundraising efforts in the United States that involved millions of dollars going to the Lebanese-based international terror group, and not the loss of secrets.

This official effort to downplay the seriousness of the case focused on three other figures linked to Prouty: Samar Khalil Nabbouh; Prouty's sister, Elfat Nadim El Aouar; and El Aouar's husband, Talal Khalil Chahine.

Nabbouh, a Marine Corps captain, played a key role in helping Prouty gain citizenship on the way to becoming a mole. She lived with Prouty and likewise entered into a fraudulent marriage to evade U.S. immigration law. She also defrauded the FBI into hiring Prouty by providing references for her in 1998, according to prosecutors. In December 2007, Nabbouh, under her married name, Samar Khalil Spinelli, pleaded guilty to conspiring with Prouty, El Aouar, and Chahine to commit citizenship and passport fraud.

In 2006, Chahine and El Aouar were charged in the Eastern District of Michigan with tax evasion in connection with a scheme to conceal more than $20 million in cash received from Chahine's chain of restaurants in the Detroit area, La Shish, and to route funds to persons in Hezbollah in Lebanon. They were not charged directly for any involvement with the terrorist group.

But court papers in the case revealed that Chahine was Prouty's main connection to Hezbollah. He had married Prouty's sister in August 2000, in a ceremony conducted according to the tenets of Shia Islam. A month later, Prouty accessed classified information on an investigation into Hezbollah and Chahine, El Aouar, and herself.

Prouty's brother-in-law was a Hezbollah fundraiser. In August 2002, El Aouar and Chahine attended a fundraising event in Lebanon where the keynote speakers were Chahine and Sheikh Muhammad Hussein Fadlallah, Hezbollah's ideological leader. The Treasury Department's Office of Foreign Assets Control (OFAC) listed Fadlallah as a specially designated terrorist, which made any financial transactions with Fadlallah illegal. Yet Chahine, according to one federal court document, "sat to the right of Fadlallah, a position of prominence in the Middle East, spoke from the same podium as Fadlallah, and conferred with him privately. Chahine was the representative at the event of a worldwide group of fundraisers. The government is in possession of a videotape of this event as well as still photographs showing El Aouar and Chahine's participation." Moreover, Fadlallah was under the personal protection of Imad Mughniyeh, the Hezbollah terrorist blamed for killing more Americans than any other terrorist but Osama bin Laden. (Mughniyeh, who organized the bombing that killed 241 U.S. troops in Lebanon in 1983, was killed in a car bombing in Beirut in February 2008.)

Officials close to the case and court documents revealed that Prouty is believed to have spied for Hezbollah through Chahine. Law enforcement and intelligence officials said Prouty looked in on Hezbollah investigative files in 2002 and 2003 when she was an FBI agent, even though she was not working Hezbollah cases and therefore did not have a "need to know." At the time, Chahine was under investigation by the FBI for his ties to Hezbollah's moneymaking operations in the United States, including gathering donations from wealthy contributors and through criminal activities. Officials believe Prouty illegally entered the Hezbollah files to find out what the FBI knew about Chahine.

Chahine fled the United States after being charged; years later he was still a fugitive, believed to be in Lebanon. El Aouar, meanwhile, was sentenced to eighteen months in prison on the tax-evasion charges, and in February 2008 was sentenced to an additional three months in prison and stripped of her U.S. citizenship for the naturalization fraud.

To counterintelligence and law-enforcement officials, the Prouty case is alarming because she in essence committed espionage on behalf of a terrorist organization by sharing FBI data on Hezbollah with Chahine at a time that she knew of his ties to the terrorist organization.

Counterintelligence officials conducted a damage assessment of the case to determine the extent of Prouty's compromises to Chahine and possibly others with links to Hezbollah. The government also examined whether the leaks undermined efforts to counter Hezbollah, in terms of identifying its members in this country and of monitoring its extensive fundraising activities. Details of the damage assessment could not be learned. "The damage as we see it is that the information has been compromised and accessed unlawfully with bad intent," one law-enforcement official told the *Los Angeles Times*.

What worries intelligence and counterintelligence officials is that Prouty obtained data from FBI files that would allow the terrorist group to identify human-source agents providing information to the U.S. government on Hezbollah. Given Prouty's connection to Chahine, U.S. intelligence officials privately believe that the classified information she accessed very likely was supplied to Iran's Ministry of Intelligence and Security (MOIS). Officials said that MOIS, which closely monitors Hezbollah, would never miss a chance to gain access to Prouty and her information.

Publicly FBI officials sought to downplay the damage by saying there was no direct link between Hezbollah and Prouty. In response to that claim, one intelligence source quipped, "Sure, they could not find her Hezbollah ID card."

The no-direct-link spin was echoed by the same intelligence official who took the legalistic approach to describing the charges against Prouty. Asked about the Hezbollah penetration, this official said no one has "proved" that Prouty shared information with Hezbollah or that she did anything wrong while at the CIA.

Here was the bureaucratic mindset at work: even as many U.S. officials acknowledged that shocking security lapses allowed penetration by a deadly terrorist organization—a penetration that in most other nations would result in firings and reforms—intelligence bureaucrats dismissed the entire affair as nothing more than a minor security problem and looked to move on as quickly as possible. In the FBI and CIA bureaucracy, the bureaucrats are fond of saying, "We may not always be right, but we are never wrong."

As for the background checks, this intelligence official said the FBI's preemployment background check would have covered Prouty's first years in this country, including the marriage, and "they didn't find anything wrong." The CIA, according to the official, "didn't seem to dig through that period on its own, apparently trusting in the FBI's ability to do a background investigation." So the CIA gave a Hezbollah spy access to some of its most secret counterterrorism information and simply "trusted" the FBI to do a thorough background check. This is clear evidence that the intelligence system is broken.

But CIA director Michael Hayden bristled at suggestions from this author that the director seemed more interested in press leaks than strategic damage caused by spies. "Director Hayden views counterintelligence as decisive to the agency's health and success," a CIA spokesman said. "The CIA constantly looks for ways to bolster its counterintelligence posture. But people need to recognize that recruiting in the pools of talent we need most comes with potential risks, as does virtually everything associated with foreign intelligence. You can't be bold and avoid risk. You have to manage it—and we do." The statement of course ignored the fact that there is little risk to conducting adequate background checks on prospective employees.

The CIA, the spokesman said, cooperated with prosecutors in the case, and "this agency, like any intelligence organization worth the name, views with extreme seriousness any potential compromise of its sources and methods." But then the spin: "You can't let your theories and suspicions get too far ahead of your facts. There's been enough of that already in the public commentary on this case. Strong counterintelligence is grounded in reality."

The spokesman's comments about counterintelligence and "reality" were an indication of the liberal views of senior intelligence bureaucrats, who despise the very concept of counterintelligence. They do not want a strong counterintelligence function because it complicates the collection of "positive" intelligence. No one in the intelligence agencies wants someone looking over his shoulder and second-guessing whether their sources are good.

The officials who were disappointed in the weak plea deal in late 2007 were even more disturbed by the sentencing Prouty received in May 2008. Before Prouty's sentencing, her lawyers wrote a memorandum stating that she should not be sentenced as "a spy, a mole or a penetration [agent] of the U.S. government." The document quoted a senior U.S. official who said there was "no evidence" she was a spy.

The lawyers insisted that Prouty was a loyal American who served her country in both the FBI and CIA, including a stint in Iraq. To support their case, they presented a letter CIA director George Tenet had written to Prouty in 2002 praising her for work with the CIA, and a February 2000 note from FBI director Louis Freeh thanking her for helping arrange his visit to the United Arab Emirates. Freeh wrote, "You embody the FBI's motto—Fidelity, Bravery, Integrity—and the Bureau is fortunate to have an employee of your caliber."

The spin worked. On May 13, 2008, U.S. District Judge Avern Cohn gave Prouty a slap on the wrist: he revoked her citizenship and fined her $750, but gave no jail time. This soft sentence was a slap at prosecutors and intelligence officials who knew the real story of Prouty. Cohn criticized the government for suggesting Prouty was a Hezbollah mole and claimed that she did not compromise any investigations. Letters from current and former FBI agents and CIA officers swayed the judge, who could have sentenced Prouty to sixteen years in jail.

It was merely another failed FBI counterintelligence investigation and prosecution, and it angered many U.S. intelligence and counterintelligence officials. One counterspy said the case was another example of the destructive impulse of government intelligence bureaucrats to "appease, apologize, and accommodate."

Fred Burton and Scott Stewart, writing for the strategic analysis service Stratfor, believe that the Prouty case highlights Hezbollah intelligence-gathering inside the U.S. intelligence community. "The evidence, allegations, and related cases suggest that Hezbollah has established a sophisticated intelligence apparatus that reaches into the United States," they stated. "Moreover, it is possible—though certainly not proven—that Spinelli and Prouty used their positions in government agencies to provide Hezbollah with sensitive information. If these women were indeed Hezbollah plants, the magnitude of the information they provided to Hezbollah and Iran could be similar in importance to the information Robert Hanssen provided to the Soviets and Russians—and the damage could prove to be just as great."

Indeed. Significant evidence indicates that through Chahine, Prouty compromised both FBI and CIA intelligence on Hezbollah. This is a disaster that will plague U.S. intelligence for years to come. What potential source would provide information to either agency if he knew that his life would be risked so easily by politically correct leaders more concerned with diversity in their agencies than in spying on foreign terrorists?

The answer is simple: no one.

The Truth About Curveball

Had the bureaucrats not opposed good counterintelligence, the entire case of the German intelligence agent and Iraqi defector who fooled the CIA about one element of Iraq's WMD program would never have happened, and a major embarrassment to the U.S. government would have been averted.

Rafid Ahmed Alwan was an Iraqi national who defected to Germany in 1999 and claimed he had worked as a chemical engineer at a plant that manufactured mobile-biological-weapons vans as part of an Iraqi WMD program. There was only one problem. The defector, codenamed Curveball, was a fabricator, and CIA analysts accepted his information uncritically.

My own experience with Curveball demonstrates how severely broken U.S. intelligence agencies are. In late 2001, I learned from U.S. intelligence officials that detailed intelligence reports were circulating within the CIA and elsewhere showing that Iraq under Saddam Hussein had purchased several mobile biological weapons vans from Russia. I did not know the information had come from Curveball. But in seeking comment for the story for an article in the *Washington Times,* I was informed by the CIA that publishing the information would harm national security by exposing a defector. After editorial discussions at the paper were held, a decision was made to publish the story, regardless of the CIA's concerns. But the CIA director at the time, George Tenet, appealed to Vice President Dick Cheney, who then contacted senior editors at the *Times* and urged them not to publish the story. As a result, the story was voluntarily withheld from publication. In exchange for holding the story, Cheney agreed to an interview with me that appeared in the *Times* on December 19, 2001.

I had almost forgotten about the mobile-van story when on February 5, 2003, Secretary of State Colin Powell addressed the United Nations Security Council on Iraq's disarmament obligations under Security Council Resolution 1441. "One of the most worrisome things that emerges from the thick intelligence file we have on Iraq's biological weapons," Powell stated, "is the existence of mobile production facilities used to make biological agents." The secretary then proceeded to produce detailed color slides on the mobile biological vans.

A short time later I contacted the CIA. The *Times* had been asked to withhold the information from publication on national security grounds, and now just over a year later the government disclosed it for the world to see at the United Nations. What was going on? I asked. The response from a CIA spokesman indicated how severely crippled U.S. intelligence agencies had become. "You can publish the story now, if you like, but if you do so, you will be completely wrong," the spokesman said. With that confusing remark, I left the story alone.

It would take the Iraq Survey Group, the intelligence unit headed by David Kay, to expose Curveball as a fabricator in its final report made public in 2004. Curveball was finally exposed on CBS's *60 Minutes* in November 2007; a former CIA official was quoted as saying that Curveball was motivated to fabricate the intelligence in order to gain permanent residence status in Germany. The CIA analysts who uncritically accepted his bogus intelligence apparently were never reprimanded.

It took the CIA until May 2004 to formally dismiss Curveball as a fabricator and his information as false. On April 8, 2005, CIA Director Porter Goss ordered an internal review of the matter to try to find out how Curveball fooled the intelligence community, but the results were never made public. George Tenet and his former CIA deputy John McLaughlin defended themselves by saying they were never told of German doubts about Curveball's credibility. Former CIA European division chief Tyler Drumheller, however, told the *Los Angeles Times* that "everyone in the chain of command knew exactly what was happening." Once again, there was no accountability for failures, even though these intelligence errors had contributed to war and subsequent counterinsurgency.

Counterintelligence had been making a comeback as an important intelligence check for a short time between 2005 and 2006 when Michelle Van Cleave, a Reagan administration national security official, headed the little-known Office of the National Counterintelligence Executive, or NCIX. Van Cleave worked hard to reform the broken counterintelligence system that was dominated by CIA and FBI bureaucrats who viewed the intelligence function as a problem. She won backing for a new, presidentially backed counterintelligence strategy that called for taking the battle against foreign spies and terrorists to the enemy, getting into their intelligence-gathering systems, and breaking them down.

But Van Cleave and her deputy, Kenneth deGraffenreid, were forced out by the bureaucrats who opposed their aggressive approach. In their place came Joel Brenner, a likable lawyer who was sent over to the offices of NCIX in Crystal City, Virginia, just over the 14th Street Bridge from Washington, to halt the aggressive programs. "He was told basically to do nothing," one intelligence official told me. The bureaucracy had struck back by using the newly formed Office of the Director of National Intelligence, under State Department career Foreign Service officer John Negroponte, to limit NCIX. Negroponte solidified State Department and Foreign Service control over U.S. intelligence agencies—with disastrous results.

The Graybeards

Pete Hoekstra, a Republican congressman from Michigan who is also vice chairman of the House Intelligence Committee, says that all one needs to do to see how broken the intelligence system is today is to look at the current leadership of the main agencies. All are antireform bureaucrats whose careers were made by not making waves, by following the old and unsuccessful patterns of intelligence-gathering that produced one intelligence failure after another, culminating with the surprise attacks of September 11 and the failure to properly gather intelligence on Iraq's weapons of mass destruction.

Four senior intelligence bureaucrats assumed key positions of leadership in early 2007 following the ouster of Porter Goss as CIA director. Goss, the former Florida Republican congressman and a former CIA operations officer, had been assigned the task of reforming the CIA. Bureaucrats, sensing that Goss might actually reform the agency and fire people who were incompetent, instead launched a concerted campaign to discredit him and his aides. These four officials were Defense Secretary Robert Gates, a former CIA director; CIA director Michael Hayden, a former National Security Agency (NSA) director; Director of National Intelligence Michael McConnell, also a former NSA director; and retired Air Force lieutenant general James Clapper, who moved into the powerful position of undersecretary of defense for intelligence, after heading the National Geospatial-Intelligence Agency (formerly known as the National Imagery and Mapping Agency).

Intelligence bureaucrats opposed to reform rejoiced at the ascension of the four officials. "The boys are back in town," was the headline on an article in the U.S. Naval Institute's magazine *Proceedings* lauding their elevation to power. The reporter, Shane Harris, described the scene at Bolling Air Force Base on February 20, 2007, as McConnell, a retired vice admiral and intelligence contractor at Booz Allen Hamilton, was sworn in as the second DNI. Gates and Hayden sat in the front row for the ceremony. As Harris put it, "Like all three men, the graybeards of intelligence across the country were smiling: their own were back in charge."

But the graybeards are the problem. They are the ones who have continued to bring about intelligence failures and inefficiencies ranging from extremely damaging spy cases that lasted for decades, to failed $2 billion spy satellites, to the failure to win passage of new electronic eavesdropping legislation needed in the battle against international terrorists and foreign spies.

Gates's predecessor, Defense Secretary Donald Rumsfeld, was skeptical publicly and harshly critical in private about U.S. intelligence agencies. Rumsfeld had chaired a commission that looked at missile threats to the United States and concluded that a major National Intelligence Estimate was wrong when it said no nation would threaten the continental United States with a long-range missile for fifteen years. The Rumsfeld Commission's July 1998 report stated that "the threat to the U.S. posed by these emerging [missile] capabilities is broader, more mature and evolving more rapidly than has been reported in estimates and reports by the Intelligence Community." The report earned Rumsfeld the enmity of the career intelligence bureaucrats. But Rumsfeld was right. A month after the report's release, to the surprise of the world, North Korea conducted its first successful test of a long-range missile called the Taepodong-2.

Gates, on the other hand, was the intelligence bureaucrats' bureaucrat. In 1996, the former CIA director headed a special panel of his own that examined the NIE on the missile threat. This panel was sponsored by the Senate Intelligence Committee. Gates said to me at the time that based on the scope of the estimate's inquiry, the analysts could have made an even *stronger* case that no nation would threaten the continental United States with a missile for fifteen years.

He also said there was no evidence of politicization—even though liberals within the CIA disclosed the first details of the estimate to Senator Carl Levin, Michigan Democrat, who used the NIE to argue against a provision of the fiscal 1997 defense authorization bill that called on the Clinton administration to deploy missile defenses. (Levin and the bureaucrats failed to defeat the legislation, but President Clinton vetoed the bill because of the missile defense provision.) Gates instead blamed intelligence managers' "hands-off approach" and conceded only that the estimate "was politically naïve and not as useful as it could have been." He insisted that it was "not a politicized estimate," since the analysts reached proper conclusions to the questions posed.

The only problem was that those conclusions were wrong. Gates had allowed institutional loyalty to the bureaucrats at CIA to cloud his judgment.

His deference to the bureaucracy was no accident. He had been shaped by the bruising Senate confirmation battle over his nomination as CIA director in 1987. During that fight, which ended when Gates withdrew his nomination over criticism of the CIA role in the Iran-Contra affair, the intelligence bureaucrats turned on Gates with a vengeance, telling the Senate Intelligence Committee that he was a lapdog for Reagan administration CIA Director William Casey. Melvin Goodman—a CIA bureaucrat who was part of the CIA's SOVA division, which was categorically wrong about the Soviet Union and missed its coming collapse—accused Gates of politicizing intelligence, claiming that the nominee had ordered analysts to produce an intelligence report that fit Casey's and Reagan's hardline views.

During his December 2006 confirmation hearing for defense secretary, Gates showed that he had learned his lesson. He was asked about the bureaucracy and whether his past experience would help him deal with vital issues of war and peace. Referring to the 1987 nomination fight, he said he had learned how all different parts of the government "need to work together to get anything done." In government "it's personal relationships that matter," he said. As for "bureaucratic infighting," Gates said that he didn't "come to this as a particularly naïve person in terms of how to get things done in this city" and therefore he knew to "respect the professionals."

That last element was key, he said, because "when you treat the professionals in an organization with respect and you listen to them and you pay attention to them, I think everybody is better served. They were there before you got there, they'll be there after you leave, and if you don't make them part of the solution, they will become part of the problem."

But the bureaucrats now are part of the problem, because, as with the Iran NIE, they have subverted the intelligence community to the point that the bureaucrats are dictating policy and ignoring the wishes of the elected officials, especially when those officials are conservative Republicans.

Gates also made sure to distance himself from his predecessor. He was deferential toward Congress, noting the need for consultations, for a lack of surprises, and for treating people's views with respect—all veiled criticisms of Rumsfeld. He also said, "What I don't like is off-line intelligence organizations or analytical groups," which was a shot at Rumsfeld for setting up a group of policy specialists to conduct analysis of global terrorist groups and their linkages. Gates explained, "I would far rather depend on the professional analysts at DIA and at CIA and at the other agencies, and work to ensure their independence than to try and create some alternative someplace. And so I think that relying on those professionals and making it clear from my position, if I'm confirmed, that I [will] expect them to call the shots as they see them and not try to shape their answers to meet a policy need."

Left unsaid was that Rumsfeld had set up those groups of four specialists because he had found bias among the "professionals" Gates was so ready to appease and let "call the shots as they see them." Douglas Feith, undersecretary of defense for policy, dispelled the widespread lies and myths about the Policy Counterterrorism Evaluation Group (PCTEG) that he assigned to look at international terrorism and Iraq. The group, headed by David Wurmser and Michael Maloof, two specialists on terrorism, produced a set of briefing slides on the financial, operational, ideological, and other links among international terrorists. Feith disclosed in his book *War and Decision* that out of 150 slides, only 9 mentioned possible contacts between Iraq and al Qaeda. Feith dismissed the critics who said the work of the PCTEG was designed to circumvent other intelligence work and stated that all the information was gathered *from* the intelligence community. "The Wurmser-Maloof work was professional, carefully researched, organized, and well presented," Feith said. "I know of no one who has ever made a case that the work was bad or was a manipulation of intelligence."

A former Defense official involved with intelligence matters under Rumsfeld said the entire episode of the Pentagon alternative analysis of intelligence reflected a covert attack by bureaucratic intelligence on Pentagon conservatives. "Before 9/11 the CIA produced volumes of reports linking al Qaeda and Iraq," this official said. "But after 9/11, they tried to pretend the links never existed." The reason? CIA liberals knew the al Qaeda–Iraq connections would be a legitimate basis for taking military action against Saddam Hussein's regime and sought to avert the use of military force.

While Gates is technically in the policy arena as a cabinet official, his demeanor is that of an intelligence analyst, which is how he spent his career. He is fond of saying that when an intelligence analyst smells flowers, he looks for a hearse. What he means is that intelligence analysts by culture tend to adopt pessimistic views that color their reports. The same outlook is present in the other main figures dominating the Washington intelligence and policy scene, especially Michael McConnell.

Like his predecessor John Negroponte, McConnell came to the job of DNI as a bureaucrat with a liberal bias and would end up being a disaster for U.S. intelligence reform efforts. Though he was a three-star admiral in the Navy, conservatives note that McConnell does not appear to be a military warrior and instead appears weak and vacillating, the quintessential bureaucratic trait. Also, along with Gates and his former boss, Colin Powell, whom he worked for when Powell was chairman of the Joint Chiefs of Staff, McConnell is part of the conservative-haters club among the national security and foreign policy elites.

McConnell turned down the job of DNI when it was first offered to him in September 2006, at a time when Rumsfeld was still running the Pentagon and thus had control over most of the U.S. intelligence community budget. But after Rumsfeld was forced out by the White House two months later and was replaced by Gates, Vice President Cheney again asked McConnell to take up the DNI post. "My first phone call was to Secretary Gates," McConnell told the *New Yorker.* Gates too had earlier turned down the DNI job, when it went to Negroponte. "Mike had a lot of the same concerns I had with the 2004 act [that created the DNI position], in terms of the ability to get things done," Gates said in the *New Yorker* article. "Under the legislation, the DNI had the responsibility for executing the intelligence budget and assuring that everybody in the community obeyed the law, but he didn't have the authority to fire anybody." The situation is the same today, meaning that the bureaucracy remains out of control of political appointees. So why not appoint sympathetic bureaucrats to run it? That is exactly what happened.

McConnell and Gates were back in the saddle and Gates told McConnell that another member of the club, former Defense Intelligence Agency director James Clapper, would be undersecretary of defense for intelligence, the key position that would give the bureaucrats ultimate control over both budgets and policy. To cement the bureaucratic takeover, in May 2007 McConnell named Clapper the director of defense intelligence under his office. Clapper, then, is "dual-hatted."

Clapper moved quickly once he was undersecretary. One of his first steps was to dismantle the Counterintelligence Field Activity (CIFA), a dedicated unit Rumsfeld established to analyze the threat posed by foreign spies. CIFA was never given operational authority and had organizational and leadership problems. But it was a unit devoted solely to identifying and countering spies and thus provided a center of gravity for the entire U.S. government counterintelligence system. Clapper placed the remains of CIFA within the Defense Intelligence Agency, a move designed to make sure it would not be effective. CIFA was despised by both the FBI and CIA counterintelligence units, bastions of bureaucratic resistance to tough counterintelligence since the 1970s, when counterintelligence was downgraded from a strategic tool to a security support function.

Rounding out the foursome was Michael Hayden, another career intelligence bureaucrat. Like McConnell, Hayden had run the National Security Agency. He also served as the first deputy director of national intelligence under Negroponte. Gates described the way this foursome would work together at the top of the intelligence community: "I thought that, between Hayden, McConnell, Clapper, and myself, we could reach an agreement on some of the issues that hadn't been resolved by the legislation."

Gates and McConnell both believed that having like-minded officials in charge of reform efforts would protect the intelligence community from the kind of radical reforms that were being called for by critics, like Hoekstra, both in Congress and outside government. But they were wrong. The Gang of Four succeeded only in maintaining a deeply rooted status quo, and thus the chance for meeting the urgent requirement for fixing U.S. intelligence was lost.

"Wall-to-Wall Knee-Jerk Liberals"

To critics of the intelligence community coup, the most striking thing about the bureaucrats is their lack of warrior ethic. Even though all four have military backgrounds, they are a far cry from some of the military's more famous warriors. Admiral William "Bull" Halsey, for instance, understood that the key lesson of war is that when you kill enough of the enemy, they will stop fighting. During World War II, Halsey encouraged those under his command to "Kill Japs! Kill Japs! Kill more Japs!" Air Force general Curtis LeMay, who directed World War II bombing against Japan and was in charge of U.S. strategic nuclear arsenals until 1957, was dubbed "Bombs Away LeMay" by critics because he believed strongly in the use of strategic bombing. LeMay opposed plans for nuclear strikes only on missiles. He wanted to kill Russians in any nuclear exchange.

The bureaucrats chosen to run U.S. intelligence, by contrast, have shown themselves to be more interested in political correctness and "diversity" among their personnel than in national security. Diversity is a good thing for intelligence if you can bring in people who will enhance the primary mission: stealing enemies' secrets. But if diversity means allowing Hezbollah spies to penetrate and steal the nation's secrets, or bringing in less-than-qualified intelligence personnel to meet predetermined political objectives, it is extremely damaging. That is especially true because it can hinder agencies from questioning people's motives and loyalties, something that is the bedrock of counterespionage and finding terrorists.

Former CIA operations officer Charles McCarry, now a novelist, best characterized the liberal political orientation of the U.S. intelligence community when he told an interviewer, "I never met a stupid person in the agency. Or an assassin. Or a Republican."

"No Republicans?" the interview asked. "Are you serious?"

"I'm serious. They were, at least in the operations side where I was, there were wall-to-wall knee-jerk liberals. And they were befuddled that the left outside the agency regarded them as some sort of right-wing threat. Because they were the absolute opposite, in their own politics."

Unfortunately, liberal policy criminals aren't confined to the intelligence community. They're spread throughout the national security apparatus, secretly undermining U.S. policy.

Some, in fact, operate right inside the White House.

LIBERAL POWER IN THE

WHITE HOUSE

N
o single agency of the federal government is capable of producing more damage from the policies of misguided liberals and bureaucrats than the staff of the White House, especially the National Security Council (NSC). The NSC is the most important—and most powerful—of the national security agencies in government. From the NSC staff, appointments are vetted and blocked, policies are formulated and undermined, and officials can wield the power of the presidency with almost no constraints.

The White House of President George W. Bush was meant to be the center of pro-American, pro-liberty ideas and policies. Instead, Bush's presidency was hijacked—not by neoconservatives, as is often alleged, but by a combination of liberal Democrats left over from the Clinton administration and liberal Big Government Republicans who came to Washington intent on supporting big spending programs and boosting trade and business with little or no regard for the consequences to U.S. national security. The combination proved fatal for his presidency, as liberal, anticonservative policies came to dominate.

The Bush administration failed to properly formulate and implement the policies needed to put the president's pro-freedom, pro-international democracy ideas into action. That failure resulted quite simply because Bush picked the wrong people for the government's most important policy positions. From that signal failure, everything would eventually unravel.

Roll Call

The roll call of Bush White House officials is littered with anti-conservative figures who undermined official policy, as outlined in the president's speeches and public statements, and ultimately undermined U.S. national security.

First there was Condoleezza Rice, a classic RINO, or Republican In Name Only. An academic with close ties to Stanford University, one of the most liberal educational institutions in the country, Rice dominated national security policies from the White House as national security adviser during Bush's first term before becoming secretary of state. She backed the president on developing missile defenses, one of the few accomplishments that will have a lasting positive impact. But her overall tenure was marred by the fact that she brought to the White House some of the most misguided anticonservative liberals—both Republican and Democrat. She and the president failed to understand the strategic principle of government that picking the wrong people results in the wrong policies.

Rice's deputy, lawyer Stephen Hadley, took over the national security adviser post in the second Bush term and continued the liberal, pro-bureaucrat policies of his predecessor.

Andrew Card, a liberal Republican, spent years blocking conservative policies as White House chief of staff. His successor, former Goldman Sachs executive Josh Bolten, was no better.

Frances Fragos Townsend, the White House counterterrorism coordinator, was a Clinton administration Justice Department official directly linked to the misguided "wall" imposed to prevent information sharing between intelligence and law enforcement, a flaw that was a major cause of the failures to stop the 9/11 attacks.

Dan Bartlett, a Texas-born aide, was among the small circle of advisers who dominated the president's policies. Bartlett began his White House career as deputy to presidential adviser Karen Hughes, a key liberal Republican close to the president. Bartlett moved up in the ranking to become White House communications director, and then, in 2005, he gained even more power when he assumed Hughes's old post as counselor to the president. As the chief White House official in charge of strategic communications, Bartlett led the planning and formulation of policy "of the President's agenda," according to his official biography. And he was one of the most visible anticonservative activists in the White House.

Three months after leaving the White House, Bartlett exposed his liberal political outlook in a speech to the U.S. Chamber of Commerce. Instead of criticizing Democrats, Bartlett turned his fire on Republicans, vehemently criticizing conservative former senator Fred Thompson as a "dud" candidate and dismissing former governor Mitt Romney as someone who could not get elected because he is a Mormon. Bartlett said he liked candidate Mike Huckabee, a fellow Big Government Republican.

Bartlett also went to work with another conservative-hater, Mark McKinnon, a Democrat who signed on with Bush in 1997 when Bush was governor of Texas. McKinnon helped Bush get elected and worked as the chief media adviser for Senator John McCain's 2008 presidential campaign. But McKinnon showed his true colors in February when he vowed to step down from the McCain campaign if Senator Barack Obama won the Democratic nomination, since "it would be uncomfortable for me" to attack Obama, whom he said he liked "a great deal."

As communications director and counselor to the president, Bartlett was in charge of the voice and vision of the presidency. He made sure the president's message was delivered through the State of the Union address, televised press conferences, statements to the press, and radio addresses. He worked closely with the various agencies of government to make sure that the message was delivered. But while Bush's message was made public, it was never translated into policies, because there was no way for the wordsmiths to penetrate into the bureaucracy. That was a job for the NSC staff, and those officials simply ignored Bush's messages and gave free reign to the policies of the liberal bureaucrats. As long as there were no conservative policies, Bartlett and his ilk were content to let the bureaucrats have their way.

Bartlett's anticonservative influence also changed President Bush's speeches. Soaring rhetoric on advancing freedom and democracy against the forces of the "axis of evil" gradually gave way to liberal bromides and platitudes that rang hollow. In perhaps his most stirring State of the Union speech, in January 2002, President Bush rallied the nation to face Islamist extremism: "We've come to know truths that we will never question: evil is real, and it must be opposed. Beyond all differences of race or creed, we are one country, mourning together and facing danger together. Deep in the American character, there is honor, and it is stronger than cynicism. And many have discovered again that even in tragedy—especially in tragedy—God is near." His 2005 speech called for America to stand with the allies of freedom to support democratic movements in the Middle East and beyond, with the ultimate goal of ending tyranny in the world. In 2006, Bush rallied the nation to combat the evil of "radical Islam."

But by his last State of the Union address in 2008, the rhetoric of earlier years had vanished. The president, the focus of hatred and anger over the Iraq War, looked and sounded defeated. Gone were references to radical Islamists. Instead he used the politically correct term "terrorists," as if the terrorist danger were secular. The toll began to show on his face and in his voice. He delivered a flat speech that was read with little passion and with a sense of resignation. He spoke very little of Iraq, noting only the progress made and the difficult challenge ahead. On Iran, the president called on the leaders in Tehran to "come clean" about its nuclear program and "verifiably suspend your nuclear enrichment so negotiations can begin." But the president must have known that in the nuclear standoff with Iran, he had been sabotaged by his own intelligence community, which only weeks earlier had issued the highly politicized National Intelligence Estimate that tied his hands. On other vital national security issues, the president was silent. For example, he made no mention of North Korea and ending its nuclear program, the six-nation talks were deadlocked, and multiple concessions could not move the Communist regime in Pyongyang. On this and other vital issues, the bureaucrats had prevented the United States from taking decisive action.

Perhaps no official in the White House better represented the faux conservatism of the liberal Republicans than speechwriter Michael J. Gerson, who worked for Bush for seven years, five of them in the White House. Upon leaving the administration, Gerson ended up in the bastion of anticonservatism, the Council on Foreign Relations, and as a columnist for the liberal *Washington Post* and *Newsweek* magazine. Gerson published a book in late 2007, entitled *Heroic Conservatism,* which showed that his ideas were anything but conservative. For Gerson and the people who controlled the policies in the Bush White House, "heroic conservatism" or "compassionate conservatism" was a stalking horse for liberal policies—using the government to help those in poverty, reforming prisons and mental hospitals, waging the struggle for women's rights and civil rights, and so on. It was merely political opportunism to get votes from liberal Republicans.

Even more important, Gerson's book showed that it was the so-called compassionate conservatives who did the most to attack true conservatives. As John Podhoretz, a conservative editor of *Commentary* magazine, noted, "What is perhaps most interesting and unusual about *Heroic Conservatism* is that its argument is aimed less at Bush's political and ideological opponents on the Left than at American conservatives." That is because Gerson is the leading ideologue of Republican conservative-haters, who see true conservatives, those who follow the commonsense populist conservatism of Ronald Reagan, as the enemy.

Podhoretz went on to reveal the ultimate problem with the Bush presidency: "the gap between the lofty principles expressed in speeches and the often compromised policies enacted by officialdom." In other words, the president was content to set policy in his speeches, but was unable to convert those principles into action because his White House was compromised, by enemies of the very principles he so frequently espoused.

The most important failure of the president's liberal advisers like Bartlett and the "communicators" who favored never conducting a political attack or even playing political hardball was on the issue of the Iraq War. On one critical political issue after another, the liberal communicators counseled the president not to challenge his Democratic critics. Thus the White House did not defend the sixteen words in his 2003 State of the Union speech on intelligence about Iraq's seeking uranium ore from Niger. In fact, it actually offered an *apology* for the Niger episode—even though a 2004 British intelligence report concluded that Bush's sixteen words were "well founded" and a U.S. Senate Intelligence Committee report similarly found that at the time of the State of the Union it was "reasonable for analysts to assess" that the Iraqis may have sought uranium in Niger. Worse, the White House did almost nothing to counter Democrats' constant criticism of the Iraq War.

As one insider put it, "Around 2004, a decision was made that we would look forward, not back. That was the point that we went from defending ourselves [in Iraq, Afghanistan, and elsewhere] to promoting democracy. The Democrats, on the other hand, played to history and we got lambasted." The naïve White House aides thought the president could stay above the fray but the result was a disaster. Like the bureaucrats, the communicators favored a policy of appeasing the Democrats, who could not be appeased and simply continued attacking. The president's approval rating continued to sink.

One White House official said the communicators' worst strategic blunder was the failure to mount an effective political defense of the Iraq War. That failure would have lasting political consequences for

Republicans, but more important, it led the entire country to doubt the cause of removing Saddam Hussein from power in 2003 and seeking to create a central point for the promotion of democracy and liberty in the Middle East. "The White House decided that it would not look back on the Iraq War," said the official. "The result is we lost the political battle for the war."

Clarke's Outrage

As if the liberal Republicans were not bad enough, the Democratic holdovers made things even worse. The main case is that of Richard Clarke, a liberal Foreign Service officer known to coworkers as a self-promoting careerist who cared more about his personal fortunes than those of the country. Clarke rose quickly in the ranks of the State Department and ended up as chief of counterterrorism at the NSC staff for both President Bill Clinton and, for a time in the beginning, President George W. Bush. But when his 2004 book, *Against All Enemies,* was published, there was no criticism of Clinton and plenty of Bush, whom he falsely accused of not being aggressive in going after al Qaeda and Osama bin Laden in the weeks before the September 11 attacks.

Clarke's attacks on Bush and his administration are the most important example of why such "holdover" officials should be barred under law from continuing in their politically sensitive positions of power when a new administration takes office. The fact that Condoleezza Rice kept him will no doubt be identified by future historians as one of the biggest failures of the Bush administration. Clarke later complained that the Bush administration demoted him from the top counterterrorism job to a new position of combating cyber attacks, but the White House should have sent him packing altogether.

Clarke's case also shows the power of liberal bureaucrats to shape public opinion. His book became a manifesto for anti-Bush liberals, both inside and outside the administration, who shared his view that the war in Iraq was a mistake that undermined the war on terrorism. Clarke launched public attacks throughout the election year of 2004 and his appearances on national media were frequent.

His comments became fodder for the left-wing advocacy group MoveOn.org, which portrayed him as a Bush insider blowing the whistle on the administration. The group claimed that citing Clarke enabled it to raise hundreds of thousands of dollars for anti-Bush commercials. MoveOn said, for example, "George Bush shamelessly exploited 9/11 in his campaign commercials. Now, Richard Clarke, his former counterterrorism chief, said: 'I find it outrageous that the president is running for re-election on the grounds that he's done such great things about terrorism. He ignored terrorism for months when maybe we could have done something to stop 9/11.'"

Clarke, who said he voted for Al Gore for president in 2000, also maintained that Bill Clinton did more against al Qaeda than Bush, a laughable claim. He insisted that he had provided memorandums to senior Bush officials urging decisive action against al Qaeda but that his warnings were ignored.

To expose Clarke, the White House authorized the release of a transcript of a background briefing Clarke had given to news reporters. During the briefing, Clarke stated that Bush decided to step up the war against al Qaeda by changing the Clinton policy of trying to "contain" the group to a policy of "eliminating" the group. The transcript also revealed that Bush increased the intelligence budget for covert action operations against al Qaeda by a factor of five.

In truth, it was not Bush but Clinton who failed on several occasions to get bin Laden when he had the chance, as even Clarke had to acknowledge.

After the bombing of the USS *Cole* in Yemen in October 2000, the Pentagon would not use special operations forces or bombing raids against al Qaeda bases in Afghanistan because Clinton's military and intelligence leaders felt there was not enough evidence of an al Qaeda hand in the *Cole* attack. As Clarke admitted, the CIA also refused to go after bin Laden during the Clinton administration; the official reason the agency gave was a lack of funds, but, Clarke wrote, "Another way to say that was that everything they were doing was more important than fighting al Qaeda." Clinton administration weakness also led to the cancellation of a planned CIA operation to capture bin Laden in Kandahar in 1998. According to U.S. officials involved, the U.S. government developed a plan in 1997 and early 1998 to capture bin Laden in Afghanistan. A CIA aircraft was set to carry out the snatch operation by flying in from a nearby country and picking up the al Qaeda leader. But risk-averse CIA leaders, including CIA director George Tenet, rejected the plan on May 29, 1998.

Clinton missed another chance to get bin Laden when the al Qaeda leader was in Sudan in 1996. The government in Khartoum offered him up to the United States in an effort to improve relations, but the Clinton White House refused. Clarke admits this as well, although he makes the outrageous claim that it was *Republicans* who were to blame because they had put Clinton under a microscope and he feared acting would lead to political attacks. Despite the Clarke spin, there is no question that the Clinton administration can be blamed squarely for not stopping bin Laden despite several opportunities and is thus far more culpable than Bush for any failures related to September 11.

To further the claim that Bush was bent on invading Iraq from the start, Clarke also promoted the myth that there was no connection whatsoever between al Qaeda and the Iraqis. He stated that "all agencies and departments" of the bureaucracy agreed on this point. Clarke made this assertion again and again, despite the fact that CIA director George Tenet had written a letter in 2002 affirming that there was intelligence of "senior-level contacts between Iraq and al Qaeda going back a decade," and stating that "Iraq has provided training to al Qaeda members in . . . poisons and gases and making conventional bombs." Douglas Feith, undersecretary of defense for policy from 2001 to 2005, revealed in his book *War and Decision* that the CIA was politically motivated to downplay, dismiss, and even ignore solid intelligence of Iraq–al Qaeda linkages, which were confirmed through the CIA's own reporting. "For the past decade, according to the cited CIA documents, Iraqi intelligence officials had been meeting with senior al Qaeda personnel and providing al Qaeda with support, including safe haven, travel documents, and training in sophisticated explosives," Feith wrote about intelligence reports his staff analyzed in 2002.

And later, new documents would emerge to disprove the claims of Clarke and the bureaucrats, who had moved to the autopilot analysis of no linkages between al Qaeda and Iraq.

Evidence of the linkages surfaced in early 2004, not from U.S. intelligence files but from the Iraqi National Congress headed by Ahmed Chalabi. I obtained a copy of a 1993 document from the Iraqi Intelligence Service (IIS), Saddam Hussein's intelligence agency. The twenty-page report, written in Arabic and labeled Top Secret, lists all those whom IIS agents considered "collaborators" with the service. Page 14 of the document states that one of the collaborators is "Saudi Osama bin Laden." Bin Laden is described as "a Saudi businessman" who is "in charge of the Saudi opposition in Afghanistan." The report adds, "And he is in good relationship with our section in Syria." The document is signed "Jabar," an Iraqi intelligence official.

Yet Clarke, the insider, lionized Bill Clinton and trashed George W. Bush and his administration, dismissing Vice President Dick Cheney as a right-wing extremist and defense secretary Donald Rumsfeld as uninterested in countering terrorism.

Joshua Muravchik, an American Enterprise Institute scholar, deftly countered Clarke's claim that the United States made a mistake by invading Iraq and that U.S. forces should have been limited to Afghanistan. "The Bush strategy has been at once much more ambitious and much more realistic: to try to change the underlying *political* conditions of the region by, in brief, promoting democracy," Muravchik said in an article in *Commentary* magazine. "The first test of this strategy is Iraq; there is no assurance that it will work, but in contrast to Clarke's blather it is the quintessence of seriousness."

Muravchik noted that Clarke's claims that Clinton was stronger on terrorism than Bush are pure fiction. "There is no truth to it," he stated. "A president who is being frustrated by his bureaucracies can always use the bully pulpit to rally public opinion. But Clinton's state-of-the-union messages to Congress hardly made any reference to terrorism at all, never mentioned al Qaeda or Afghanistan, and cited bin Laden only once, in 1999, after the African embassy bombings that were known to be his work."

But the bureaucrats' spin was ultimately what mattered. Piece by piece they were weakening U.S. efforts in the war on terrorism.

Rand Beers's "Defense"

Richard Clarke was not the only liberal to undermine the White House on terrorism. Rand Beers was another liberal State Department bureaucrat who had worked on the Clinton administration National Security Council staff. In 2002 he was appointed the NSC's director for combating terrorism, replacing Clarke.

Beers no doubt promoted himself for the Bush White House by playing up his experience on the NSC staff under Ronald Reagan and George H. W. Bush. But he had come on board at the end of the Reagan administration, when the NSC staff shifted dramatically leftward under Chief of Staff Howard Baker, a liberal Republican who purged the staff of conservatives. Beers replaced Oliver North, who had been caught up in the Iran-Contra arms-for-hostage scandal.

George W. Bush's team should have paid closer attention to Beers's time in the Clinton administration, where he served on the NSC until 1998. He was a key official then, when the Clinton administration was accused of using Chinese money that was funneled into the 1996 presidential campaign.

In June 1996, Beers, the NSC intelligence director, was informed by the FBI that the People's Republic of China was suspected of funneling money illegally into the Clinton reelection campaign. Beers later claimed that FBI agents asked him not to report the information about the Chinese influence buying, and he insisted that he therefore did not brief President Clinton or National Security Adviser Sandy Berger on this issue. The FBI, however, denied Beers's claim. "The FBI placed no restriction whatsoever on the dissemination up the chain of command at the NSC," the Bureau said in a statement. "Briefing senior NSC staff is the long-established procedure for the FBI to provide sensitive information to the NSC." Beers represented the worst of the State Department bureaucrats whose careerist and liberal political agendas trumped U.S. national interests.

So how did he come to be the Bush White House's NSC director for combating terrorism? The exact story is not known, but it seems obvious that Condoleezza Rice, then the national security adviser, was to blame for the blunder. It was Rice who announced Beers's appointment. The announcement, made on August 19, 2002, was met with little fanfare, but the appointment would seriously damage the Bush administration.

Beers betrayed President Bush in 2003 by resigning in protest five days before the March 2003 invasion of Iraq and then publicly denouncing the administration. "The administration wasn't matching its deeds to its words in the war on terrorism," he told the liberal *Washington Post* for a long profile piece that portrayed him as a hero. "They're making us less secure, not more secure." Beers added, "As an insider, I saw the things that weren't being done. And the longer I sat and watched, the more concerned I became, until I got up and walked out." Beers's foolishness is captured in his conception of the deadly business of countering Islamic extremism: "Counterterrorism is like a team sport. The game is deadly. There has to be offense and defense. The Bush administration is primarily offense, and not into teamwork."

He claimed that the administration failed to focus on the root causes of terror, the typical liberal excuse for not fully understanding the nature of the Islamist extremist threat. To liberals, ending the plight of Palestinians or ending the poverty of the Arab world are the only solutions. What Beers and those in the bureaucracy utterly fail to understand is that the war against terrorism must be fought ideologically, with specific ideas that can be used to counter the false and misguided ideas of the extremists.

News reports played up Beers's protest resignation and his attacks on the administration. Although he was a registered Democrat, the media portrayed him as a career professional who was not a political activist. Thus reports trumpeted what the *Washington Post* called the "astounding" news that the "lifelong bureaucrat" and "unlikely insurgent" quickly signed up with liberal Democrat John Kerry's presidential campaign as a national security adviser. Beers became Kerry's senior foreign policy adviser throughout the 2004 campaign.

Eventually Beers went to work as an adjunct lecturer at Harvard University's John F. Kennedy School of Government.

There, he taught a seminar with none other than Richard Clarke.

Fran's Wall

President Bush must have been completely blind to what was going on in his own NSC staff, because even after the disasters of Clarke and Beers, yet another liberal Clinton holdover was appointed to the NSC staff for counterterrorism. This time it was Frances Fragos Townsend, who worked in the intelligence policy office at the Clinton Justice Department. Condoleezza Rice appointed Townsend to replace Beers on May 27, 2003.

It is truly astounding—and frightening—that Townsend could become the Bush administration's most senior domestic counterterrorism official, since she was to blame for some of the most disastrous policies that ultimately contributed to the September 11 attacks. Clarke, Beers, and Townsend represent true "policy criminals" who should never have been chosen for sensitive assignments at the highest levels of the national security policymaking establishment.

Townsend, a former organized crime prosecutor in New York, got her start in Brooklyn first under liberal district attorney Elizabeth Holtzman in 1985, and then under U.S. Attorney in Manhattan Rudy Giuliani, a Big Government Republican. She was working for liberal Democrat Jo Ann Harris at the U.S. Attorney's Office in New York in 1993 when Janet Reno, Bill Clinton's attorney general, picked Harris to run the Justice Department's Criminal Division. Harris brought Townsend with her to head the international law-enforcement office. In March 1998, Townsend took over the traditionally nonpolitical post of director of the Office of Intelligence Policy and Review (OIPR). The OIPR conducts the strategically important role of checking and seeking approval of electronic surveillance in both criminal and foreign intelligence investigations.

When John Ashcroft took over the Justice Department under President George W. Bush he immediately recognized Townsend as part of the problem and dismissed her from OIPR. She then moved quietly to the U.S. Coast Guard, where she was named head of intelligence in January 2002.

According to officials who worked with Townsend at OIPR, she was considered an abrasive control freak who, one official told me, managed the office "by decibel"—a reference to her frequent outbursts at subordinates. But that was just a small part of the problem that Ashcroft recognized.

Townsend was notorious in national security circles for contributing to the Clinton administration's pro-China policies. While at OIPR she was criticized in a Justice Department internal report for turning down an FBI request for a wiretap on Los Alamos National Laboratory scientist Wen Ho Lee, who was suspected of supplying China with some of the most sensitive nuclear weapons secrets. The delay undermined and ultimately destroyed the FBI's spy probe. Apparently,

Townsend did not want the Lee case to upset relations with China. Then in 2000 Townsend listed democratic and friendly Taiwan as one of the FBI's hostile intelligence threats, along with Russia, China, North Korea, the Federal Republic of Yugoslavia, Serbian-controlled Bosnia, Vietnam, Syria, Iraq, Iran, Libya, and Sudan.

But the most damaging aspect of her tenure at Justice was her role in erecting the "wall" that prevented communications between U.S. intelligence and law enforcement officials—and that ultimately led to the September 11 intelligence failures. In 1995, Attorney General Reno issued the directive that restricted FBI agents from talking to intelligence officials. But in fact the wall was, as one official told me, "Fran's creation." Prosecutors complained that when Townsend became head of OIPR in 1998, she kept the wall of separation between law enforcement and intelligence-gathering under the Foreign Intelligence Surveillance Act (FISA). Townsend stuck to the letter of the strict separation that prevented prosecutors from having a hand in intelligence-gathering in national security investigations.

Both the Government Accountability Office and the 9/11 Commission blamed Townsend's OIPR and its narrow interpretation of FISA for the intelligence failures related to the September 11 attacks, specifically the failure to track down two of the terrorists, who had entered the country prior to the attack. The problem was that the OIPR made the wall practically impenetrable. As the 9/11 Commission's report concluded, "the Office of Intelligence Policy and Review became the sole gatekeeper for passing information to the [Justice Department's] Criminal Division," even though "Attorney General Reno's procedures did not include such a provision." The commission said OIPR kept a lock on a vital national security tool. "The office threatened that if it could not regulate the flow of information to criminal prosecutors, it would no longer present the FBI's warrant requests to the FISA court," the report said. "The information flow withered."

In fact, Ashcroft fired Townsend largely because of her history of blocking electronic surveillance requests, and because the chief judge of the FISA court, Royce Lamberth, was not happy with her work at OIPR. According to *U.S. News & World Report,* Townsend claims that she tried to persuade Lamberth to lower the wall but so angered the FISA court judge that he blocked her from coming to meetings to discuss the wall and how it was hampering FBI wiretapping in national security probes. Lamberth was angered by Townsend because she failed to prevent the FBI from presenting false information to the wiretap court in dozens of FISA applications. According to *U.S. News,* Lamberth told Aschcroft he had lost faith in Townsend and as a result Ashcroft wanted her ousted. She was reported to be "furious" but ended up as assistant commandant of intelligence at the U.S. Coast Guard.

Ashcroft's concerns were well placed: The OIPR's wall led the FBI to be so overly cautious that, as *U.S. News & World Report* noted, "in July and August of 2001, FBI intelligence analysts prohibited their own criminal-case agents from searching for two men on the government's terrorist watch list who they knew had entered the United States."

Amazingly, that shocking failure didn't matter to the Bush White House by the spring of 2003. Nor did the fact that Bush's own attorney general, John Ashcroft, had recognized Townsend's problems early on and dismissed her because of them. Nor did Townsend's role as a close adviser to Janet Reno.

When I contacted Townsend about her experience as Reno's trusted aide in the Clinton administration, she insisted that she was a lifelong Republican. Apparently the Bush White House took that sort of claim at face value, as it made the shockingly irresponsible decision to elevate her to its most crucial counterterrorism post.

The damage done to the Bush presidency by the likes of Clarke, Beers, and Townsend only mounted. Liberals in the White House, led by people like Dan Bartlett, would use the criticism to orchestrate the ouster of defense secretary Donald Rumsfeld and deputy defense secretary Paul Wolfowitz, two effective conservative opponents of the liberal bureaucracy. By 2005, the stage was set for a major shift in policy.

The shift was solidified in November 2006 after Republicans were repudiated at the polls. Rumsfeld resigned on November 8, 2006, marking the shift away from conservative, hard-line policies on the war on terrorism, Iraq, North Korea, Iran, Syria, the spread of dangerous weapons around the world, and other issues. The president would begin trying to fashion a "legacy" with some positive accomplishment, despite the worsening of the war in Iraq. Policies toward China, which had been quietly weakened over the previous five years, changed sharply in favor of doing business with China and deemphasizing U.S. support for the democratic government in Taiwan. "What's changed today is the election is over, and the Democrats won," Bush told reporters at a White House news conference on November 8.

The nominee named to be the next defense secretary was Robert Gates, a nonwarrior, a retired intelligence bureaucrat with little understanding of defense and military issues. The ouster of Rumsfeld was engineered quietly by Josh Bolten, a liberal Republican who was preparing for a Democratic takeover of Congress before the election, when he had assigned aides Karl Rove and Joel D. Kaplan, National Security Adviser Stephen Hadley, and counselor Dan Bartlett to prepare for the political shift.

Vice President Dick Cheney was sidelined by the scandal involving his top national security aide, I. Lewis "Scooter" Libby, who was forced out of his job in October 2005 and convicted of lying to government investigators over the leak to the press of the identity of Valerie Plame as a CIA officer. Libby's departure weakened Cheney's hand in policy. So once Rumsfeld departed, the White House and the government bureaucracy were effectively in liberal hands.

Hiring Bad People

The war on terrorism was not the only place that liberals and bureaucrats subverted the presidency. Liberals in the Bush White House also produced an immoral, business-above-all foreign policy of actually helping antidemocratic regimes like those in China and Russia.

The central figure in this regard was Josh Bolten, a former Goldman Sachs executive who became the White House chief of staff in April 2006 after Andrew Card resigned. Bolten handpicked another Goldman Sachs bigwig, Henry Paulson, the international investment and banking firm's chief executive officer, for the powerful post of secretary of the treasury that summer. The White House was not deterred by the fact that Goldman Sachs had made a profit of $963 million alone from an investment in the Industrial and Commercial Bank of China, the largest state-owned bank.

Sure enough, Paulson, with Bolten running interference for him in the White House, reoriented U.S. policy toward China in ways that seemed aimed more at helping Goldman Sachs and other American companies make money than at protecting U.S. national security. Liberal Republicans' new mantra was "what's good for China is good for the country," and the bureaucrats went along. As former Pentagon official Frank Gaffney put it, Paulson became "China's man in the Cabinet."

Bolten was the quintessential Big Government Republican whose interest in business overshadowed U.S. national security needs. He had been executive director of legal and government affairs for Goldman Sachs in London from 1994 to 1999. He first signed on with Bush as policy director for the president's election campaign from 1999 to 2000; he was appointed deputy chief of staff for policy in January 2001, and in 2003 he became director of the Office of Management and Budget. A former trade official in the administration of President George H. W. Bush, Bolton also burnished his liberal credentials as a State Department lawyer and as an aide to former secretary of state Henry Kissinger on a commission on Central America.

Bolten got the chief of staff position after the liberal camp within the White House, headed by Dan Bartlett, waged political warfare against the president's more conservative staff, especially presidential adviser Karl Rove. Bartlett had shown his loyalties by cooperating with reporter Bob Woodward on his 2002 book, *Bush at War*, and quietly attacking Rumsfeld and other administration conservatives. Liberals like Condoleezza Rice, at the time national security adviser, were presented in the most flattering light in the book.

The disputes led President Bush to replace Card, a mild-mannered liberal Republican business executive whose main claim to fame was not waging political warfare but serving as secretary of transportation in the administration of President George H. W. Bush. His business orientation made him ill-suited for the high-pressure political environment in Washington.

But the effect of choosing Bolten as Card's replacement was only to push the White House more toward a business orientation and away from the conservative policies and philosophy that guided the president. Bolten defended nonpolitical and anticonservative policies and appointments as part of an effort to "professionalize" the White House. In reality, his efforts undermined the president's goals and the administration's efforts.

A biography of President George Bush published in the fall of 2007 highlights the division between the president wanting one policy and the bureaucracy carrying out another. Bush told biographer Robert Draper that he had ordered that the Iraqi army be kept intact after the March 2003 invasion. "The policy was to keep the army intact; didn't happen," Bush said. When asked to explain why if the policy was to maintain the Iraqi army that the chief administrator in Iraq, L. Paul Bremer, ordered the 400,000-man army disbanded in May 2003, Bush replied, "Yeah, I can't remember, I'm sure I said, 'This is the policy, what happened?' . . . Again, [National Security Adviser Stephen] Hadley's got notes on all this stuff."

The fateful decision was carried out because State Department bureaucrats had made the decision to disband the military, leading to chaos and an insurgency that is going on today. According to senior Bush administration officials, the Pentagon had supported a plan by retired Army general Jay Garner, the first post–Iraq invasion leader of the Office of Reconstruction and Humanitarian Assistance, to keep the Iraqi army intact, despite its past association with corruption and atrocities. The idea was to use the Iraqi military to help with reconstituting a new government, and most important, to avoid having U.S. forces become an occupation force. But the Iraqi army fled after the fall of Baghdad in April 2003, and rather than try to put the force back together, Bremer, the State Department bureaucrat, disbanded the military under advice from Walter Slocombe, who had been Bill Clinton's undersecretary of defense for policy. Both Bremer and Slocombe, an adviser to the Iraqi defense ministry under the Coalition Provisional Authority, were approved for their positions by Rumsfeld, who once again was given bad advice by the liberals he trusted and relied on.

Liberal policy subversion also crept into the White House through two other Clinton administration holdovers: Maureen Tucker, an NSC staff member, and Newell Highsmith, a lawyer on detail to the White House from the State Department. Both officials had been leading proponents of the Clinton administration's 1998 decision to grant Loral Corp waivers allowing the company to export sensitive technology to China. The technology transfers involved in the space cooperation, which were opposed by conservatives in the Pentagon at the time, ended up permitting China to obtain strategic missile technology that improved Chinese missiles aimed at U.S. cities.

The liberal officials stuck to similarly dangerous positions after Bush took power. For example, they fought against national security officials who wanted to follow the law and impose sanctions on companies involved in deadly transfers of weapons and technology. One Bush administration official told me, "Tucker and Highsmith also worked against [WMD] sanctions during the Bush administration. Tucker chaired an NSC panel on sanctions. Highsmith was the State lawyer on proliferation."

Tucker managed to go on to a senior post in the State Department within the office of Undersecretary of State for International Security and Arms Control John Rood.

"Tucker illustrates a serious problem in the Bush administration—its tendency to retain and hire bad people who do not share the president's views," the official said.

The late Constantine Menges wrote in his book *Inside the NSC* how staffing the National Security Council with State Department Foreign Service officers and other political opponents hurt American foreign policies.

"The Bush NSC is déjà vu all over again," the official said, paraphrasing baseball great Yogi Berra. "The Clinton administration removed everyone they thought might have Republican leanings.

"This administration retained Clinton appointees such as George Tenet, Rand Beers, Richard Clarke, and Maureen Tucker," he said. "It also gave most NSC staff jobs to State officers."

It is clear that the administration's failure to get political appointees and bureaucrats to line up behind the president has caused serious damage to U.S. national security. The problem has been especially bad because it is directly linked to similar renegades in the Pentagon.

6

THE PENTAGON PUZZLE PALACE

The Defense Department and the U.S. armed forces are the front line in protecting the United States from its enemies, whether from Islamist extremists bent on destroying the country, or Chinese Communists who view the United States as their main enemy to be vanquished. But that key line of defense has been severely compromised.

Over the past twenty years, bureaucrats and their liberal Democrat and Republican allies have caused enormous damage to American security by stripping the Pentagon of its warfighting ethos, infusing feminism and immorality into policies, and stripping hundreds of millions of dollars from needed defense spending to boost left-wing environmental policies.

The damage continued even after President George W. Bush came into office. Bush's Pentagon regime, led by defense secretary Donald H. Rumsfeld, deputy defense secretary Paul Wolfowitz, and a few key aides, did try to reverse some of the Clinton administration's disastrous policies and programs, and to work around the career bureaucracy. But they ended up making a series of key blunders that completely undermined their policy efforts: they appointed to several key political positions liberal Republicans who were not committed to the administration's national security objectives.

Rumsfeld, one of the first Bush Cabinet officials appointed, was a defense hawk who took over the Pentagon at a time when adult supervision in U.S. defense and national security affairs was sorely needed. Eight years of the Clinton administration, with its deep defense budget cuts, its left-wing policies loosening restrictions on homosexuals in the military, and its weakness and vacillation toward growing international terrorist attacks against American forces in Yemen, Saudi Arabia, and elsewhere had taken a toll. Both the civilian and military ranks were facing a leadership crisis, as liberals within the Clinton Defense Department and White House launched a systematic campaign to promote liberal or left-leaning military officers in an effort to liberalize the conservative armed forces. The politicization produced the likes of Marine Corps general Anthony Zinni, Army chief of staff General Eric Shinseki, Army general Wesley Clark, and chairman of the Joint Chiefs of Staff John Shalikashvili. All were averse to using American power around the world and opposed to committing troops or even using force unless the risks were minimal.

America's enemies had grown bolder as a result, as became crystal clear on September 11, 2001. Rumsfeld, already committed to what he termed defense "transformation," redoubled his efforts. But he faced an extremely difficult internal political battle against the entrenched "Clinton generals" and the Pentagon bureaucracy. Unfortunately, the Rumsfeld team was also undermined from within—by a network of "special assistants" and political appointees who proved to be incompetent.

The Cambone Failures

Rumsfeld made a particularly big mistake when he brought in Stephen Cambone as one of his closest aides. A liberal Republican, Cambone had never held senior positions in government, but he had worked for defense secretary Dick Cheney from 1990 to 1993. More important for his career in the Bush administration, he had been the staff director for Rumsfeld on the 1998 Commission to Assess the Ballistic Missile Threat to the United States. He came to the Pentagon early in Rumsfeld's tenure as principal deputy undersecretary of defense for policy, and despite his lack of government experience, the highly ambitious official rose through the ranks under the defense secretary's protection.

Officials who worked with Cambone described him as a "BENS" Republican, for the liberal group Business Executives for National Security. That organization favored doing business around the world over making the protection of U.S. national security a prime objective.

Cambone quickly developed the reputation as the defense secretary's hatchet man. He was reviled in many areas of the Pentagon because of his lack of experience and because he was given to loud tirades during meetings with underlings. He often berated senior military officers, including generals and admirals, and in general showed little respect for the military. Yet whenever he met with Rumsfeld, he was said to become a mild-mannered bureaucrat.

Cambone also clashed with Douglas Feith, who occupied the important position of undersecretary of defense for policy. Feith, a lawyer who had worked for the Reagan administration on the National Security Council staff and at the Pentagon, came under fire from critics of the administration as a "neoconservative" who had engineered the Iraq invasion, when in reality he was just one of several key players. Nevertheless, in reaction to the Iraq War going badly, Feith was replaced in 2005 by a career Foreign Service officer, Eric Edelman, who proceeded to orient Pentagon policies in favor of the liberal, appeasement-oriented policies of his home agency, the State Department.

Even worse, Cambone caused serious damage to national security by ending some of the most important defense and intelligence programs, according to officials who worked with him. He carried out unreasonable cuts in U.S. force structure that officials told me will have a lasting negative impact on U.S. military power. The cuts were so severe that the United States could now be faced with the difficult task of not being able to prevail in a future war with a foe like China, and these critics blame Cambone for contributing to the failures.

Another Rumsfeld special assistant, Larry Di Rita, defended Cambone from his critics. He acknowledged that Cambone was pressing ahead to cut troop strength and weapons programs and that these efforts upset generals and admirals opposed to the reductions. But, Di Rita insisted, "Change agents bring change, and that is understandably unsettling to some." According to Defense officials, Rumsfeld was partly to blame, because he insisted on not getting into the details of such changes, choosing to focus on grand strategy rather than tactics. The shortcoming was a major failing of the conservative defense chief.

By 2003, Cambone had maneuvered his way to becoming the first ever undersecretary of defense for intelligence. The new post reflected Rumsfeld's belief that he needed a "czar" to oversee the big-budget intelligence agencies at the Pentagon, which consumed some 80 percent of the U.S. intelligence community's $43.5 billion annual intelligence budget. The defense secretary insisted that beefing up defense-related intelligence capabilities become a major priority.

A May 8, 2003, memorandum from Deputy Defense Secretary Paul Wolfowitz gave Cambone's undersecretariat control over 286 people and all policies related to intelligence, counterintelligence, and the assistant secretary for command, control, communications, and intelligence, or C4I, which in the past had always been the top Pentagon intelligence official. Three deputies were created, one each for intelligence warning, warfighting and operations, and counterintelligence and security.

The memorandum said that the new undersecretary would "exercise authority, direction, and control over the Defense Intelligence Agency (DIA), the National Imagery and Mapping Agency (NIMA) [later renamed the National Geospatial Intelligence Agency], the National Reconnaissance Office (NRO), the National Security Agency (NSA), the Defense Security Service (DSS) and the DoD Counterintelligence Field Activity (CIFA)." The new undersecretary would see that "these organizations . . . have adequate acquisition-management structures and processes in place to deliver intelligence programs on time and within budget."

So as "USD-I," Cambone oversaw a bureaucratic empire that provided him with sweeping power over the intelligence bureaucracy. Yet he failed to complete any major intelligence upgrades or reforms of the kind Rumsfeld sought. Defense intelligence agencies, both civilian and military, were left largely intact and badly in need of reform. Most of the Pentagon intelligence money was spent on the rather mundane but vastly expensive National Reconnaissance Office, which developed, in deepest secrecy, spy satellites and launched them on boosters.

Cambone acted recklessly when he moved rapidly to take over and eliminate a number of the Pentagon's special access programs (SAPs), which are considered the most sensitive intelligence secrets in the U.S. government. SAPs are so secret that U.S. government officials are actually permitted to lie about the programs in order to protect their "operational security." One example of a SAP was the program run during the 1980s that identified a key electronic vulnerability in Iraq's air defense radar, which ultimately allowed U.S. forces to destroy the radars during the 1991 Persian Gulf War. Officials said that Cambone's irresponsibility with strategic defense and intelligence policies will come to haunt the Pentagon for years to come.

If Cambone did not achieve much with the power he had as USD-1, that did not stop him from trying to exercise even more power within the Pentagon. He was not content with controlling intelligence and also sought to control policy related to special operations forces. In the summer of 2004, Congress, after consulting with Cambone, tried to add new restrictions to the military's use of special operations forces by requiring a presidential order before deploying commandos in routine but hidden activities. The restrictions were outlined in a classified Senate report that was part of the annual intelligence authorization bill for fiscal 2004.

These restrictions would have added a new burden to the most important strategic element of Rumsfeld's strategy in the war against Islamist extremists around the world. Rumsfeld wanted *fewer* restrictions, since he aimed to transform the U.S. Special Operations Command (SOCOM) from a "supporting command"—one that supports other warfighters—to a "supported command," or a leading warfighting component of the U.S. military. Only months earlier, Rumsfeld had told Congress that the Bush administration wanted to dramatically expand the commando force with an additional $1.5 billion, nearly 2,000 more troops, and more authority to go after terrorists. Instead, Cambone moved to make it harder to use the forces.

Defense officials sounded the alarm when they learned about the restrictions, which were dubbed the "Cambone understanding." A former special operations officer who opposed the rules said that the new restrictions meant "that things that special ops used to do will now require sending a 'finding' to [Capitol Hill] before doing anything." The existing intelligence report language from 1991 excluded special operations forces from the legal finding requirements.

"We want to be able to deploy [special operations commandos] in minutes and hours instead of days and weeks," said the former special operations officer. "And this will get us delays. It will make it hard to kill terrorists by turning over deployment decisions to the Senate."

Instead of firing Cambone for the incompetence, Rumsfeld and his aides sought to defend him, saying the rules were due to a "misunderstanding" between Cambone and several senators. But the Senate report singled out Cambone by noting that "the committee commends the designee for undersecretary of defense for intelligence for agreeing to these conditions."

After I reported on this debacle for the *Washington Times,* Rumsfeld let it be known that if the restrictions were ultimately contained in the final bill, the president would veto it. They eventually were removed, and a disaster was averted.

One reason Cambone did not succeed in reforming the intelligence system was that he remained extremely deferential to the CIA.

Officials who worked with him described his relations with the agency as slavish. In fact, they told me they suspected he was kowtowing to the agency in hopes of becoming the CIA director in the future.

The only minor successes within the newly created intelligence office were accomplished by Army lieutenant general William G. "Jerry" Boykin. Boykin, who got into trouble by casting the war on terrorism in religious terms, was a true warrior, a member of the Army's legendary Delta Force who knew how to employ special forces in the war on terrorism, despite having to work under Cambone.

Cambone's work was so ineffective that when Robert Gates was nominated to replace Rumsfeld as defense secretary in late 2006, he told senators during his confirmation hearing that he did not like "offline intelligence organizations or analytical groups." Sure enough, he replaced Cambone with a longtime antireform intelligence bureaucrat, James Clapper, a former director of the Defense Intelligence Agency (DIA).

As undersecretary for intelligence Cambone also displayed a political bias in favor of liberal bureaucrats. In 2006, the Justice Department finally prosecuted what many intelligence officials identified as a notorious pro–China influence agent, former DIA analyst Ronald Montaperto—whom this author first identified as a suspected Chinese agent back in 2000. Montaperto, who worked on Chinese affairs, had denied being a Chinese mole and, alarmingly, had held on to his security clearance. He was finally caught in a sting operation carried out by the Naval Criminal Investigative Service (NCIS), which fooled him into revealing that he had supplied Top Secret intelligence data illegally to two Chinese military intelligence officers.

Montaperto found supporters among pro-China officials in the U.S. intelligence community, including Deputy National Intelligence Officer for East Asia Lonnie Henley, who wrote a pre-sentencing letter to the judge on behalf of his good "friend." Montaperto was never charged as a spy and faced only relatively minor charges of mishandling classified documents. Prosecutors never explained why they didn't charge him as a spy. They only claimed that Montaperto admitted passing the information, and therefore he was treated lightly. But the fact is that his final plea agreement stated that he knowingly provided classified information to Chinese military intelligence agents. He did not admit providing secrets to China until fooled into doing so by the NCIS.

At the time of the case, Cambone was the senior Pentagon intelligence official and could have weighed in on the case. Instead, he remained silent. The failure to properly highlight Montaperto's crime and expose his high-level supporters in the intelligence community would have long-term negative consequences, as I will show later. The liberal bureaucrats at the Pentagon and CIA closed ranks in defending Montaperto, claiming he was a victim of U.S. government "McCarthyism." But retired FBI counterintelligence chief David Szady stated that Montaperto "is guilty as hell and gave a lot to the Chinese. If he had it, they got it. . . . He did get off easy based on what we know he did."

By late 2006, Cambone had left the Pentagon. About a year later he took a high-paying position with QinetiQ (pronounced "kinetic"), a British-owned defense and intelligence contractor. In January 2008, just two months after his hiring, QinetiQ announced that its Mission Solutions Group had signed a five-year, $30 million contract to provide security services for the Pentagon Counterintelligence Field Activity office—an office Cambone had overseen while at the Pentagon. It was the ultimate example of a liberal bureaucrat cashing in on his government experience.

Henry's Reorg

Another staffing mistake Donald Rumsfeld made was to bring on Christopher Ryan Henry as deputy undersecretary of defense for policy in 2003. Henry had worked for the contractor SAIC and the think tank the Center for Strategic and International Studies, and was a career military officer with no policy experience. His political experience consisted of working for a Democratic member of Congress—something he did not reveal to the Pentagon when he was hired, according to Pentagon officials.

So Henry was ill-suited for this top policy position. How, then, did he get the job?

It is possible that Rumsfeld offered him the job at least in part because Henry's wife, Delonnie, had become the defense secretary's key administrative assistant. Delonnie Henry had worked with Rumsfeld in the 1990s when he chaired the 1998 Commission to Assess the Ballistic Missile Threat to the United States, and when Rumsfeld became secretary of defense he brought Delonnie into his immediate Pentagon office as a confidential assistant. Henry reportedly received his appointment after he and his wife planned to move out of the area, which would have deprived Rumsfeld of his assistant.

Despite Henry's lack of experience, he was given the extremely important task of undertaking a major reorganization within the Office of the Secretary of Defense. His decisions had dire consequences. The reorganization was so badly done that it placed responsibility for nuclear weapons and missile defense policies under the assistant secretary for special operations and low-intensity conflict. Thus it diminished the importance of both strategic nuclear arms and missile defenses.

Along with his predecessor Stephen Cambone, Henry was distrusted by many Pentagon officials. Both Cambone and Henry undermined Donald Rumsfeld's policies, according to officials I spoke with. When Rumsfeld resigned, it looked as if Cambone and Henry would be heading out the door (though as it turned out Henry would stay on at the Pentagon). A sizable contingent of Pentagon officials welcomed the prospect of their departure. "I think everyone in the building is breathing a sigh of relief that they'll be gone," one veteran official said. "They did serious harm to national security."

In the summer of 2008 the Pentagon inspector general launched an investigation into whether Henry had misused government travel for personal reasons. Henry quietly let it be known he was resigning. In an interview with the author, he downplayed the inspector general probe, saying that such allegations are made frequently and usually end without any action. He also defended his policy reorganizations as "beneficial" and dismissed critics as "single-issue advocates."

Defense officials said that Henry's departure had come too late, since he had already undermined defense policies.

Special Ops Turf Wars

Within the military and civilian ranks, the liberals and bureaucrats fought against Rumsfeld's plans to increase the use of special operations forces in the war on terrorism and for other missions. Rumsfeld, as noted, wanted to transform special operations commandos from warfighting supporters to front-line covert warriors in the war on terrorism.

Specifically, he took steps to give the U.S. Special Operations Command new powers to plan and execute operations to kill or capture terrorists. Prior to 9/11 the command, which had 46,000 troops, was basically a training unit that provided expertise and equipment but rarely was used for combat, paramilitary operations, intelligence-gathering, or covert action. Rumsfeld was fond of pressing the general in charge of the command early in the Bush administration, General Charles Holland, "Have you killed any terrorists today?" The dig highlighted perfectly Rumsfeld's frustration with the special operations forces, who had become accustomed to playing the role of trainers and military support providers and were resisting, for bureaucratic reasons, efforts to take the lead in the war on terrorism. Conventional-forces generals and admirals resisted the changes as well, since Rumsfeld's plan would encroach on their turf.

Rumsfeld ultimately thwarted his own plans through a series of ineffective appointments. Stephen Cambone was one. Another was

Thomas W. O'Connell, a former Army paratrooper and intelligence specialist who was named assistant secretary of defense for special operations and low-intensity conflict in October 2003. As a soldier O'Connell had fought in wars in Vietnam, Grenada, Panama, and Southwest Asia and had experience in thirty-three countries. During the Vietnam War he was part of the CIA-led Phoenix Program, which targeted Vietcong. He also was a manager at the defense contractor Raytheon and spent three years in the 1990s as a CIA officer. But he was unschooled in the ways of Washington policymaking and as a result he was unable to get U.S. special forces and special operations commandos to make the transition from trainers to warfighters.

After three years of Pentagon turf wars, the military bureaucrats won the battle, defeating the defense secretary's plan for giving the better-equipped and better-trained commandos more power in the war on terrorism. The Unified Command Plan 2004, signed by President Bush on March 1, limited SOCOM's role to "synchronizing" operations against terrorist networks. The only concession the order made was to give SOCOM authority for conducting what the military called "operational preparation of the environment," a bureaucratic way of saying commando forces would be involved in more direct intelligence-gathering. The change was significant in that it gave commandos authority to operate in nonwar zones, despite opposition from State Department bureaucrats. Still, the focus of commandos' activities remained as in the past—on training, planning, and conducting psychological operations, with limitations on the use of special operations forces for actual counterterrorism operations.

The real power to lead military operations remained with conventional-forces commanders. The result was that more than seven years after the 9/11 attacks, bin Laden and his main deputy Ayman al-Zawahiri remained at large and continued to lead the al Qaeda terrorist group, despite the fact that getting both terrorist leaders was the highest priority of both the military community and the intelligence community.

The Consummate Bureaucrat

By 2006, Donald Rumsfeld, Paul Wolfowitz, Douglas Feith, and most of Rumsfeld's other key aides had been ousted from the Pentagon. The final shakeup was orchestrated by White House chief of staff Josh Bolten, the former Goldman Sachs executive who took over in April 2006 and proceeded quietly to purge conservatives from the administration.

To counter any leftover Rumsfeld influence in the Pentagon, the consummate bureaucrat was chosen to be the new secretary of defense: Robert Gates. Gates was a career CIA analyst who had worked for Bush's father, President George H. W. Bush, on the National Security Council staff from 1989 to 1992. Then he became CIA director, a position he held until 1993.

When Gates took over as defense secretary in late 2006, there was hope that he might get rid of some of the liberal Republicans who had worked against Rumsfeld. One was Tina W. Jonas, who became the Pentagon's top budget official in 2004. A former House Appropriations defense subcommittee staff member under Representative Jerry Lewis, California Republican, Jonas was disliked by many conservatives who worked with her. Prior to taking the Pentagon comptroller post, Jonas worked at the FBI as its chief financial officer.

Defense officials hoped that Gates would get rid of Jonas because her rude treatment of her staff led at least fifteen senior budget officials to resign during her several years at the Pentagon. They simply refused to work for her. But Jonas quietly lobbied friends on Capitol Hill, hoping that members of Congress would put in a good word for her with Gates so that he would keep her on. Gates did.

Gates had an opportunity to make improvements by replacing Thomas O'Connell, but the replacement he chose was far from an improvement. For the assistant secretary position he selected a career CIA bureaucrat, Michael G. Vickers, who took over the office in July 2007. The Pentagon plucked Vickers from the Center for Strategic and Budgetary Assessments, an anticonservative think tank loaded with Big Government Republicans and Democrats. And as a CIA officer during the Reagan administration, he was, according to administration officials, one of the worst agency opponents of President Reagan and his pro-freedom policies. Yet he was chosen to take over one of the most important posts in the war on terrorism.

The selection was not accidental. He was chosen because, as a CIA bureaucrat, he would not upset the entrenched bureaucracy, who wanted nothing to do with the reform-minded Rumsfeld and the more conservative members of his team.

Vickers declined to be interviewed by this author, but he spoke to the *Washington Post* in a bit of self-promotion. The liberal *Post* portrayed Vickers as an unsung hero of the war on terrorism. The "top Pentagon adviser on counterterrorism strategy," the article said, was "working to implement the U.S. military's highest-priority plan: a global campaign against terrorism that reaches far beyond Iraq and Afghanistan."

The piece came out in December 2007, when the film *Charlie Wilson's War* was in theaters. The movie, about Congressman Charles Wilson, is a liberal revisionist history of the Cold War. It makes Wilson, a hard-drinking, liberal Democratic congressman from Texas, and his CIA buddies—including Vickers—the heroes of the Cold War who by themselves led and won the rebel war in Afghanistan against the Soviet Union. The film makes little or no mention of the contribution of Reagan and his advisers. The *Post* article bought the revisionism, lauding Vickers as the "principal strategist" for the 1980s CIA paramilitary program that assisted the Afghan mujahideen against the Soviet army. "Not a lot of people thought we could drive the Soviets out of Afghanistan," Vickers told the *Post*.

According to Reagan officials, Vickers's comments are pure fantasy. The CIA fought against the Reagan administration's efforts to arm the Afghan resistance and instead simply used them as fodder against the Soviet army, trying to bleed the Soviets through a war of attrition rather than seeking to actually win against them. It took conservatives led by CIA director William Casey, Defense Secretary Caspar Weinberger, Defense Undersecretary for Policy Fred Iklé, and his deputy Michael Pillsbury to force the CIA bureaucrats to back the Afghans. "The CIA was literally ordered to develop a plan for the Afghans to win, and despite their resistance, they eventually did it," said one senior intelligence official involved in the operation.

Reagan conservatives bristled at the erroneous portrayal of history on display in *Charlie Wilson's War*. Not only did it falsely depict Wilson and a few key allies as the true reason the Soviets were defeated in Afghanistan, the Reagan-era officials said, but it also initially promoted the left-wing myth that the CIA-led operation funded Osama bin Laden and al Qaeda and ultimately produced the attacks of September 11, 2001. Bin Laden, the officials said, never got CIA funding or weapons, and was not directly involved in Islamist extremist activities until years after the Afghan operation, when Soviet troops withdrew in 1989. Some of the more outrageous of these elements were removed from the film before its release.

The movie also fostered the notion that Wilson and his CIA cowboy collaborator, Gust Avrakotos, were enthusiastic backers of supplying advanced U.S. Stinger antiaircraft missiles to the Afghan rebels. Fred Iklé told me the CIA initially fought against sending Stingers, while Wilson was lukewarm on the matter. Both later supported the plan once rebels began downing Soviet gunships with them.

"Senior people in the Reagan administration, the president, [CIA director] Bill Casey, [Defense Secretary Caspar] Weinberger, and their aides deserve credit for the successful Afghan covert action program, not just Charlie Wilson," an angry Iklé said in an interview.

The officials blamed the anti-Reagan slant of the film on the movie's screenwriter, Aaron Sorkin, the Hollywood liberal who regularly attacked conservatives on his television drama *The West Wing*, also known as *The Left Wing* because of its liberal bias.

A Harvard University study confirms the Reagan officials' claims and reveals that Vickers's self-serving comments are false. The report, entitled "Politics of a Covert Action: The U.S., the Mujahedeen, and the Stinger Missile," was conducted by researchers at the John F. Kennedy School of Government. It states that CIA officials vigorously opposed the Afghan covert-action program because they feared it would trigger a world war and because they did not want the Pentagon encroaching on CIA turf.

One key official identified in the report is CIA officer Thomas Twetten, the Near East operations chief from 1983 to 1986. Twetten, the report says, worked against political appointees in the Reagan administration who favored helping the Afghans win. He dismissed the Reagan officials as "strange people developing strange ideas."

"There was a concern [during the Reagan years] between what I call sensible bureaucrats, having been one of them, and the rabid right," Twetten said, referring to Reagan administration policymakers. Twetten later was promoted to the highest position in the Directorate of Operations, the agency's all-important espionage and covert-action branch.

Contrary to the film's claims, the Harvard study reveals that CIA officials, led by Twetten and another officer, William Piekney, the station chief in Pakistan, opposed sending Stinger missiles to the Afghan rebels for political reasons. They feared that the move would expose the CIA's hand. The report states that the anti-Stinger CIA officials did not even admit that Pakistani president Zia ul-Haq requested the missiles for the Pakistan military and the Afghan rebels.

Twetten, in particular, told one interagency meeting that Zia did not want the missiles, a statement that was contradicted by several other participants in the debate. The report quotes Michael Pillsbury as saying that mid-level CIA officers "were openly defying President Reagan's signed directives and most likely belonged to the opposition political party." According to Pillsbury, "These officers acted in a near-mutiny by exploiting their monopoly on access to [Pakistani intelligence] and Zia about the sensitive Afghan program to deny information to their own [director of central intelligence], and to [the Department of Defense] and the [National Security Council]."

The Harvard report provides a devastating indictment of the CIA bureaucrats' treachery and infighting.

Vickers is a clear example of someone who is the wrong person to get the job done in the war on terrorism. Three years after new authorities were granted for special operations forces to go after terrorists, the commandos remain hobbled by weak Pentagon leaders like Vickers.

The bigger problem is that Defense Secretary Gates has shown no stomach for refocusing the Pentagon's efforts to combat terrorism. During his confirmation hearing he said that he had learned the hard way at the CIA to avoid upsetting career bureaucrats. "When you treat the professionals in an organization who . . . perform the mission of the organization with respect, and you listen to them and you pay attention to them, I think that everybody is better served," he said. "They were there before you got there, they'll be there after you leave, and if you don't make them a part of the solution, they will become a part of the problem."

What Gates failed to understand is that the bureaucracy has become the central problem in the Pentagon, as in other key government agencies.

In any case, Gates himself became part of the problem. As noted in Chapter 1, his May 2008 comments advocating negotiating with, making concessions to, the radical Iranian regime of Mahmoud Ahmadinejad—a public statement that ran directly counter to the president's stated policy on Iran—could have been a firing offense.

And that was just part of it. Gates also favored closing the U.S. military prison at Guantánamo Bay, Cuba, which critics had said was unconstitutional and inhumane for keeping terrorists in the facility. That notion was exploded in April 2008 when a terrorist who had been released from "Gitmo" and sent to Kuwait carried out a suicide bombing in the northern Iraqi city of Mosul.

Representative Pete Hoekstra, Michigan Republican and ranking member of the House Permanent Select Committee on Intelligence, said the attack by Abdallah Salih al-Ajmi, who was held at Guantánamo for three and half years before being released, "demonstrates the difficulty of the detainees in Gitmo." This was not an isolated problem either: as many as seven other former Gitmo prisoners were found to have returned to the battlefield.

"Once again," Hoekstra told me, "a detainee may have been given the benefit of the doubt, released, and returned to the battlefield and attacked innocent people and our troops. These are dangerous people."

Destroying "Soft Power"

Ask anyone in a senior policy position in the Pentagon about the main components of the war on terrorism and they will tell you there are three parts. The first is the "kinetic" or direct military combat element, most obvious in Iraq and Afghanistan. Next is the law-enforcement intelligence component, most visible in domestic security. Last is the war of ideas, the ideological component of the war.

It is this last element that was destroyed and rendered useless by liberal Republicans and their supporters in the Pentagon. Chief among them was Victoria Clarke, a liberal Republican who was assistant secretary of defense for public affairs until her abrupt resignation in July 2003.

A look at Clarke's political contributions shows she is clearly a Big Government Republican. Clarke gave cash to the likes of liberal Republicans Rudy Giuliani, John McCain, Senator Arlen Specter of Pennsylvania, and William Weld, the former governor of Massachusetts who ran unsuccessfully for the Senate in 1994.

Pentagon officials said that Clarke was single-handedly responsible for forcing the dismantling of a key strategic office that was—and is—urgently needed to wage a war of ideas against Islamist extremism. That war of ideas was never properly emphasized: while the U.S. government spends upwards of $12 billion a month on the war on terrorism, mainly for military operations in Iraq and Afghanistan, it has spent less than $50 million on "soft power" counterideology programs. But the Clarke disaster made the problem much worse.

It was Clarke who had put out the word privately to her friends in the liberal press that the Office of Strategic Influence (OSI), which was to have led the Pentagon's soft-power drive, had planned to use "disinformation," or false and misleading information, in planting stories in foreign media. Liberal bureaucrats seized on the reports of OSI's disinformation component to wage a nonstop political campaign to subvert the much-needed office. And then the *New York Times* ran the fateful article on OSI in February of 2002.

Douglas Feith, the undersecretary of defense for policy from 2001 to 2005, in his book *War and Decision* blamed Clarke for undermining the OSI effort. As a result of losing OSI, the ideological component of the war on terrorism was left to the Pentagon public affairs office and the State Department's public diplomacy office. "Neither office was equipped to promote initiatives to fight jihadist ideology," he wrote. Feith also told me that he was frustrated by Pentagon bureaucrats unable to grasp the urgent need to conduct a strategic counterideology campaign. Feith said the military bureaucrats even lobbied successfully to prevent the use of the term "war of ideas" because it implied another level of warfighting for the military, something the nonwarrior bureaucrats opposed.

Rumsfeld, whose dislike of the press is legendary and dates to his days as an official in the post-Watergate administration of President Gerald R. Ford, was forced to cave in to pressure from liberal Republicans and bureaucrats. He closed the office in February 2002, saying the office had been irreparably damaged by "inaccurate speculation and assertions" in news reports that it might engage in spreading false information. OSI, he said, never would have spread misinformation, but the media reports and commentary subverted any hope that the mission of the office would succeed. "While much of the thrust of the criticism and the cartoons and comment has been off the mark, the office has been damaged so much that it could not operate effectively," he said.

The office was to have been headed by Air Force brigadier general Simon "Pete" Worden, an aggressive, forward-thinking conservative who understood well the need for an information-warfare component of the war on terrorism. Worden wanted to use the Internet and other clandestine operations to attack terrorists and their ideas at both the source and the dissemination points.

As Rumsfeld expected, the responsibility for providing an ideological counter to Islam fell to the State Department, which, as noted in Chapter 3, produced more failure to wage ideological warfare.

The bureaucrats had won one of the most significant behind-the-scenes battles, one that has had a lasting effect in prolonging the death and suffering of Americans in the war on terrorism.

Pentagon efforts in the war of ideas continued to fail. In October 2006, shortly before Rumsfeld resigned, a memorandum leaked to the press revealed that the Pentagon was trying to step up a public relations effort to "correct the record" on the war in Iraq specifically and the war on terrorism generally. The memo said the Pentagon planned a "rapid response" unit similar to those used by the Clinton administration for its political campaigns. The author of the memorandum was Assistant Secretary for Public Affairs Dorrance Smith, a liberal Republican whom White House liberals had sent to the Pentagon to try to control Rumsfeld.

The effort was another lame effort to try and spin the press, rather than wage ideological war.

The rapid-response office was shut down by Gates shortly after he came into office. But Gates quickly recognized that the government was hamstrung by a lack of organizations capable of waging ideological war. In November 2007, he called for using soft power to defeat terrorism. "Based on my experience serving seven presidents, as a former director of CIA and now as secretary of defense, I am here to make the case for strengthening our capacity to use 'soft' power and for better integrating it with 'hard' power," Gates said. But he offered no concrete steps on how to do it.

Letting Down the Troops

Bureaucratic bungling and liberal incompetence in the Pentagon has had an even more direct—and even deadlier—effect on U.S. troops.

The problem is that Pentagon bureaucrats have resisted providing troops in the field with much-needed equipment, including mine re-sistant, ambush-protected vehicles, known as MRAPs. Democrats have often tried to use the equipment issue as a political issue against Re-publicans, but the real story reveals that it is liberal bureaucrats who are responsible for this disturbing failure.

The Bush administration recognized this problem early on. In 2004, Deputy Secretary of Defense Paul Wolfowitz established the Joint Rapid Acquisition Cell, or JRAC, to get urgently needed sup-plies and equipment to U.S. warfighters precisely because the tradi-tional Pentagon acquisition processes were so slow and cumbersome.

But even after the JRAC was set up, the Pentagon had a difficult time working around the bureaucracy. One official in the office of the undersecretary for Acquisition, Technology, and Logistics (AT&L) said, for example, that the person "who controls all personnel assets in AT&L . . . stonewalled the JRAC for almost one year on acquiring one personnel space. This while at the same time filling positions in offices with little to no connection to the 'current fight'!"

In May 2007, Defense Secretary Gates made MRAP production the Pentagon's highest priority and said in a memo that the Army was not buying enough. Said one Pentagon official, "The current political lead-ership in AT&L instead threw the MRAP issue over to the traditional 'Acquisition people' in AT&L asking that they form a working group to study what the impediments were to expediting this program. This research had already been done! Bureaucratic foot-dragging such as this has delayed this program only further, [and] internecine warfare and a lack of political leadership and engagement within the highest level of the AT&L acquisition organization has only hurt our warfighters."

The Pentagon was looking to fund 18,000 MRAPs, but early budgeting would have provided about 8,000. Gates pressed for the MRAP production to be stepped up in 2007, and while more than 14,000 vehicles were ordered, by the spring of 2008 there were 4,200 in Iraq, and 1,200 in Kuwait waiting to be delivered.

The Marines also were exposed for bureaucratic bungling. They, too, dragged their feet on MRAPs needed for Marines in Iraq. In January 2008, a report by Franz Gayl, an employee in the Plans, Policies, and Operations Department of the Marine Corps Headquarters, disclosed that urgent appeals from Marines in Iraq for MRAPs in 2005 were ignored. "If the mass procurement and fielding of MRAPs had begun in 2005 in response to the known and acknowledged threats at that time, as the USMC is doing today, hundreds of deaths and injuries could have been prevented," Gayl's report stated. "The urgency of the request to [Chairman of the Joint Chiefs of Staff] was unmistakable."

Who's in Control?

The Pentagon is supposed to be America's first line of defense, but again and again the people in control have undermined rather than enhanced our national security. That's because the people who are really in control are different from the ones who are nominally in control. The Pentagon remains in the hands of liberal bureaucrats.

7

THE SELLOUT OF

FORMER OFFICIALS

O n March 11, 2008, at the height of a highly charged presidential election campaign in which the war in Iraq was one of the most hotly debated issues, the senior commander of U.S. military forces in the Middle East—the officer charged with leading the war on terrorism—abruptly resigned. Admiral William J. "Fox" Fallon quit as commander of U.S. Central Command (CENTCOM), claiming that a magazine article discussing his liberal, antimilitary position on the Bush administration's Iran policy had become a "distraction." Fallon had quit in the middle of a war.

By quitting when and how he did, Fallon undermined the commander in chief he was sworn to serve, and gave aid and comfort to the opponents of the war.

Admiral Fallon represented the worst of the nonwarrior tradition among a generation of military officers whose careers blossomed during the Clinton administration. From 1993 to 2001, military officers, whether they realized it or not, were subjected to a Clinton administration litmus test, which transformed the officer corps into politically correct nonwarriors who support the advancement of women, regardless of competency or skills, and who sought to modify rules barring homosexuals from serving in the military.

The frightening truth is that even now these "Clinton generals" continue to dominate the ranks of the U.S. military.

Fallon the "Good Cop"

The article that spawned the Fallon controversy ran in *Esquire* magazine. "The Man Between War and Peace," written by former Naval War College professor Thomas P. M. Barnett, portrayed Fallon as the "good cop" seeking to block warmongering conservatives in the Bush administration from taking a hard line on Iran.

Fallon's resignation statement artfully sought to mask the liberal admiral's antiwar views. He stated that recent press reports suggested "a disconnect between my views and the president's policy objectives" and that the differences "have become a distraction at a critical time and hamper efforts in the CENTCOM region" (CENTCOM covers from North Africa through Pakistan). Fallon insisted that there was not such a disconnect, but "the simple perception that there is makes it difficult for me to effectively serve America's interests there." It was "best to step aside," he said, and let Defense Secretary Robert Gates and other military leaders "move beyond this distraction."

What kind of warrior would quit the most important position in the military in a time of war over a magazine article? It strains credulity to the breaking point. If Fallon had had any political conviction or belief in the rightness of the cause of fighting terrorism and creating a stable democratic Arab state in the heart of the Middle East, he would never have quit.

After the resignation, senior defense and military officials privately expressed their concern that Fallon was not simply ill-suited for running CENTCOM but had actively opposed the president's policies.

President Bush had nominated Fallon as CENTCOM commander just two months after he had made a stop in Hawaii, where Fallon was serving as commander of the Pacific Command. Bush was impressed with Fallon during that meeting, so much so that apparently he did not fully explore Fallon's personal views on the war in Iraq and Afghanistan. Nor did he seem to examine Fallon's stance or other crucial issues like how to address the threat from Communist China.

As it turned out, Fallon's views were at odds with the president's. Fallon soon clashed with Bush's ground commander in Iraq, Army general David Petraeus. Admiral Fallon opposed the plan Petraeus implemented to help stabilize wartorn Iraq, the troop increase that became known as the "surge." General Petraeus and the Bush administration carried out the plan in the face of vehement protests from antiwar Democratic political leaders and especially from liberal bureaucrats who viewed the war as lost and who only wanted to pull out troops and leave Iraq worse off than it was under Saddam Hussein.

Fallon, according to senior Bush administration supporters who spoke for him in private, wanted to pull most U.S. troops out of Iraq by 2009, a position favored by liberal Democrats. He also wanted to shift the focus from Iraq to Pakistan and Iran—Iran in purely diplomatic terms and Pakistan as a place that was becoming more of a safe haven for al Qaeda in the ungoverned tribal areas. "He didn't support the surge because he was opposed to the concept of a 'long war,' " said a senior administration official.

Of course, the surge that Fallon and so many others opposed proved remarkably effective in curtailing the insurgency in Iraq.

Later, in September 2007, Fallon gave an interview to the pro-terrorist television news station Al Jazeera, which the Pentagon had once considered bombing. In the interview he took a soft line on the Islamic Republic of Iran and thereby undercut the Bush administration's official policy on Iran. Fallon argued against not only the use of force, but even the *threat* of the use of force—the only leverage available for pressuring Tehran into giving up its illegal uranium enrichment program.

"This constant drumbeat of conflict is one that strikes me as not helpful and not useful . . . ," Fallon told Al Jazeera television. "I expect that there will be no war [with Iran] and that is what we ought to be working for. . . . We should find ways through which we can bring countries to work together for the benefit of all. . . . It is not a good idea to be in a state of war. We ought to try and to do our utmost to create different conditions." The four-star admiral said he favored a "combination of strength and willingness to engage," a position in line with liberal arms-control and foreign policy advocates who favor "dialogue" and "diplomacy," even when the enemy is guided by fanatical Islamists like Mahmoud Ahmadinejad, who has threatened to wipe Israel from the map.

Fallon represented the generation of military leaders who have turned out to be weak-willed and more akin to diplomats than warriors. In fact, while at the Pacific Command, Fallon proposed easing restrictions on military exchanges with China and even made an uninvited trip to Beijing, where he got a chilly closed-door reception from senior Chinese military leaders.

The White House, however, blamed not Fallon himself but the media for the problems. Asked about the CENTCOM commander's resignation, White House spokeswoman Dana Perino said that the "perception" of policy differences between Fallon and President Bush built up "through reading about it in the Fourth Estate." In reality, the press had nothing to do with it. The White House spin machine was covering up for the president's blunder in picking an incompetent, liberal admiral as his war commander for Middle East forces.

Playing Politics

Democrats seized on the Fallon resignation as evidence that the Bush administration was stifling dissent among senior military leaders over Iraq. Senate majority leader Harry Reid of Nevada led the way by announcing that the admiral's departure was "yet another example that independence and the frank, open airing of experts' views are not welcomed in this administration."

Senator Barack Obama, campaigning for the Democratic presidential nomination, accused the Bush administration of punishing officers who opposed the president's policies. "Under this administration, too often we have seen civilian control turned into an expectation that the uniformed military will be punished if they tell the president what he needs to know, rather than what he wants to hear," Obama said. "When I am president, the buck will stop with me, but we will restore trust and open dialogue between the military and civilian leadership."

Hillary Clinton also used the Fallon resignation to try to propel her presidential campaign. She praised Fallon as "a voice of reason in an administration which has used inflammatory rhetoric against Iran." She added, "I am asking that the Senate Armed Services Committee hold hearings into the circumstances surrounding his departure." The hearings never took place, because the Pentagon blocked Fallon from testifying, noting that he was no longer in charge of the Central Command or the war in Iraq because of his resignation. Senator Clinton also said that the Bush administration should not use Fallon's resignation as an excuse to "ratchet up tensions with Iran," and instead she urged diplomacy, including direct talks with the radical Islamist regime in Tehran.

Fallon's resignation highlighted the unprecedented use of former military officers in the presidential campaign, as both Republicans and Democrats moved to line up former generals, admirals, and other officers to try and burnish their credentials for the post of commander in chief. What is most disturbing is that the "formers" were engaging in partisan politics and undermining the long tradition within the military of maintaining an apolitical posture that would benefit not only future senior leaders but also keep the military free of negative political influences.

The politicization of the military through former officials actually began during the 1992 presidential campaign, when former Joint Chiefs of Staff chairman Admiral William Crowe backed Vietnam War draft-dodger Bill Clinton against World War II combat pilot George H. W. Bush. Crowe said at the time that he sought nothing in return for backing Clinton. Clinton, however, considered the Crowe endorsement crucial to his victory and rewarded the admiral with a plum appointment as ambassador to Britain.

By the time the 2008 campaign rolled around, both the Obama and Clinton campaigns were bragging about the numbers of former military leaders who supported them. For Obama, the most senior former officer to support him was retired Air Force general Merrill "Tony" McPeak, who was the Air Force's chief of staff and a Joint Chiefs member during the presidency of Bush's father. McPeak became an Obama campaign cochairman and, outrageously, blamed President Bush for Iran's bad behavior. "Iran is a big enemy of al Qaeda," McPeak told the *Washington Times*. "They were a big enemy of the Taliban. They cooperated with us quite completely in the initial phases of our Afghanistan operation. And it was us that insulted them by including them in the 'axis of evil' and making sure they understood we didn't like them very much."

The truth is that Iran is a terrorist state sponsor of the first order and has continued to supply arms, explosives, and training to insurgents and terrorists that are killing U.S. forces in Iraq. Iran also harbored al Qaeda members, claiming falsely that it had placed senior al Qaeda leaders under house arrest. McPeak said he switched parties from Republican to Democrat because he opposed the president's 2003 invasion of Iraq.

A day after Fallon resigned, Obama appeared at a ballroom in the Chicago History Museum, American flags arrayed in the background, to announce that a group of former generals and admirals had endorsed him for president. One retired admiral, Robert Williamson, all but accused President Bush of misusing force and failing to get the best possible information before taking military action. Another retired general, Air Force brigadier general James Smith, told the gathering that Obama would be different because he would be using "multinational relationships," an echo of the Clinton administration policy of aggressive multilateralism that essentially turned over U.S. global action in many cases to the United Nations.

Republican presidential nominee John McCain, too, was able to muster the support of more than one hundred retired military officers. A former Navy pilot and prisoner of war during the Vietnam War, McCain easily won the support of many current and former military officers, most of them, not surprisingly, former Navy officers. They included Admiral Leighton "Snuffy" Smith, who led operations in southern Europe and the Balkans. "This nation is at war and we'd better damn well understand that fact," said Smith. "John McCain understands it, and he is the only candidate that has not wavered one bit in his position regarding the importance of victory in the war against Islamic extremism or in his commitment to the troops who are doing the fighting." Others included retired Marine Corps Commandant General P. X. Kelley; Admiral Frank Kelso, former chief of Naval Operations; and former Army general Norman Schwarzkopf, CENTCOM commander during the 1991 Persian Gulf War.

The Revolt of the Generals

The politicization of the military mushroomed in 2006 after a group of former high-ranking military officers took the extraordinary step of going public to criticize the Pentagon leadership in the middle of a war. The effort focused on Secretary of Defense Donald Rumsfeld, who was eventually pressured out by the White House. The so-called revolt of the generals was an ugly episode that will be remembered for lowering the apolitical stature of the American military leadership, especially during time of war.

In April 2006, a group of six former officers called on Rumsfeld to resign, stating that the defense secretary was guilty of poor war planning for Iraq after Saddam Hussein was deposed, not sending enough ground troops, and a failure to anticipate the insurgency. They also charged that Rumsfeld had intimidated senior officers and meddled in war planning.

Among the six protesters was retired Marine General Anthony Zinni, who was unusual in that he was a politically liberal Marine general in a mostly conservative Corps. Zinni had served as CENTCOM commander in 1998 and was one of the most obvious examples of a "Clinton general." It was under his command that the military carried out the limited bombing campaign against Iraq called Operation Desert Fox, which coincided with the House of Representatives' impeachment hearings of President Clinton. To any observer, the bombing raid was an obvious attempt by Clinton to distract attention from his personal problems. Yet Zinni never spoke out or resigned over that disgraceful misuse of military power. He reserved his ire for Republicans, notably Rumsfeld, whom he accused of wanting to disband the Army.

Zinni was from the nonwarrior culture of generals who believed that there was never a time when military force should be used. When it came to the Middle East, he favored "stability" over change, even when a stable Middle East was a breeding ground for terrorists, including those that attacked the United States. Zinni suffered from the same disease common among State Department bureaucrats: clientitis. From being around Arab and other leaders in the Middle East and South Asia, he lost sight of the need to transform the region politically and economically as a way to mitigate its problems.

The other retired officers who broke ranks in time of war were Army general John Batiste, who headed the Army's First Infantry Division during the 2003 Iraq invasion; Army major general John Riggs; Army major general Charles Swannack; Army major general Paul Eaton; and Marine lieutenant General Gregory Newbold, the former

Joint Staff director of operations, who in 2002 declared that U.S. bombing raids had "eviscerated" the power of the Taliban. A few days after that comment, Rumsfeld publicly chastised the craggy Marine general for overstating the effect of the initial airstrikes. The defense secretary was right; he understood that it was way too soon to count the Taliban as defeated. Sure enough, the Taliban would launch counterattacks in 2007 and by 2008 had imported many of the deadly Islamist tactics used elsewhere: suicide car bomb attacks and roadside improvised explosive devices.

When Newbold retired in late 2002, Rumsfeld made fun of the general by showing a video of the comment and then later saying on a television show that he was surprised a Marine even knew what the word "eviscerated" meant. But the general could not take the joke and eventually turned on Rumsfeld. Perhaps not surprisingly, when the revolt of the generals occurred, the mainstream media floated dubious charges that Rumsfeld was insensitive to subordinates.

Overall, the generals' criticism was a disgraceful display of undermining civilian authority. Military tradition held that officers who disagreed with their orders would quietly resign. But these men were not content simply resigning. They felt the need to make a very public display of protest—knowing full well that they would be used to further partisan agendas. To the grandstanding former generals, it was important to make political points and settle old scores against their civilian bosses.

Air Force general Richard B. Myers, the chairman of the Joint Chiefs of Staff during the George W. Bush administration, explained the dangerous precedent the generals' revolt was setting. "I think what we see happening with retired general officers is bad for the military, bad for civil-military relations, and bad for the country," Myers said. The retired generals' criticism was "inappropriate because it's not the military that judges our civilian bosses," he added. "We'd be in a horrible state in this country, in my opinion, if the military was left to judge the civilian bosses, because when you judge Secretary Rumsfeld, you're also judging the commander in chief, because that's the chain of command, and that's just not appropriate."

Likewise, Marine Corps lieutenant general Michael P. DeLong, who was deputy CENTCOM commander during the invasions of Iraq and Afghanistan, said, "When we have an administration that is currently at war, with a secretary of defense that has the confidence of the president and basically has done well—no matter what grade you put on there, he has done well—to call for his resignation right now is not good for the country."

President Bush mounted a defense of Rumsfeld, stating publicly that he supported his defense chief, but the bureaucracy and the liberal Republicans continued working to subvert the conservative Rumsfeld and his aides and supporters in the Pentagon.

The real reason the former generals spoke out had less to do with policy and war planning than the long-running bureaucratic battle to prevent Rumsfeld from reorganizing the military, especially the Army. He sought to transform the Army from a large, land-based service equipped with armored forces, heavy and difficult to move and suited to waging conventional maneuver warfare, into a rapidly deployable, highly mobile force more suited to countering terrorism and the proliferation of weapons of mass destruction.

Army chief of staff General Eric Shinseki, a political liberal, had sought to block Rumsfeld's changes. He told Rumsfeld that he would help make him look good to Congress if the defense secretary would leave the Army alone and not change the current large-division-oriented structure, according to defense officials close to Rumsfeld. Shinseki cultivated liberal Democrats on Capitol Hill and could have deflected some of the criticism of Rumsfeld. Rumsfeld refused, and Shinseki would go on to encourage dissension among the Army's senior officer corps against Rumsfeld, and indirectly President Bush, according to Defense officials. So the Army seized on the formers' revolt to discredit Rumsfeld. It was insubordination bordering on sedition, and was made worse because it undermined popular support for the war among the American people.

The revolt triggered widespread political attacks on the Bush administration and its conduct of the war in Iraq, Afghanistan, and elsewhere. One former official who used the generals' revolt for political gain was Richard Holbrooke, a former senior State Department official and an adviser to Hillary Rodham Clinton's presidential campaign. Holbrooke went public in an opinion article in the *Washington Post* to state that he expected "more generals" to voice their criticism of Rumsfeld, including those on active duty, until it "consumed" the defense secretary. Holbrooke seemed to delight in urging U.S. military leaders to trash their civilian commanders, including a president and vice president elected by the American people.

Eventually, of course, the insubordination succeeded in knocking off Donald Rumsfeld. He resigned in November 2006.

Subversion Confessed

The generals' revolt of 2006 was by no means the only case of disloyal former officials witnessed in recent years. The leadership crisis facing the United States is epitomized by the case of retired Air Force general George Lee Butler, who served as commander of the U.S. Strategic Command and thus would have been in charge of conducting nuclear warfare.

In early 1993, when he was commander of the Strategic Command, General Butler stated that in the future, U.S. nuclear weapons might not be targeted only against the former Soviet Union and other strategic enemies; they might, he said, be called on to take out nuclear, chemical, or biological weapons of rogue states or terrorists. "Our focus now is not just the former Soviet Union but any potentially hostile country that has or is seeking weapons of mass destruction," Butler told the *New York Times*. He noted that traditional nuclear deterrence "may not work" against terrorist states and suggested that he was actively revamping the nuclear war plan to be more responsive to these new threats.

Butler, it turns out, was not a warrior at all, and it is scary to think about what would have happened had a nuclear war broken out when he was in charge of Stratcom. After retiring in 1994, Butler revealed himself to be a nuclear pacifist. Yes, the commander of U.S. nuclear forces was opposed in principle to the development and maintenance of nuclear weapons.

Significantly, Butler did not change his mind on nuclear weapons only after he left the Strategic Command. In fact, he has taken pains to stress that his opposition to nuclear weapons developed even before he was put in charge of the U.S. nuclear arsenal. In an essay he wrote in 2007 for Santa Clara University's Markkula Center for Applied Ethics he described his pacifist, anti–nuclear weapons views as "not an epiphany, not some road-to-Damascus revelation." Butler explained that before he became Stratcom commander in 1991 he "had developed a series of reservations and doubts" about nuclear weapons "that progressively deepened."

He added, "I had no basis for understanding whether these concerns proceeded from a lack of information and insight, or whether they were rooted in the reality of bureaucratic processes run amok, by the intrusion of the self-serving profit interests of the military-industrial complex, by the collision of cultures and turf in the Pentagon for budget dollars, or simply by the towering forces of alienation and isolation that grew out of the mutual demonization between the U.S. and the Soviet Union over a period of forty-five years. I just didn't know."

Becoming Stratcom commander and learning the ins and outs of the U.S. nuclear weapons program only "accelerated and confirmed my worst fears and concerns." He said he found the United States to be "in messianic pursuit of a demonized enemy."

These comments provide a clear indication that the military and government bureaucracy had failed in one of its most important responsibilities: making sure that the people put in charge of defending the nation believe in defense of that country.

More important, the military has prided itself on making sure that the people put in charge of nuclear weapons are the best and the brightest, and Butler's comments reveal that he was neither. He was a pacifist military commander who believed it was immoral to use the very weapons he might have been ordered to use.

Butler, who founded the Second Chance Foundation to fight the "nuclear danger," admitted in his essay that he was never prepared to carry out the orders of the president to deliver a nuclear attack even if word of a Soviet nuclear strike on the United States had reached his command. "For three years I was required to be within three rings of my telephone so that I could answer a call from the White House to advise the president on how to respond to nuclear attack," he wrote. He noted that he "had to be prepared to sign the death warrant of 250 million people living in the Soviet Union. I felt that responsibility to the depth of my soul, and I never learned to reconcile my belief systems with it. Never."

He continued, "In those responsibilities of commander of the forces responsible for the day-to-day operational safety, security, and preparation to employ those weapons, I was increasingly appalled by the complexity of this ballet of hundreds of thousands of people managing, manipulating, controlling, and maintaining tens of thousands of warheads and extremely complex systems that flew through the air, were buried in the bowels of the land, or patrolled beneath the seas of the world."

Butler was not a passive opponent of U.S. defense. During his three years as Stratcom commander he actively subverted U.S. nuclear policies, and he now admits that he had made a private decision to "end the madness" of nuclear deterrence. "So in those three years I did what I could to cancel all of the strategic nuclear modernization programs in my jurisdiction, which totaled $40 billion. I canceled every single one of them. I recommended to the president that we take

bombers off nuclear alert for the first time in thirty years, and we did.
I recommended that we accelerate the retirement of all systems designed to be terminated in present and future arms control agreements,
and we did. We accelerated the retirement of the Minuteman II force.
We shrank the nuclear warplanes of the United States by 75 percent.
By the time I left my responsibilities, those 12,500 targets had been
reduced to 3,000. If I'd had my way and I'd been there a while longer,
I would have worked to reduce them to zero. Ultimately I recommended the disestablishment of my command. I took down its flag
with my own hands."

The more important question to ask now is where were the president, his advisers, the senior Pentagon leaders, and congressional over-
seers? How could they have not seen what was going on? Butler's
misguided belief that nuclear weapons were unjustified morally reveals
him to have been unfit for command of the U.S. nuclear arsenal and
warfighting plan, and certainly of questionable loyalty to the uniform
he wore and the country he swore to defend. Butler's four-year tenure
as the most senior nuclear warfighter spanned both the first Bush administration and the Clinton administration and demonstrated the
principle that picking the wrong people for important positions leads
to wrong policies.

Butler is typical of a U.S. officer corps that has remained disdainful of the concepts of patriotism, love of country, and the idea that liberty and freedom and the American way of life are worth fighting for
and ultimately worth dying for.

Asked about Butler's nuclear pacifism, Air Force general Kevin P.
Chilton, who became head of the Strategic Command in October
2007, told reporters in March 2008 why he disagreed with the likes of
Butler and other antinuclear generals.

"So long as there are other countries in the world that possess
enough nuclear weapons to destroy the United States of America and
our way of life, we will have to deter those types of countries," Chilton
said. "So I am not in favor of unilateral disarmament. I think so long

as we possess nuclear weapons it is our responsibility to treat them appropriately, safely and securely, and to make sure that we are ready to use them, because that is the deterrent force that we provide."

Chilton said that he too ultimately would like to see the world get rid of nuclear weapons. "I'm a father, too, of children that I would love to have grow up in a nuclear-free world. Absolutely. I don't want to equivocate on that at all." But he added, "I also want them to grow up free. . . . As long as we have other nations out there with nuclear capabilities I've described that threaten our freedoms, then I think we need to have a nuclear deterrent force that can do the mission of preserving our freedoms."

Such real-world considerations are lost on Lee Butler and other naïve former military officers who have injected themselves into partisan political debates.

The Case of Kissinger

No other former U.S. government official has been more a part of the bureaucracy and its maintenance as a policy tool for misguided policies that are undermining America than Henry Kissinger.

According to U.S. government officials familiar with China affairs, Kissinger was known to accompany the chief operating officers of large U.S. corporations who would fly into Beijing aboard shiny corporate jets and get special government permission to land in Beijing. Kissinger would then use his influence to get meetings with top officials of the Chinese Communist Party, all the while pretending not to be engaged in business.

After the meetings, Party officials would quietly spread the word to the Chinese state-run enterprises to close on favorable contracts and deals with the corporations. Officials said within the U.S. intelligence community, this kind of activity is a known method for how China buys influence: by providing lucrative business contracts. The unspoken conditions for the deal are that the beneficiaries can voice no public criticism of the Beijing government and its communist system.

One U.S. Defense official revealed that seven prominent Americans, including former Cabinet secretaries, made millions of dollars in deals with Chinese companies through the Kissinger connections. The identities of the seven could not be learned.

In 1982, the former secretary of state for President Richard M. Nixon founded Kissinger Associates in New York City, a multimillion-dollar international consulting firm that has provided a home for many liberal Republicans cycling in and out of the government bureaucracy. To take just one notable example, L. Paul Bremer joined Kissinger Associates after a career in the Foreign Service; Bremer eventually went back into government to head the Coalition Provisional Authority in immediate post–Saddam Hussein Iraq, where, as noted in Chapter 7, he made the disastrous decision to disband the Iraq army, leaving the country in turmoil for years afterward.

Kissinger Associates' clients include some of the most powerful companies in the world, including American Express, American International Group, Atlantic Richfield, JPMorgan Chase, Coca-Cola, Fiat, Heinz, Hollinger, Merck, and Volvo. The U.S. and foreign companies are worth billions of dollars and pay millions to Kissinger and his stable of former officials for advice, door-opening, and consulting. The business has become so important to Kissinger that he resigned his post as cochairman of the 9/11 Commission rather than divulge his secret list of clients, as Democrats demanded.

Kissinger has thrived on secrecy; it was his watchword as a government official and has been his watchword as he became an international deal maker as well. Few details of his client list and paymasters were ever made public. One of the few public references that identifies how Kissinger cashed in on his connections to foreign and U.S. leaders for his business was Walter Isaacson's biography, *Kissinger*. Isaacson, the former *Time* magazine editor and former head of CNN, conducted extensive interviews with the former secretary of state for the book. His chapter on Kissinger Associates reveals how in the aftermath of China's 1989 military crackdown on unarmed protesters in Beijing's Tiananmen Square, where hundreds if not thousands were killed or injured, Kissinger launched a public relations campaign against U.S. sanctions, at the same time that he was representing major U.S. corporations doing business or seeking deals with the Communist government. The sanctions were imposed and remain in place, but it was an example of the kind of immoral foreign policy promoted by Kissinger.

The Tiananmen case is an example of why Kissinger has become well known for his close relations with the Chinese government. For a fee, in the range of tens of thousands to hundreds of thousands of dollars, Kissinger will introduce clients who want to do business in China to senior Chinese officials. For example, he might set up his clients with a meeting with Chinese president Hu Jintao; the clients are photographed with the Chinese leader and then use the photos to cement lucrative contracts with state-run Chinese companies. Similar door-openings take place in oil-rich regions of the Middle East, including Saudi Arabia.

Details on Kissinger's work with China are the most secret of his business dealings, but Isaacson provided some examples. Back in 1987, Kissinger brought in Robert Day, the CEO of the Trust Company of the West, a client, to meet with senior officials of the Chinese regime, then led by Deng Xiaoping. In 1988, Kissinger brought David Rockefeller of Chase to meet Deng. After the bloody Tiananmen crackdown, Kissinger client Maurice Greenberg, when he was chairman of the insurance giant AIG, was brought to China to meet Deng. Kissinger also was behind the visit to China in 1989 by another protégé, then–national security adviser Brent Scowcroft, who traveled secretly to Beijing to reassure China's Communist rulers that the deadly crackdown would not disrupt U.S.-China relations.

Kissinger's political influence has extended into the highest levels of the U.S. government as well. In fact, while the secretive Kissinger managed to keep his influence on George W. Bush's administration quiet for years, it turns out that his advice proved instrumental—and ultimately destructive—to Bush policy. Kissinger's role as counselor to President Bush and Vice President Dick Cheney was not exposed until reporter Bob Woodward's book *State of Denial* was published in 2006. Woodward revealed that Kissinger was not only a secret adviser but was in fact the former official the president and vice president most frequently consulted. As a result of Kissinger's advice, the Bush administration shifted sharply in the direction of foreign policy "realism," the term most associated with immoral and valueless policies. In the case of the Bush administration, the Kissinger policy led to the shift in favor of the business-first approach to world affairs, and of course that had the most negative impact on U.S. policy toward China, perhaps the most serious and dangerous foreign affairs issue that America will face for the next ten years.

Numerous Kissinger protégés have populated the ranks of senior government officials. For example, John Negroponte, the deputy secretary of state and the former director of national intelligence, was once a Kissinger aide. Another protégé, Peter Rodman, worked for Kissinger Associates and later served as the George W. Bush administration's assistant secretary of defense for international security affairs, the key position controlling Asian security policy. As the assistant secretary in charge of Pentagon China policy, Rodman was a Kissingerian when it came to military exchanges with China, viewing them as benign even though they were one-sided in helping Beijing's military gain valuable warfighting secrets. Defense Secretary Donald Rumsfeld was skeptical of the Chinese, taking a more realistic approach to the situation, but he was outflanked by Rodman. The Chinese military continued to steal information about the U.S. military during its visits, while denying U.S. military visitors a comparable chance to learn about the Chinese military.

Kissinger Associates' main director, J. Stapleton Roy, is not surprisingly a liberal former State Department bureaucrat, who for years headed the department's intelligence section. Roy took part in an Oxford-style debate with me and several others in New York City in May 2007 and tipped his hand on how he has been systematically downplaying the threat from China, thus allowing Kissinger Associates to continue making millions from its China business.

During the debate, Roy dismissed the threat from China as the stuff of "fantasy fiction." "Nothing sends shudders up my spine so much as contemplating sinister Chinese scheming to control the world," he said. Roy then repeated almost verbatim the latest propaganda line emanating from Beijing under Hu Jintao, that China had "abandoned Marxism and Leninism and class struggle" in favor of "market economics and the promotion of a harmonious society." In summing up, Roy once again rejected the idea that China could pose a real threat, saying, "Dragons are mythological creatures."

This answer glossed over the many dangers that China represents (dangers that will be discussed in the next chapter), and said nothing about the Beijing government's systematic efforts to extend Chinese power and undermine that of the United States. Roy represented the ultimate strategic objective of the Kissinger worldview: At all costs, China's international behavior and human rights abuses must be ignored or downplayed to preserve business relations. The strategy is the most subversive and dangerous threat facing long-term U.S. national security interests.

To cover his political bases, Kissinger in 1999 joined forces with Bill Clinton's first White House chief of staff, Mack McLarty, to form a subsidiary in Washington, D.C., called Kissinger McLarty. By the mid-2000s, this Kissinger Washington operation was a who's who of State Department bureaucrats and liberals. They included Alan Larson, the undersecretary of state for economic, business, and agricultural affairs during both the Clinton and Bush administrations; Frank

Wisner, ambassador to India from 1994 to 1997; Donna Hrinak, former envoy to Brazil, Venezuela, and Bolivia; and Will Itoh, former ambassador to Thailand. Others included former secretary of state Lawrence Eagleburger, former United Nations ambassador Bill Richardson, and former National Security Council European Affairs director Donald Bandler. As part of the Kissinger operation, all provided intelligence on world affairs for Kissinger McLarty, which sells strategic advice, foreign affairs information of interest to businesses, and of course, lobbying with a special emphasis on opening doors. In early 2008, Kissinger and McLarty split.

Russian state-run press reports indicate that another key Kissinger client is the Russian government. And where did President George W. Bush's special assistant for Russian affairs, Thomas Graham, go to work after leaving his highly sensitive government position in 2007? Kissinger Associates.

Henry Kissinger's power and influence have been enhanced by his appointment to numerous government advisory boards and panels that have not required him to disclose his clients. One of the most important was his seat during the 1980s on the President's Foreign Intelligence Advisory Board, a board of experts that had access to the most sensitive U.S. intelligence. In 1989, the *New York Times* cited a former member of the intelligence board saying that Kissinger, "using his authority as a board member, frequently reviewed intelligence documents outside the regular board meetings." The *Times* also reported that "the former official said he believed that Mr. Kissinger's association with the board gave him benefit because he could not have separated the insights gained from his access to United States intelligence data from his continuing analysis and advice to clients." Kissinger's lawyer, Michael T. Masin, dismissed the suggestions of improperly benefiting from U.S. intelligence information as "outrageous." But this was just one item in a long trail of questionable activities and apparent conflicts of interest involving the powerful former secretary of state.

No Enforcement

The examples of these former officials demonstrate that legal or ethical standards of conduct are not being enforced, either by the executive branch or by the Congress. Congress has an oversight responsibility but has been severely remiss in dealing with the life-and-death issues related to the selection of government leaders. Our elected leaders have failed to grapple with what has happened to our government, which has come to be dominated by bureaucrats who have lost sight of the purpose of their work: protecting, defending, and promoting the interests and values of the American people.

8

THE CHINA SYNDROME

No single national security issue facing the United States, other than the global war on Islamist extremists, is more important—or more dangerous—than confronting China's rise as a global power. Today, China, a nuclear-armed Communist dictatorship despite its market-oriented economic reforms, poses the most serious threat to future U.S. security in Asia and the world. China is working covertly to weaken the United States by backing America's enemies, including Iran, Syria, and North Korea, and working together with states such as Russia to realign the international balance of power. The ultimate goal is to ensure that China, not the United States, is the world's sole superpower.

The China threat is dangerous enough. But it is made much worse because U.S. bureaucrats in both the intelligence community and the government policymaking offices are complicit with this Chinese strategy. For at least the past decade, bureaucrats at all levels of government have subverted U.S. policy toward China, based on the false liberal assumption that conservative Americans pose a greater danger to U.S. security than the Communists in Beijing.

Beijing's influence on the U.S. government is so pervasive that most Americans remain entirely ignorant of the danger. A community of current and former officials, known derisively as "Panda Huggers" for their pro-China views, has gained enormous influence over U.S. policies and programs related to China through a carefully orchestrated program of vetting and if necessary blocking appointments of significant government officials, both bureaucratic and political. By targeting government, both personnel and policymaking, the pro-China crowd has advanced the Beijing government's clever strategic deception scheme, which portrays China as a benign, non-Communist power.

The three streams of pro-China influence, from both government and the business community, have successfully misrepresented the nature of the threat to the United States posed by Beijing and thus prevented the U.S. government from preparing itself to adequately defend against China's rise and its anti-American subversion. They include:

- The Panda Huggers, who believe their mission is to provide support to China, whose system and government they admire, and to oppose all U.S. government policies and programs they regard as leading to a confrontation or a cold war.

- Lobbyists, including former senior officials like Henry Kissinger and his protégés, who exert enormous influence on U.S. leaders and are motivated both by misguided policy and by the search for power, influence, and money. Many work privately for China and see nothing wrong with assisting a foreign government.

- Business power brokers, like the Bush administration treasury secretary Henry Paulson, who as chief executive officer of the international investment bank Goldman Sachs made hundreds of millions of dollars in profits in China during the early 2000s, yet was placed in charge of most U.S. policies toward China with little regard for the dangerous conflict of interest. These Sinophiles, seeing an unparalleled market opportunity in China's 1.3 billion consumers, turn a blind eye to China's dangers, its growing military, its dangerous arms transfers, and its massive human rights abuses. With little or no concern for U.S. national security interests, they have ended up bankrolling an emerging and threatening Communist global power.

The story of this subversion can be traced to the liberals' reaction to the rise of the new conservatism in the 1980s—a conservatism that was unafraid to identify the Communist threat in frank, unapologetic, and unequivocal terms. President Ronald Reagan set the tone for the new conservatives when he called the Soviet Union the "evil empire," with a clear implication that this source of evil in the modern world must be defeated and replaced with a democratic system. It was for the time revolutionary rhetoric, and it was backed with policies that had not been seen since anti-Communist Democrats populated the CIA during the 1960s before being forced out and retiring. President George W. Bush followed this unapologetic model with his identification of Iraq, Iran, and North Korea as an "axis of evil," but over the years of his administration he quietly backed away from the term—and from taking a hard line on these threats.

The pro-China forces have responded to nongovernment forces as well. Specifically, the new conservatism was led by talk radio, and its undisputed leader, Rush Limbaugh. Later, as the Internet emerged in the 1990s as a powerful information tool, Internet pioneer Matt Drudge helped expose news that the mainstream media had long ignored. And last, the conservative-oriented newspaper the *Washington Times* provided the first institutional balance to the liberal-dominated mainstream press and, more important, served as a bridge between the old media of the liberal establishment and the new media represented by talk radio and the Internet.

As a long-time *Washington Times* national security reporter, I have become a central figure in what I term the bureaucrats' China policy crimes story and have been singled out as such by the Chinese government. By policy crimes I mean programs and policies that undermine

American power and influence and limit the pro-democracy, anti-Communist foreign policies. The official Chinese state-run press declared me the number one "anti-China expert" in the world, ahead of several current and former U.S. and foreign government officials. In my defense I tell Chinese Communist visitors and liberal pro-China activists that I am very much "pro-China," in that I support the Chinese people in their search for freedom. I explain that my issue with China is their government and Communist political system and that I am very much *anti–Chinese government,* because of its repressive totalitarian system.

The reason liberal bureaucrats have reacted so strongly to conservatives is that conservatives pose a great threat to their agenda—feckless arms control toward Russia, appeasement toward China, and a subtle anti-Americanism that views not foreign states as the main source of the world's ills but the United States itself. These self-styled anticonservative internationalists view the traditional concepts of patriotism and love of country as outmoded and even dangerous to their liberal agenda, which promotes globalization and the value-neutral perspective that nations can get along if they simply engage in international commerce and diplomacy.

Beginning around 2000, the liberal China hands in the bureaucracy decided they could no longer stand by and be passive observers; the conservatives had to be politically discredited. The mantra of the Sinophiles was first set out several years earlier by Joseph S. Nye Jr., a former assistant secretary of defense and former chairman of the National Intelligence Council, which is linked to key U.S. policy failures in the 2000s.

In 1995, Nye set up the straw-man argument that with the demise of the Soviet Union, conservatives in the United States needed a new enemy and that enemy would be China. Nye, the Sultan of Oman Professor of International Relations at the John F. Kennedy School of Government at Harvard University, advocated kid-glove treatment of the Chinese. In a long article that appeared in the July/August 1995 edition of the journal *Foreign Affairs,* Nye stated that the best course of action to promote U.S. national security in Asia, and with regard to China in particular, was a policy of "deep engagement." He argued against creating a NATO-like alliance in Asia because it would be misperceived by China. Nye wrote that it would be "wrong to portray China as an enemy," since "enmity would become a self-fulfilling prophecy"—merely characterizing Beijing as an enemy would lead to policies that alienated the Chinese and prevented them from "becoming a responsible great power in the region." He concluded, "The Clinton administration's policy of engagement is a far better approach to dealing with emerging Chinese power."

Thus was born the appeasement policy to all things Chinese. Nye's argument resonated with the pro-China academics who would come to populate both the intelligence agencies and key policy slots in the State Department, the Pentagon, and the rest of the government.

The "China Is Not a Threat" Mantra

The obsession among liberal bureaucrats with preventing China from becoming a U.S. enemy has reached absurd proportions. It is seen in the frequent comments of the nation's highest officials aggressively insisting that "China is not a threat" or "China is not an enemy."

A list of some of these statements is instructive, and alarming, as they mirror the false propaganda campaign emanating from Beijing for the past three decades:

- President George W. Bush, May 5, 2006: "First of all, I wouldn't call China an enemy." (Bush's rhetorical praise for China peaked in October 2002, when he welcomed President Jiang Zemin to his ranch and declared the two countries "allies" in the fight against terror, a claim that is false.)

- Former secretary of state Colin Powell, June 13, 2005: "I, for one, do not see China as an enemy that is emerging, as a threat that is emerging, but as a nation taking its rightful place in the world."

- Secretary of State Condoleezza Rice, July 10, 2005: "There is no doubt that we have concerns about the size and pace of the Chinese military buildup . . . [but] that does not mean that we view China as a threat."

- Defense Secretary Robert Gates, December 21, 2007: "I don't consider China an enemy."

- U.S. Pacific Command commander Admiral William J. Fallon, September 12, 2005: "We do not see an enemy to China."

- CIA Director Michael Hayden, March 11, 2007: "It is not inevitable that [China] will be an enemy."

And so on. The drumbeat of apologies for a brutal Communist dictatorship is deeply troubling. How did these senior officials come to voice, in almost the exact same terms, statements denying any China threat? It begins with the State Department and U.S. intelligence bureaucrats who have deceived their superiors about the nature and intentions of China.

The Tilelli Commission

The first signs of the bureaucrats' China subversion were discovered by Senator Richard Shelby, a Democrat turned Republican who headed the Senate Intelligence Committee from 1995 to 2003. Shelby and a key staff aide, Peter Flory, recognized that the highly classified reports on China produced by the CIA and other U.S. intelligence analysts exhibited an unusual bias.

"What we're interested in is good analysis," Shelby told me in

2000. "The nation depends on it, but it has to be good, it has to be accurate, it has to be unbiased." Shelby, unlike other government officials, recognized early on that China's rapid industrialization and development signaled that "China is going to be our biggest challenge, militarily and economically, down the road," meaning in ten or twenty years.

Flory noted that the current generation of China intelligence analysts were educated and trained after President Richard Nixon made the historic opening to China and thus came up in an environment in which China was regarded as a "sort of benevolent panda bear."

"I'm not saying these are bad people deliberately doing bad things, but those sort of baseline assumptions have crept in" to the analysts' reports, Flory said at the time. "And it's hard for a lot of people to conceive of China as a threat because we've viewed them generally as benign. Not only benign, but sort of on our side against the Soviet Union all those years."

Worried that intelligence analysts were getting China wrong, just as the CIA missed the Soviet Union in the late 1980s, Senator Shelby tried to press the intelligence community to do more "contrarian" and "alternative" intelligence analysis on China—specifically, as it related to the security issues and China's military buildup. He wanted the analysts to look at "nonlinear" developments such as strategy, and "wild cards"—things that are variables with regard to the development of China's forces.

The analysts refused. Worse, the bureaucracy viewed Shelby's attempt to get honest China assessments as a conservative effort to politicize intelligence and, back to Nye, turn China into an enemy.

To counter this resistance, Shelby added language to several classified intelligence authorization bills directing intelligence analysts to be more focused on unconventional ways of looking at China and its military and intelligence capabilities. "What we're trying to do is make sure that process is carried through with respect to China in certain specific ways by directing certain specific tasks to be looked at in alternative and contrarian ways," Flory said.

Shelby fought for two and a half years to pressure the analysts to do better and more competitive intelligence analysis. A rare success was forcing the CIA to set up a secret blue-ribbon commission of specialists to review CIA analysis on China. The twelve-member panel was formed in late 2000 and headed by retired Army general John Tilelli, a former commander of U.S. forces in Korea, who was a good soldier but was no intelligence analyst and had no comprehensive understanding of the level of resistance within the intelligence analytical community to doing fair and honest assessments of China.

The CIA, led by longtime analyst Dennis Wilder, a leading voice for those who believed China had to be protected from conservatives, counterattacked by stacking the Tilelli Commission with Sinophile specialists who were sympathetic to the skewed views of the China hands. Wilder maneuvered to place CIA supporters on the commission, including Davidson College professor Shelley Rigger, who identified herself on a website as a "CIA consultant," undermining her credibility for the supposedly impartial, "outside" commission work. Another member, retired Air Force colonel Larry Mitchell, also was a paid CIA consultant. The commission was "assisted" by James Harris, head of the CIA's Strategic Assessment Group. Harris, like Wilder, was a former China division chief and had a reputation as a pro-China analyst.

At first, Wilder also succeeded in blocking commission members from studying highly classified raw intelligence reports, the most important requirement for judging finished reports. But under pressure from several commission members with intelligence experience, CIA Director George Tenet eventually permitted some commissioners to view raw reports. Among the commissioners with intelligence backgrounds were former CIA officer James Lilley, Heritage Foundation China hand Larry Wortzel, and Peter Rodman, who would go on to be assistant defense secretary for international security affairs, with authority over China policy. Rodman, as noted in Chapter 9, was a protégé of Henry Kissinger who hid his pro-China views carefully while at the Pentagon.

The Tilelli Commission finished its work in the summer of 2001. According to officials involved, its still classified report identified an "institutional predisposition" on certain issues related to China. In other words, a bias. But the analysts were so upset with the report that they insisted it be kept secret. After I published reports about the commission findings, the CIA sent a deliberately misleading note to all agency employees on the findings of the China Futures Panel. Tilelli said that the commission found "no politicization or bias by analysts in their reporting." However, the statement did not dispute the finding of an "institutional predisposition."

The bureaucrats had successfully dodged a congressional bullet. They were able to water down the final report to the point that its chairman could state, inaccurately, that there had been no finding of politicization or bias, despite reporting institutional predisposition.

In the aftermath of the commission, intelligence analysts were to become even more powerful. They initiated a series of seemingly innocuous changes in the production of intelligence estimates.

Wilder Runs Wild

Dennis Wilder, critics say, maneuvered through the bureaucracy like riding a Jet Ski on a calm lake. According to these critics, the damage to U.S. national security that he caused during his time at the CIA as the top analyst on China military affairs and later at the pinnacle of power as the National Security Council staff director for Asia was substantial and will be lasting. No single American official in the past twenty years has done more to propagate false and misleading views on China than Wilder. He blocked key personnel appointments in both the intelligence and policy area, shifted the entire U.S.

government position toward the highly damaging notion of "protect-ing" China from conservatives and other anti-Communists, and weak-ened U.S. support for a key ally in democratic Taiwan.

The Wilder policies exploited traditional Republican pro-business ideas and the desire to tap into the 1.3 billion people in China as the market of the future. Within a period of several years, Wilder had managed to turn the president and his administration from focusing on the growing threat of a rising China to making Taiwan the prob-lem. He portrayed Taiwanese president Chen Shuibian, who left office in 2008, as the source of danger in East Asia because of Chen's belief that Taiwan is a separate nation and not a part of China, as Beijing claims. In 2001, President Bush declared that the United States would do whatever it takes to help Taiwan defend itself, ending Clinton-era strategic ambiguity about relations with the island government. But by 2008, the president and his key advisers were openly critical of Taiwan and were denying Taiwan's request for needed U.S. defense items, including newer versions of F-16 warplanes needed to bolster its forces against the rapidly growing Chinese military threat across the 100-mile-wide Taiwan Strait.

And it was not only Taiwan. Wilder, from his NSC perch, blocked Japan's request to buy the new F-22 fighter, the long-range stealth fighter bomber, because its capabilities would give Japan a deep-strike capability against China, and, ever the Sinophile, Wilder did not want to upset Beijing, according to defense officials close to the interagency discussions.

Wilder moved into the strategic NSC slot in 2005 following the departure of Michael Green, a Japan specialist. He beat out several can-didates who, while not exactly conservatives, were not believers in the false theory of treating China as a normal, allegedly non-Communist friendly nation. And more important, they did not view conservative China hands as the enemy. Wilder's patron was Brent Scowcroft, an-other protégé of Henry Kissinger, who had been NSC adviser under President George H. W. Bush. Scowcroft, a so-called foreign policy realist, had opposed U.S. intervention in Iraq in 2003, and back during the elder Bush's presidency, in 1989, had been the architect of a disastrous secret visit to China to assure Chinese leaders that the administration was still friends with the Communist regime despite the Tiananmen Square massacre. Wilder, with the CIA at the time, had helped arrange that visit. As the CIA's top China analyst in the late 1990s, Wilder worked closely with Bill Clinton's NSC China specialist Kenneth Lieberthal.

While Wilder was at the CIA, his management of China analysis triggered more than a half-dozen formal complaints from analysts to the agency's ombudsman for politicization, according to intelligence officials familiar with the complaints and those who made them. Among the intelligence reports he was accused of skewing or suppressing were analyses of China's worsening human rights record; a report by a retired Navy captain warning in the late 1990s about China's rapid military buildup; and a report that stated China was rapidly developing its scientific and technical base, with help from American corporations. Most analysts would have been fired under such a barrage of criticism, but Wilder survived the complaints by going after the complaining analysts and moving them out of the China analysis section to other posts related to non-China subjects.

The intelligence bias complaints against Wilder were made public shortly after President Bush was reelected in November 2004. Critics were trying to derail his anticipated promotion and to boost the candidacy of another ex-CIA specialist, Richard Lawless, who had won praise for his relatively tough handling of China issues as a deputy assistant defense secretary, despite working under Rodman. The conservatives hoped that the new CIA director, Porter Goss, would take action to recall Wilder to CIA, but officials familiar with the issue at the time said Goss did not want him back at the agency. So Wilder remained at the NSC staff and eventually got the strategic post of Asia director. Wilder, through associates, denied that the complaints were made against him or that he eliminated the problems by transferring the analysts to non–China-related positions. But the conservatives were adamant: Wilder had a secret record of skewing intelligence analysis on China, and specifically China's military.

In January 2005, President Bush declared in his inaugural address and the State of the Union message that his administration was committed to the global promotion of democracy and freedom. But thanks to Wilder that effort excluded Communist-ruled China. Pro-democracy Chinese dissidents, such as Wei Jingsheng and Yan Jiaqi, were blocked from visiting the White House through the efforts of Wilder. Instead, Wilder got the administration to support Communist leaders. For example, he arranged the 2005 meeting between White House National Security Adviser Stephen Hadley and Chinese Communist Party official Zheng Bijian, the alleged reformer and a key architect of China's strategic deception operation to fool the West into believing that China's ruling Communist Party would initiate democratic reforms. The truth, as revealed in an official Chinese government white paper from 2006, is that the regime will never adopt Western-style democracy and that democracy is limited to Marxist-Leninist Communist Party members.

The Zheng meeting was the most significant of a series of White House visits Wilder arranged for Chinese Communist and military officials.

Getting It All Wrong

By 2008, after nearly eight years under a supposedly Republican administration, the China apologists within the bureaucracy had taken almost complete control of U.S. policy toward Beijing. They also controlled the information that is used to formulate those policies. Any government official who challenged the pro-China views of these Sinophiles was targeted by the clique dubbed the Panda Huggers.

Surprisingly, the intelligence and policy clique was forced to ad-

mit they got it wrong in a stunning, highly classified intelligence report produced in 2005 and disclosed to this author.

The government report was produced by several current and former intelligence analysts for the director of national intelligence, the
intelligence chief whose position was created in the aftermath of the
failures relating to September 11 and Iraq weapons of mass destruction. The report stated that U.S. intelligence analysts missed more
than a dozen Chinese military developments over a period of nearly a
decade, including:

- China's development of a new long-range cruise missile
- the deployment of a new warship equipped with a stolen
  Chinese version of the U.S. Aegis battle management
  technology
- deployment of a new attack submarine known as the Yuan
  class that was missed by U.S. intelligence until photos of the
  submarine appeared on the Internet
- development of precision-guided munitions, including new
  air-to-ground missiles and new, more accurate warheads
- China's development of surface-to-surface missiles for targeting U.S. aircraft carrier battle groups
- the importation of advanced weaponry, including Russian
  submarines, warships, and fighter-bombers

The report mentioned the word "surprise"—which intelligence is
supposed to avoid at all costs—more than a dozen times to describe
the failures to anticipate or discover Chinese military developments.

Of course, the analysts responsible did not blame themselves. The
pro-China bureaucrats cleverly deflected criticism by placing the blame
on intelligence collectors—the spies on the ground or in the region—
who failed to obtain solid information on the Chinese. The CIA operations officers involved in China affairs were livid upon learning they
had been blamed for the intelligence failures on China's military, and

they fired back at the analysts, whom they blamed for playing down and ignoring their intelligence reports. The report also cited excessive secrecy on China's part for the failures.

But in reality the lapses resulted from the bias of the pro-China analysts and the effort not to portray China as a threat or enemy. As one intelligence official put it, "This report conceals the efforts of dissenting analysts [in the intelligence community] who argued that China was a threat." The official added that covering up the failure of intelligence analysts on China would prevent a major reorganization of the system.

A former U.S. official said that the report should help expose a "self-selected group" of specialists who fooled the U.S. government on China for ten years. "This group's desire to have good relations with China has prevented them from highlighting how little they know and suppressing occasional evidence that China views the United States as its main enemy."

Likewise, an intelligence analyst said that the intelligence failures on China resulted because key analysts were "carrying out their own private foreign policy" aimed at minimizing China's military buildup.

A number of U.S. intelligence analysts who did not share the accommodationist view wondered why they had been excluded from contributing to what came to be viewed as the China failures report. The fear among the China analysts was that the report, labeled "Top Secret" and designated "HCS," for humint (human intelligence) control system, would trigger a far-reaching review similar in scope and aggressiveness to the presidential panel that probed intelligence failures related to Iraq's weapons of mass destruction. Copies of the 95-page report and associated briefing slides were recalled from a limited distribution and were locked away to prevent congressional oversight panels from seeing them. Analysts who had not been allowed to share their views suspected that the entire report was part of an effort to cover up past intelligence failures on China.

Participation in the study had indeed been limited to current and former officials who were sympathetic pro-China analysts. The main drafter was Robert Suettinger, who was a National Security Council staff member for China during the Clinton administration, which skewed U.S. policy in favor of Beijing, and the U.S. intelligence community's top China analyst until 1998. Other authors included longtime CIA analyst on Asia John Culver; former Defense Intelligence Agency analyst Lonnie Henley, who critics in the intelligence community said was notorious for his role in seeking to downplay intelligence that highlighted the military threat from China; and John F. Corbett, a former Army intelligence analyst and attaché in Beijing who spent part of his career as a China policymaker at the Pentagon during the Clinton administration.

Suettinger was linked to the 1996 Chinese fundraising scandal that embroiled the Clinton administration, which accepted large donations from people linked to Chinese military intelligence. Suettinger approved a visit by Democratic Party fundraiser Johnny Chung in 1995 with a group of Chinese officials. Suettinger, as the national security official in charge of China affairs, wrote a memo that defended the visit by Chung, who pleaded guilty in 1998 to making illegal campaign contributions, by stating that the visit would not cause "any lasting damage to U.S. foreign policy." He added, "And to the degree it motivates him to continue contributing to the [Democratic National Committee], who am I to complain?"

Suettinger would go on to head a special counterintelligence unit at the CIA devoted to looking at Chinese aggressive intelligence activities, a mission for which he was ill-suited. He ended up missing—or ignoring—a series of highly damaging spy cases that would surface in the mid-2000s.*

Lonnie Henley was a close friend of convicted former Defense Intelligence Agency analyst Ronald Montaperto, who was caught supplying highly classified intelligence information to Chinese military

---

*See my 2006 book *Enemies: How America's Foes Steal Our Vital Secrets, and How We Let It Happen* (Crown Forum).

intelligence officers but convicted of lesser charges of mishandling classified documents.

Henley's views on China were disclosed to a semisecret Internet forum known as Chinasec on June 9, 2005, when he wrote to another liberal China hand, Michael Swaine, and disclosed China's thinking on when would be the best time for a surprise attack on democratic Taiwan. "There is no good time," Henley said. "If you want to achieve surprise, given the People's Liberation Army's normal rhythms of conscription and annual training, July-August is the best. But that's typhoon season. Late spring is the best weather, but you either attack during a low point in annual readiness cycles, or you make a highly visible departure from normal patterns—troops held on active duty past their normal demobilization date, etc. And you still have the problem units massing together and clustering near the coast at a time of year when they'd normally be doing dispersed small-unit training close to home. Very little chance of surprise in a spring attack. The third possibility is a deliberate, long-term shift in annual cycles, to break up the patterns and make it easier to conceal attack preparations. Often forecast, but no sign of it yet, and the new pattern would have to prevail for several years before our alarm levels subsided to normal. So the PLA doesn't have an ideal answer on what time of year would be best to attack. My money would be on July-August, in hopes of achieving surprise and establishing a fait accompli before the U.S. arrives in force. And just pray to Mao there isn't a typhoon." It was signed "Lonnie."

By outlining in detail what he knew about China's plans for a surprise attack, Henley was, critics said, discussing sensitive but unclassified information that if provided to China would assist them in using disinformation prior to any real invasion of the island.

Henley stated in an e-mail to the author that the Chinasec electronic e-mail group was not a "public Internet forum" and that the group's rules prohibited members from publicly disclosing e-mails. As a result, he said, claims by critics that Henley might have risked helping the Chinese conduct a surprise attack on Taiwan were "inaccurate and misleading." But the fact that his e-mails leaked out shows that the forum was not secure, and could have been subject to aggressive Chinese electronic intelligence-gathering.

Henley, who was working for the CIA contractor Centra in 2005, returned to government in the Bush administration, despite his anti-conservative views. In 2006, he went to work for liberal pro-China analyst Thomas Fingar, who became the power behind the throne of Director of National Intelligence John Negroponte and then his successor, retired admiral J. Michael McConnell. From his perch as the top analyst, Fingar installed his pro-China friends in high places. Henley became the deputy national intelligence officer for East Asia, but was denied the top NIO Asia job after writing the letter of support for Montaperto, according to U.S. officials familiar with the matter. Critics say he played a major role in developing the U.S. intelligence community's pervasive soft-line analyses of China's military, in keeping with the widespread self-deception within both the intelligence and policy communities that if China is treated as a threat it will become a threat. Henley later stated that his letter to the judge in support of Montaperto was intended to attest to Montaperto's character during the sentencing phase of the proceeding, something that was a common procedure in criminal cases and that does not suggest any support for the underlying crime.

Disclosure of the classified report on China intelligence coincided with the first relatively tough rhetoric on Beijing voiced by Defense Secretary Donald Rumsfeld, who during a speech in Singapore mildly criticized China for hiding defense expenditures and expanding its military forces with no justification.

Nevertheless, within three years the pro-China cabal of bureaucrats had successfully maneuvered to discredit the Rumsfeld policies and to shift the administration toward appeasement—doing business with Beijing and completely ignoring China's anti-U.S. behavior. Dennis Wilder played a pivotal role in this regard. Soon after taking his

NSC post in September 2006, he made sure that the key positions related to China affairs, the deputy assistant secretaries at the State Department and Pentagon, were filled with appeasement-oriented, China-is-not-a-threat bureaucrats. The intelligence community, meanwhile, was covered by Thomas Fingar, who appointed like-minded analysts to the senior ranks of the intelligence agencies.

The Truth About China

Chinese deception has worked. Throughout the U.S. government, officials from the president to junior analysts at the CIA have been pressed into conformity to the China-is-not-a-threat theory, as well as the underlying Joe Nye straw-man doctrine that treating China as a threat will create a threat.

When China actually conducts threatening activities, the apologists in the U.S. government shift tactics. In response, the Sinophiles say little more than "We don't know why China is doing that," or "We are puzzled why China would do that," as if there is no explanation for threatening developments and activities. That type of reaction is the most serious of policy crimes.

This low-key reaction was evident even after the horror of Chinese repression in Tibet became known in 2008. It was also witnessed after Beijing conducted an antisatellite weapon (ASAT) test in January 2007—the most significant Chinese military activity of the young century. With this test, China had demonstrated a new weapon that could cripple or disable U.S. satellites, the center of U.S. high-technology weaponry and systems that handle about 90 percent of all military communications, as well as intelligence and missile guidance. The Chinese test had thus exposed a key U.S. strategic vulnerability. Said one U.S. defense official, "The ASAT test showed they are not following us [militarily] but trying to leap ahead."

U.S. intelligence agencies had advance indications of the test, in which a KT-1 space booster rocket, a version of the medium-range DF-21 missile, was launched from the Xichang space center in south-western Sichuan province. The ASAT weapon separated from the last stage in space and then destroyed the Feng Yun-1C weather satellite, launched in 1999 and orbiting over both poles, by ramming into it at high speed. U.S. officials said some 10,000 pieces of debris from the destroyed satellite will continue orbiting for forty years, posing a risk to some of the 800 satellites now in space, 400 of which are American.

Nor was this the first threatening activity in space by the Chinese. In December 2006, China also illuminated a U.S. satellite with a ground-based laser in another antisatellite test, according to a report by the congressional U.S.-China Economic and Security Review Commission.

The Bush White House and the governments of a number of other countries, including Japan, Australia, India, and Canada, protested the ASAT test. The Chinese simply stated that they had not "weaponized" space and that "China has always advocated the peaceful use of space, opposes the weaponization of space and arms races in space." These weak assurances were apparently enough for some pro-China officials in U.S. policy and intelligence circles. Internal memorandums from such officials tried to downplay the significance of the ASAT test, saying that the warhead hit a large low-earth-orbit satellite and that it would be more difficult to hit higher-orbiting and smaller systems.

But the true nature of China's position is visible for anyone to see, from reading the official press and other available writings of Chinese Communist Party officials and military writers. Such was the case in 2007 when an official of the Chinese government candidly confirmed that China is supporting U.S. enemies around the world. Yuan Peng, director of the Institute of American Studies, part of the China Institutes of Contemporary International Relations (CICIR), stated that "in the world, almost all enemies of the United States are China's friends."

It was a rare admission, but it confirmed that China's arms sales to rogue states like Iran, Syria, and North Korea are not aberrations or "puzzling" policy inconsistencies but based on a deliberate strategy of indirectly confronting the United States. Peng's institute is an entity under the Ministry of State Security, China's main intelligence service, and he made the remarks in a state-run media report. He also stated that the prospects of long-term strategic stability between the United States and China "still remain doubtful." He accused the United States of attempting to "hold up the pace and scope of China's rise by economic, social and diplomatic means."

The Goldman Gang

While the Bush administration's pro-China policies percolated quietly under Wilder and the Panda Huggers over several years, there was a tectonic shift in 2006 that accelerated the pro-China policies: the ascension of Josh Bolten to White House chief of staff in April, followed two months later by the appointment of Henry Paulson to the post of treasury secretary.

Both were former Goldman Sachs executives, and both were staunchly pro-Beijing, seeing only one thing in China: a market and not a nuclear-armed Communist dictatorship seeking to push the United States out of Asia and replace it as the dominant global power. Bolten and Paulson set their priorities immediately as doing business with China in what has been termed "unrestrained engagement"; in effect, they ignored China's repressive human rights practices and unfair trade policies. They also created a policy wall that sought to prevent U.S. national security officials from directly influencing China policy.

Before taking the Treasury post, Paulson made millions of dollars for Goldman Sachs in China, going on some seventy trips there in a decade and a half and concluding multiple deals with Chinese state-owned businesses. Yet no one in Congress bothered to question the president or his advisers as to whether placing someone with such vested interests in making money in China had a major conflict of interest. The questions were not even asked by Republicans or Democrats in the Senate who voted to confirm him.

Paulson's pro-China credentials led conservative critics to dub him "China's man in the Bush cabinet." Former Pentagon official Frank Gaffney wrote that "Henry Paulson has been Communist China's Armand Hammer," comparing the Treasury secretary to the Western capitalist enlisted by the Soviet Union to serve as a financial adviser and agent of influence in Washington and other foreign capitals. Hammer and others like him were rewarded for their support with lucrative deals for energy and natural resources while being allowed to market their products exclusively in the evil empire. It was a deal with the devil that few in the West fully understood.

"In fact," Gaffney said, "[Paulson] has been vastly more effective than Hammer ever was in promoting his clients' interests and enabling their access to Western economic assistance and high technology." Paulson adopted the view that helping China develop economically was in U.S. interests and thus that U.S. trade with China must be the centerpiece of relations with Beijing.

To that end he launched what became known as the Strategic Economic Dialogue, one of a number of showpiece dialogues between U.S. and Chinese officials that were long on platitudes but produced almost nothing of substance, at least for U.S. interests. This became the centerpiece of Bush administration China policy. One of Paulson's first appointments as treasury secretary exposed his anticonservative, pro-China position. He put Deborah Lehr, a former Clinton administration trade official, in charge of this Strategic Economic Dialogue. The White House announcement on Lehr's appointment described her as a well-known China specialist but failed to mention that she had worked at the consulting firm of Clinton administration national security adviser Samuel R. "Sandy" Berger. The architect of President Bill Clinton's appeasement policies toward China, Berger was convicted for stealing classified documents from the National Archives in an apparent attempt to hide information from the 9/11 Commission.

Paulson understood that China has a nonmarket economy with a tightly managed currency and said that Beijing was "unnaturally" integrated into the global economy on goods and services although not on capital markets and currency. But he bought into the false notion that China was no longer Communist, even though it remained structurally a Soviet-style state that was not simply nondemocratic but antidemocratic, in that Chinese rulers opposed the freedoms and liberty that are so integral to the modern Western way of life. Beijing's leaders continued to follow the dicta of Marxism-Leninism in ruling the country, and the rule of law was almost nonexistent. All this continued to happen behind China's façade of espousing wealth and markets for its mostly state-run businesses.

Without reforming China's Communist system of government, Paulson's pro-China policy bolstered the emergence of a one-party dictatorship with a socialist economy and a powerful military armed with nuclear weapons.

The treasury secretary often urged China to become more flexible, and Chinese bureaucrats met his requests with smiles and handshakes and promises of reform. But action never took place. Paulson was a liberal businessman who viewed strong conservative policies on China as "nationalism" and "protectionism" that would hinder global trade.

At a time of Paulson's unrestricted engagement with China, other parts of the U.S. government were grappling with China's technology theft and espionage, problems that were completely ignored by the pro-China team in government.

Worse, Paulson and his supporters actually facilitated China's penetration into U.S. capital and other markets. Goldman Sachs was the most aggressive U.S. investment banking firm in this regard and played a role in a number of deals that directly threatened U.S. economic and security interests. In 2005, Goldman Sachs under Paulson advised the China National Offshore Oil Corporation (CNOOC) in an attempted takeover bid of the oil company Unocal. Goldman made sure that a U.S. company that had offered to buy Unocal, ChevronTexaco, lost out to CNOOC by providing the Chinese state-owned company with the money to top the bid. Only after conservatives in the press and a few stalwarts in Congress stepped in was the deal scotched. No senior leaders of government ever bothered to ask whether it would have been good for America, both economically and from a national security standpoint, for a Chinese state-run company to buy a major oil company.

In 2006, Goldman Sachs bought into China's biggest bank, the Industrial and Commercial Bank of China, for $2.58 billion, netting Paulson himself, as CEO, a personal stake worth a reported $25 million.

These deals by Goldman Sachs were not with private companies competing in the international marketplace but with foreign government-owned entities, raising serious questions about whether doing business with China is simply a reality of the global marketplace, as the pro-China advocates claim, or business deals that are helping create a superpower dictatorship inimical to U.S. national interests. The answer is not known, because Paulson has never even been asked the questions by a press corps uninterested in such conservative-sounding topics.

Goldman Sachs also has a close relationship with Chinese billionaire Li Kai-shing, who according to U.S. intelligence officials has close ties to the Communist politburo in China, and his company Hutchison Whampoa. Li's company owns ports on either end of the Panama Canal as well as port facilities around the world that provide a strategic potential naval basing structure for China's emerging blue-water navy.

As Gaffney noted in an analysis produced by his Center for Security Policy, a 2001 Goldman Sachs annual report quoted a Hutchison Whampoa official as saying, "Goldman Sachs has been our valued counselor—advising us on key strategic transactions. . . . Goldman Sachs continues to be loyal and dedicated to our business." Goldman Sachs also helped Hutchison Whampoa in a takeover bid to buy the telecommunications giant Global Crossing, but the Pentagon blocked the sale as a threat to U.S. national security, based on concerns that China would gain access to fiber optic technology it might use against the United States militarily or through intelligence-gathering.

Paulson's Goldman Sachs China business would surface in another failed bid by China to buy a U.S. high-technology company, the first attempt by China's socialist leaders to buy into the strategically significant American high-technology sector. In September 2007, Bain Capital, an international investment firm founded by former governor Mitt Romney, quietly announced that it was brokering a deal to buy the U.S. telecommunications manufacturer 3Com for $2.2 billion. In the fine print of the announcement was the fact that included in the deal was a Chinese state-run telecommunications company called Huawei Technologies.

Most news reporters did not recognize the significance of what was happening. I was not one of them.

Huawei Technologies, often considered the Cisco Systems of China for its work with Internet and network hardware, was a major international bad actor, linking up with terrorists and rogue states throughout the world. It was founded by a former Chinese general and had close ties to the Chinese military, providing the PLA with the main elements of emerging "informationalized" high-technology communications and command-and-control networks.

In fact, Huawei fiber optic communications equipment was the target of one of the first military actions ordered by Defense Secretary Donald Rumsfeld. In February and again in August 2001, U.S. and British warplanes carried out a raid on an Iraqi air defense network that had been targeting U.S. aircraft patrolling the skies over Iraq under United Nations resolutions in place since the end of the 1991 Persian Gulf War. Some fifty jets bombed an air defense control center that was a hub for fiber optic cables that Huawei technicians had installed in violation of UN sanctions.

Intelligence reports also indicated that Huawei a year earlier had been involved in installing a telephone system in Kabul, Afghanistan, for the Islamist regime headed by the Taliban militia. Huawei had no problems working with a regime that harbored Osama bin Laden and his al Qaeda terrorist organization.

What's more, Huawei was caught stealing proprietary trade secrets from the U.S. high-tech company Cisco Systems. A 2003 report by the Pentagon's International Technology Security section, produced through Deputy Defense Undersecretary Jack Shaw, found that Huawei stole Cisco's proprietary networking-switching technology. The inquiry into this economic espionage prompted Huawei to reach an out-of-court settlement with Cisco. But in February 2008, the Justice Department and Homeland Security Department announced that they had broken a ring of Chinese counterfeiters who were trafficking in . . . knock-off Cisco Systems hardware and company labels that had been traced to China. The counterfeit network hardware included network routers, switches, network cards, and modules copied from Cisco. The global operation was codenamed Cisco Raider.

An FBI PowerPoint briefing posted on the Internet in the spring of 2008 revealed that China may be using its counterfeit Cisco Systems network routers to penetrate U.S. government and private-sector computer networks. Federal authorities in February 2008 seized some 400 counterfeit Cisco knockoffs worth $76 million. The equipment included routers, switches, gigabit interface converters, and WAN interface cards. Among the purchasers of the fake equipment were the U.S. Naval Academy, the U.S. Naval Air Warfare Center, the U.S. Naval Undersea Warfare Center, the U.S. Air Base at Spangdahelm, Germany, the Bonneville Power Administration, the General Services Administration, and the defense contractor Raytheon, which makes key missile and weapons systems.

The FBI briefing slides on the case stated that while there are "intelligence gaps" on why the Chinese made the counterfeit equipment, it could have been for profit or as part of a state-sponsored operation. Additionally, the scope of the Chinese counterfeit equipment may extend beyond routers to include fake IT equipment such as PCs and printers. Under a section titled "The Threat," the FBI described the effort as "IT subversion/supply chain attack" that could "cause immediate or premature system failure during usage." The counterfeit equipment also could be used to "gain access to otherwise secure systems" and to "weaken cryptographic systems." The briefing slide said the Chinese information-warfare efforts require "intimate access to target systems."

How could a Chinese company linked to international illegal activities, to support for terrorist regimes, and to supplies for Saddam Hussein's military even be considered for purchasing a company like 3Com, whose subsidiary TippingPoint made equipment for the Pentagon that on a daily basis was detecting and stopping hundreds, if not thousands, of attempted computer intrusions from China?

The answer was simple: Treasury Secretary Henry Paulson. 3Com's announcement of the Bain-brokered Huawei deal stated that Goldman Sachs was advising 3Com. It should not have been a surprise, considering Goldman's past service on behalf of Chinese Communist state-run companies. After the Huawei connection to the deal was exposed, publicity forced the companies involved to submit the deal for review to the Treasury-led Committee on Foreign Investment in the United States (CFIUS), which is supposed to be a national security check on foreign company purchases of U.S. firms. Paulson, the head of CFIUS, was forced to recuse himself, but his deputy, another liberal anticonservative Republican named Robert Kimmitt, was there to pick up the slack.

A classified U.S. intelligence assessment supplied to CFIUS stated the obvious: The deal as structured was not in the interest of U.S. national security, because of Huawei's nefarious past and current links to the Chinese military. 3Com offered to spin off TippingPoint as a way to win CFIUS approval, but even that offer was blocked. The reason was that Deputy Attorney General Mark R. Filip was opposed to the deal within CFIUS, which includes representatives from Treasury, Justice, State, Defense, Homeland Security, Commerce, and other agencies. Filip argued that approving the deal would undermine efforts by Justice and other agencies to go after the aggressive Chinese high-technology collectors, by legitimizing one of the most egregious violators. On March 20, 2008, 3Com announced that it was canceling the deal because of U.S. government opposition.

The small victory did not mask the onslaught of Chinese state-run penetration of the U.S. economy that is continuing today because of the out-of-control bureaucracy and the subversion by liberal pro-China activists throughout the U.S. government.

A New Low

The shame of U.S. policy toward China reached a new low in March 2008. That is when the State Department removed China from its list of the most egregious violators of human rights, claiming as evidence a dialogue with China on the issue.

Secretary of State Condoleezza Rice told reporters that "we just got China to renew or to begin again the human rights dialogue that had been in limbo for some time," as if that was sufficient grounds to ignore massive Chinese rights violations against a host of Beijing's internal enemies, ranging from Tibetan-independence advocates, ethnic Uighur dissidents seeking freedom in western Xinjiang Province, and the Falun Gong, an anti-Communist religious group. The atrocities have included harvesting body organs from imprisoned members of Falun Gong.

"The only purpose here," Rice said, "was to call out that there are some countries that are so closed, the Burmas of the world, that you have a different kind of problem when you have a country that is in many ways completely closed off to the world. But it is by no means suggesting that there is not significant emphasis on human rights problems in China."

The State Department report noted that China's human rights record "remained poor." So why take China off the list? It was craven appeasement—another victory for the pro-China faction. This act of appeasement was clearly geared toward the Olympic Games hosted by Beijing, which were to begin in August.

Days after the report was issued, China demonstrated once again that it is not even close to being the "responsible stakeholder" in the international system that the pro-China acolytes pretend it is. A demonstration by a group of Buddhist monks in the Tibetan capital Lhasa was met with violence by Chinese military and security forces. The repression of the monks triggered a popular uprising by thousands of Tibetans and spread to neighboring Tibetan cities and even to western Sichuan province. Hundreds were reported killed.

The lame Bush administration response was only to "urge restraint" on the part of the Chinese government. There was no condemnation of China or suggestion that President Bush's planned visit to the opening ceremony of the Olympic Games might be canceled.

The liberal bureaucrats in charge of the administration made no threats of sanctions, or to cut off the military exchange program between the Pentagon and China's military. Christopher Hill, the liberal assistant secretary of state for East Asia, said the Chinese military did not appear to even be directly involved, as if the People's Armed Police, the Soviet-style Communist political security forces, were a different entity from the Communist-run People's Liberation Army. Both are under control of the Communist Party Central Military Commission. The hapless Hill defended the administration policy of doing nothing. "I realize when you see people getting killed in these things, calls for restraint don't look adequate, but such is the nature of this issue," Hill said.

China continues to express its disdain for the United States and everything it stands for, and yet our self-deluded leaders refused to understand the simple truth: China views the United States as its main enemy, despite the outward appearance of seeking friendship and mutually advantageous relations. It is not interested in becoming a responsible stakeholder in a global system led by the United States, the world's sole superpower. As one Pentagon conservative China specialist put it, "China believes it cannot hold stakes with its enemy."

This simple truth is the most important point that is being denied, and hidden, by the subversive liberal bureaucracy running the U.S. government.

9

ENEMY ALLIES

The anti-American tendencies of bureaucracies are not limited to the U.S. government. One international nongovernmental organization has shown itself to be a major source of anti-Americanism: the International Committee of the Red Cross (ICRC).

The committee states on its website that it is "an impartial, neutral and independent organization whose exclusively humanitarian mission is to protect the lives and dignity of victims of war and internal violence and to provide them with assistance." Its impartiality and neutrality were meant for nation-states engaged in traditional, conventional warfare. But the ICRC, funded largely with U.S. taxpayer dollars, has become a voice of support for terrorists captured in the U.S.-led war on terrorism.

In late January 2008, ICRC president Jakob Kellenberger came to Washington and met with senior U.S. officials, including Secretary of State Condoleezza Rice, National Security Adviser Stephen Hadley, and Director of National Intelligence J. Michael McConnell. Kellenberger complained that the United States was not doing enough to protect the rights of captured terrorists held at the prison at Guantánamo Bay, Cuba, and at Bagram, Afghanistan. He criticized the United States for its interrogation methods and demanded that the 620 prisoners at Bagram and 270 at Guantánamo Bay receive trials in regular courts.

The comments angered U.S. military officials. The ICRC has positioned itself as the guardian of the 1949 Geneva Conventions because the committee, unique among nongovernmental organizations, was recognized by the conventions. But its role is merely to be an independent adviser; ultimate responsibility for implementing the provisions of the Geneva Conventions and other law of war treaties rests with governments, not the ICRC. And to U.S. officials, it seemed clear that this "guardian" of the Geneva Conventions was holding the United States to higher legal standards than exist in the 1949 treaties. Said one official, "Under the 1949 Geneva Prisoner of War Convention, prisoners of war may be held for the duration of the hostilities. They are not entitled to know when they may be released or repatriated. Thus the ICRC has demanded greater protection for al Qaeda members than the Geneva Conventions afford captured lawful combatants."

The important distinction between al Qaeda captives and lawful combatants is important, since captured al Qaeda members are legally considered "unprivileged belligerents" who do not meet criteria that would entitle them to prisoner-of-war status. So, the official said, the ICRC is "in essence demanding more 'rights' for terrorists than prisoners of war legally are entitled to, and greater protection and entitlements than any nation has provided any prisoner of war in history." In any case, the committee's complaints overlook the fact that al Qaeda detainees at Guantánamo receive better care and treatment than most prisoners of war in any armed conflict of the last century.

As this inconsistency indicates, the ICRC's record as the guardian of treaties and conventions is mixed, its position of neutrality questionable. In fact, the same ICRC that has lobbied heavily on behalf of terrorists held by the United States took no action on behalf of U.S. prisoners of war held by North Vietnam from 1964 to 1973. The Americans suffered in conditions far worse than those experienced by prisoners at Guantánamo and Bagram; they received inadequate medical care, and they endured systematic torture—evidence of which the ICRC was provided at the time. The North Vietnamese also denied prisoner-of-war status to captured U.S. military personnel. Still, the ICRC did nothing.

According to U.S. officials, when President Ronald Reagan in 1987 forwarded the 1977 Additional Protocol II to the Senate for ratification, the ICRC covertly blocked Senate action through its liberal Democratic allies in the Senate. The protocol was never ratified as a result.

In another case, ICRC officials received access to Iraqi prisoners of war held by the coalition forces in Saudi Arabia during the 1991 Gulf War, but they took no action with respect to coalition prisoners of war in Iraqi hands. Iraq finally agreed to release and repatriate coalition POWs, a process that ICRC field representatives facilitated, but the repatriation never included Kuwaiti prisoners, many of whom apparently were murdered. The ICRC neither made any inquiry as to their status nor publicly criticized Iraq's actions.

In 1999, the ICRC again showed its anti-American bias when it did nothing to protect three U.S. soldiers captured by Serbian forces. Only after U.S. diplomats demanded ICRC action did the head of the organization travel to Belgrade to visit the Americans.

In the words of one U.S. military official, the committee has also "carried out several direct attacks on the U.S. in its efforts to regulate or prohibit new weapons, an area not within its charter or mandate." The official cited an example: "Its 1992–1996 campaign to ban so-called blinding laser weapons used an argument with other governments that the U.S. was building such weapons—it was not—and that these weapons would be used against that government's military." The organization also spent $35 million in its effort to ban antipersonnel mines, likely using U.S. funds to finance a program the U.S. government opposed. And along with the group Human Rights Watch, the ICRC has since 2000 tried to ban cluster munitions, which, one defense official told me, "are a critical component in the inventory of the U.S. military and many other nations."

The U.S. government is by far the largest contributor to the ICRC, providing $217.5 million in 2006. The next largest contributor that year was Britain, with $97 million. U.S. officials said American government contributions to the ICRC are "conditional," based on the committee's adhering to its own principles of humanitarian service, impartiality, neutrality, independence, voluntary service, unity, and universality. But Congress approves the funding every year and demands little accountability for how the money is spent—perhaps because many within the U.S. bureaucracy and among Democrats in Congress agree with the organization's leftist agenda. The funding occurs largely behind the scenes, with little supervision, as one defense official noted. "All this is done through an anonymous earmark to the State Department budget by U.S. senators whom the ICRC clandestinely lobbied, two of whom sit on the Armed Services Committee," the official said, without identifying the lawmakers. "The Defense Department and the military services have no opportunity to comment on this expenditure and its deleterious effects on national security."

Further, the ICRC has involved itself in the Biological Weapons Convention (BWC) process, an area not within its mandate. The United States and other governments in the past issued diplomatic protests to the ICRC to stop interfering with the work of the BWC signatory states, but the committee has refused.

The United States has had fundamental differences with the ICRC during the global war on terrorism, since the committee has made public demands of the United States it has not made—publicly or otherwise—of other governments in other conflicts. The organization's political interference is making it more difficult for the United States to defeat the insurgents and extremists. For example, after Hamid Karzai was inaugurated as president of Afghanistan in 2004, the ICRC declared that the situation in that country was no longer an international armed conflict and thus all persons captured during U.S. military operations that began in 2001 had to be released. Fortunately, the United States rejected the ICRC's claims. The ICRC made the same declaration in regard to Iraq, and again the United States found no legal basis for that claim.

For the United States, the committee has adopted a double standard. It normally employs what diplomats call the "quiet diplomacy" of working with governments behind the scenes without public statements of criticism. But the ICRC has publicly attacked the United States regularly since 2001. In general, the organization has proved to be anything but "impartial" and "neutral." For example, the ICRC's frequent condemnations of the United States and Israel are not matched with similar criticism of Syria, Saudi Arabia, Iran, or Egypt. It has been quick to publicly condemn any U.S. military operation where there is a single civilian casualty, but remains steadfastly silent with regard to use of civilian human shields or suicide bombers by these nations either against Israel or within Iraq.

Most tellingly, the ICRC has not condemned al Qaeda's ongoing attacks and operations within Iraq and Afghanistan. Its criticism of the United States has undermined U.S. military operations and encouraged al Qaeda attacks, U.S. officials said.

The betrayal of the United States occurs overseas as well as at home.

The United States of America has many friends and allies abroad. Many are considered close. But the reality of the world today is that some foreign governments that assert they are friends of the United States are playing a deadly double game. These alleged allies voice praise and support for America, but at the same time they are involved in some of the worst acts of betrayal and violence.

Saudi Arabia is a prime example. While Saudi Arabia is providing intelligence to the United States, selectively and carefully, it is the prime mover of the global Islamist ideology of Wahhabism, the ultraconservative strand of Islam that teaches hatred of non-Muslims and democracy, and is a basis for al Qaeda's terrorist ideology. Wahhabism has caused massive death and destruction, including the killing of Americans and other innocents.

Other enemy allies include Pakistan, whose past ruler, Pervez Musharraf, has indicated that he is a supporter of the United States, but in reality he has prevented the U.S. military and the CIA from taking aggressive action in remote parts of the country where Osama bin Laden is thought to be hiding. South Korea under successive left-wing administrations became vehemently anti-American and viewed the extreme totalitarian state of North Korea as a more important friend than America. The election in 2008 of a more conservative government in Seoul is viewed as paving the way for better U.S. policies toward the Communist regime in the North. Many European governments as well, including France, Britain, and Germany, have voiced their support for the U.S. war on terrorism while in their policies revealing an anti-American side that is helping to bolster U.S. enemies.

The Europeans in particular have become a model for America-haters in the United States, especially among government bureaucrats and the academic and political elites who approve of European appeasement policies, whether they be toward Iran, Syria, or Islamist terrorists themselves.

The United States has emerged as the sole superpower at a time when global threats are becoming more deadly. But these liberal elites don't see America's role as beneficial. They are working with nations overseas to check American power and ultimately subvert the United States through the concept of "multipolarity," the notion that cutting down American power and balancing it with power from states likes Communist China and authoritarian Russia will create peace. This naïve outlook does not take into account that the spread of nuclear weapons and other deadly arms will mean that these weapons soon end up in the hands of nonstate extremists.

Witness the proliferation of advanced conventional weaponry from China. During the summer 2006 war between Israel and the Islamist extremist group Hezbollah, the terrorists obtained a Chinese-made advanced C-802 antiship cruise missile from Iran and used it to sink an Israeli patrol boat. It was the first time an advanced weapon system had reached the hands of international terrorists.

With Iran's drive for nuclear weaponry, how easy will it be for the radical Islamists in Tehran to trade a nuclear device to a terrorist group?

The Saudi Problem

Several days after the September 11, 2001, terrorist attacks, Saudi Arabia's ruling monarchy carried out what could only be called an extraordinary display of power. The Saudi ambassador to the United States, Bandar bin Sultan, the powerful prince of the Saudi royal family, received a message from the oil-rich kingdom's monarch, King Fahd. The message was urgent. Bandar needed to get all Saudi nationals, including members of the royal family who were famous for spending tens of thousands of dollars in the United States on frequent visits, out of the country.

Bandar called on Richard Clarke, the left-liberal career State Department official who was working in the White House as a member of the National Security Council staff. Clarke was the counterterrorism coordinator, and a holdover from the Clinton administration who would turn on President George W. Bush with a vengeance. Clarke would accuse Bush of not taking his warnings seriously enough about the danger of bin Laden, but he would not criticize the liberal Clinton administration for whom he worked for years and which did little or nothing to go after bin Laden despite at least four opportunities to capture or kill him for his terrorist crimes.

After hearing from Bandar, Clarke called the FBI and told the Bureau to cooperate in the evacuation of some 140 Saudis. While most Americans were stranded at airports, Saudi Arabia was able to remove these people from the United States within a week of the attacks, including some 40 members of the bin Laden family. The FBI asserted that it did not need to keep the bin Ladens in the country. But if any other nation's people had been involved in such a heinous crime, there is no question that relatives of the mastermind behind the attacks would have been kept and questioned extensively.

The Saudis were different. It didn't matter that 3,000 Americans lay dead and the World Trade Center towers and a section of the Pentagon were rubble because of the actions of nineteen terrorists—seventeen of whom were from Saudi Arabia. A simple telephone call from the Saudi ambassador subordinated U.S. interests in learning about the killers. This was the power of the Saudi kingdom and its oil supply.

Bandar told the *New York Times* that private jets were dispatched to the United States to pick up members of the bin Laden family after King Fahd had notified him that there were "bin Laden children all over America." The king had ordered Bandar to "take measures to protect the innocents."

Apparently, the Saudi ruler's view of Americans was so primitive that he believed Americans would go after the bin Ladens in anger and kill them in public, perhaps in mobs. This despite the fact that the al Qaeda terrorist leader was estranged from his wealthy Saudi family, and that most of the bin Ladens in the United States were students studying at high school or college.

The 9/11 Commission sought to dispel some of the criticism about favored treatment of the Saudis in the aftermath of the attacks. The commission's final report said it found no evidence—not that it was necessarily untrue—that Saudi nationals were allowed to depart the United States before national airspace was reopened on September 13, 2001. It also said there was no political intervention "above the level of Richard Clarke" who approved the FBI assistance to the departing Saudis.

The report quoted Clarke as saying, "I asked the FBI, [Counterterrorism chief] Dale Watson . . . to handle that, to check to see if that was all right with them, to see if they wanted access to any of these people, and to get back to me. And if they had no objections, it would be fine with me." Clarke stated that he had "no recollection of clearing it with anybody at the White House." Yet White House chief of staff Andrew Card told the commission he remembered "someone telling him" that the Saudis had requested help in getting people out of the country and President Bush and Vice President Cheney did not know about it.

The commission said it believed the FBI conducted "satisfactory screening" of the Saudis who left. But documents declassified in 2005 revealed that the FBI gave personal airport escorts to two prominent Saudi families who, along with several other Saudis, were allowed to leave the country without first being interviewed.

One document revealed that there were six flights and that the FBI questioned all and checked watchlists and determined that "no information of investigative value" was obtained. Counterintelligence specialists said the FBI was playing politics by stating it could not gather such information, since a more detailed probe would have revealed important leads.

The FBI was protecting one of the biggest secrets in the U.S. government: Saudi Arabia's provision of intelligence information to the U.S. government, a problem that has come to dominate U.S. policy and undermine American security. U.S. intelligence information is handled at several classification levels, beginning at Confidential, the least sensitive, and going to Secret and then to Top Secret. Within the Top Secret classified information there are additional compartments known as Sensitive Compartmented Information. Intelligence officials who have access to all levels, up to and including the most sensitive human-source and electronic intelligence, say that there is one further level that is beyond the reach of the uppermost ranks of the U.S. intelligence community.

It is the information channel used for information provided by Saudi Arabia.

The Saudi channel is unique in that it is based on the kingdom's sources and it is doled out only on condition that it be allowed to be seen by only a few of the most senior U.S. officials. The intelligence has not been good enough to catch or kill bin Laden. That might be because the Saudis do not want him killed. There are indications that many in the Saudi royal family are sympathetic to the terrorist leader, if not secretly supportive.

For starters, Saudi Arabia has only selectively cooperated with the United States against terrorism, despite a series of al Qaeda attacks in the kingdom in the mid-2000s that U.S. officials say has awakened the monarchy to the threat. The financial area is one place that the Saudi government has not cooperated. Riyadh has not helped with identifying charities linked to the tens of thousands of royal family members that U.S. intelligence agencies believe are covertly providing funds to al Qaeda.

Michael Leiter, the director of the National Counterterrorism Center, the intelligence component in charge of U.S. intelligence on terrorists, revealed in Senate testimony that Saudi Arabia continues to fund Islamist extremists seven years after the September 11 attacks. "The problem of terror funding from Saudi Arabia and elsewhere is very serious," Leiter told the Senate Select Committee on Intelligence in May 2008. He said that the Saudi government had disrupted major elements of the al Qaeda terrorist group but politely noted that "they continue to face challenges in stopping funding elsewhere." He declined to detail the problem in a public session, but Senator Ron Wyden, Oregon Democrat, castigated the Saudis, bluntly stating, "It seems to me they're interested in protecting their own country, but I don't see a lot of cooperation as it relates to the area outside Saudi Arabia and that this is a problem today."

Stuart A. Levey, the Treasury Department undersecretary in charge of the office of terrorism and financial intelligence, also acknowledged that Saudi Arabia is a major financier of terrorism. "Saudi Arabia today remains the location from which more money is going to Sunni terror groups and the Taliban than from any other place in the world," Levey told the Senate Finance Committee in April 2008. He blamed the closed nature of the Saudi monarchy, its failure to provide "public accountability," and its unwillingness to invest some of the hundreds of billions of dollars in oil revenue into financial investigations of terrorism on the Arabian peninsula. "What I said in 2006 about the status of their financial intelligence unit remains largely true, and there may have been improvements," Levey said, "but still Saudi Arabia has a financial intelligence unit that hasn't met the criteria for admission to the Egmont Group, which is the international organization for financial intelligence units, which has over a hundred members. So when we think about the threat in Saudi Arabia, that's a real problem."

Intelligence sharing also has been one-sided. Whenever the CIA approaches its Saudi counterparts, the Saudis demand details beyond the scope of what they need to know, prompting fears that the Saudi services are finding out things that will be used against the United States, to protect Saudi nationals involved in terrorism and to dampen international opposition to the monarchy. U.S. intelligence officials revealed that Saudi intelligence knows details of global terrorist networks that it keeps from the United States.

Saudi arrests of al Qaeda terrorists also are kept secret and the information on interrogations withheld in part or in whole, limiting U.S. intelligence efforts to track down the group and its leaders.

Intelligence officials critical of the Saudi intelligence relationship said that it is a case of the tail wagging the dog. The Saudi intelligence relationship is now dominating U.S. policy, as intelligence officials prevail in arguing against policymakers who want to put pressure on Riyadh to do more in the war against terrorism.

Fatal Flaws

There have been two fatal flaws in U.S. policy toward the Saudi kingdom: fear of losing access to oil, and mirror-imaging, or the belief, widespread in policy circles, that the Saudis think and act just like us.

The first flaw reflects a genuine problem: losing access to Saudi oil would cripple the United States overnight. The Saudi kingdom cut off oil supplies in 1973, as a result of the Yom Kippur War fought between Israel and Arab states. The action, illegal according to international law, prompted the oil crisis. Ever since, U.S. presidential administrations have looked the other way at illegal and anti-American Saudi behavior, whether it is the Saudis' medieval system based on Sharia law or their often brutal treatment of their own people (burglars have their hands cut off and women are not permitted to drive cars). As the price of oil sky-rocketed in 2007 and 2008, the Saudi oil factor loomed larger than ever.

The second flaw involves a sorely mistaken assumption. No matter what many bureaucrats would like to believe, the Saudis do not think like us.

A rare leak of intelligence critical of the Saudis exposed what U.S. intelligence officials say is the real view of the Saudi government and military toward the United States. This intelligence came to me shortly after the September 11 attacks. A Saudi air force general was over-heard in an intercepted telephone conversation telling a colleague that the deadly al Qaeda attacks were the result of America "reaping what it sows." The comment highlighted the Riyadh government's duplici-tous policy of claiming to back the United States while secretly work-ing against it, and expressing sympathy for U.S. enemies.

By March 2007, the Saudi government was no longer doing much to hide its anti-American positions. That month King Abdullah bin Abdul Aziz Al Saud, the successor to Fahd, stated clearly his opposi-tion to U.S. foreign policy when he called the American military pres-ence in Iraq an "illegitimate foreign occupation."

"In beloved Iraq, blood is flowing between brothers, in the shadow of an illegitimate foreign occupation, and abhorrent sectarianism threat-ens a civil war," Abdullah said.

The U.S. government had encountered this problem before. Ter-rorists blew up a U.S. military barracks in Dhahran, Saudi Arabia, in 1996, killing nineteen, yet Saudi authorities refused to cooperate with the United States in getting to the bottom of the murders. Former FBI counterterrorism chief John O'Neill was quoted as saying before he died in the 2001 World Trade Center attack that Saudi pressure on the State Department prevented the FBI from investigating al Qaeda links to the bombing, as well as the al Qaeda attack on the USS *Cole* in 2000.

The Saudis are playing both sides in the war on terrorism, and the reason for that is simple: Saudi national interest is limited to preventing al Qaeda from killing the ruling monarchy.

To the public, the Saudi monarchy appears as an island of stability in a sea of Islamic fervor. But the corrupt ruling House of Saud has a tenuous hold on power. As one senior U.S. intelligence official told me, understanding the Saudis' monarchy requires looking at it as similar to the British monarchy around the seventeenth century. It is a feudal system where ruling court politics drive its policies and national interests, making cooperation in the pursuit of higher international goals nearly impossible.

Unfortunately, U.S. leaders and government bureaucrats have embraced the Saudi regime and other nondemocratic governments, failing to understand that those types of states seek regime survival and are not interested in helping the United States and other countries fighting an existential battle against Islamist terrorists.

The instability in Saudi Arabia was highlighted just two months after the September 11 attacks. U.S. intelligence officials revealed to me that a terrorist tried to assassinate King Fahd as his motorcade drove through the capital, Riyadh, on November 10, 2001. The terrorist attempted to ram his vehicle into the limousine carrying the monarch. The attempt failed, as the car could not get through the heavily guarded motorcade to the king's limo. But according to a classified intelligence report, had the terrorist been driving an explosive-packed vehicle, the assassination attempt would have succeeded.

The Open Source Center, a U.S. intelligence unit located at CIA headquarters, revealed in an April 2008 report that the Saudi government has failed to pressure Sunni clerics in the kingdom into permitting greater religious tolerance, a key step toward mitigating the terror-ist threat. King Abdullah in March 2008 did call for more tolerance toward non-Muslims, but it had little effect. One sermon posted on fundamentalist Muslim website Nur al-Islam three days after the king's remark stated that "Jews, Christians, polytheists, and hypocrites are nothing more than infidels." The sermon also said that "some people's love for the infidels has reached frightening proportions." Then a rad-ical Saudi cleric, Shaykh Abd-al-Rahman Al-Barrak, issued a religious edict, or fatwa, denouncing two Saudi journalists for expressing toler-ance toward non-Muslims, and stating that those who do not recant such views must be "killed as apostates." As the Open Source Center's report noted, these comments reflect the Riyadh government's failure to tamp down religious extremism, even though the Saudi Ministry of Islamic Affairs supposedly monitors Islamic sermons and presses cler-ics to use more moderate language and topics.

The monarchy's desire to retain power has led to covert support for al Qaeda and its affiliates in terms of payments and other rewards that could be stopped if the Saudi government wanted it stopped. Likewise, if Saudi Arabia were to use its intelligence and other re-sources, finding and capturing Osama bin Laden could be done with relative ease. Alex Alexiev, a specialist on the Saudi Kingdom's terror-ist connections, has stated that the Saudi government controlled or funded, or both, nearly fifty Islamic organizations that the U.S. law-enforcement operation Green Quest has raided, shut down, or frozen the assets of since September 11.

That is how the House of Saud, which includes as many as 10,000 princes, has managed to keep enemies at bay—by doing whatever it can to play potential threats off one another.

One means the Saudis use to try to strengthen their grip on power is to funnel huge amounts of money into Wahhabi schools and clerics, both within the kingdom and abroad.

Funding Hatred

Saudi Arabia has used its vast oil wealth to influence the United States, including its government, the U.S. military, civilian policymakers, its business community, the academic world, and the news media. In late 2007, the Saudi government reported a budget surplus of $77 billion, and with oil trading way above $100 per barrel, the Saudis are loaded with cash. Rarely do critical stories about the Saudis appear in the prestige news outlets like the *New York Times,* the *Washington Post,* or CBS News. A review of the U.S. Justice Department's foreign agent registration includes a who's who of powerful law firms and public relations outlets representing the Saudis, including Patton Boggs, Hogan & Hartson, Burson-Marsteller, Hill & Knowlton, and Akin Gump Strauss Hauer & Feld. Lesser-known Saudi agents on the list include the Loeffler Group, the Gallagher Group, Qorvis Communications, Mpd consultants, and Fleishman-Hillard.

Saudi government money to the tune of around $10 million was given to the Clinton Library in Little Rock, Arkansas, and about the same amount was given to former president George H.W. Bush's center at Texas A&M University. Also, a Saudi prince donated $20 million to Georgetown University, the key educational source for Foreign Service officers; the size of the donation raised questions about whether it will influence Georgetown's teaching on the kingdom. And these are just a few of the outlets that have received millions in Saudi money. The Saudi largesse helps explain the deafening silence about the Saudis and their export of radical Wahhabism. It is Wahhabism that is at the root of concerns about Saudi Arabia.

New information on Saudi funding activities in the United States surfaced during an embezzlement case of the leader of the Islamic Center of Washington, D.C., the nation's oldest mosque, which is Saudi-funded and has sought to bring Islamic radicals into the United States to promote Wahhabism.

An Iranian-born American citizen, Farzad Darui, was dedicated to preventing radical fundamentalists from taking over the Islamic Center. As court papers in the case revealed, he became the target of a vicious campaign to discredit him, including a federal prosecution on embezzlement charges that his lawyers suspect was the work of White House officials seeking to please the Saudi monarchy.

Darui sought to prevent the Saudis, through their appointed imam, Abdullah M. Khouj, from using the mosque to fund and promote radical Islamism in the United States. Darui's court findings allege that when the Saudis hired Khouj to be the center's director in 1984, he was employed by the Muslim World League. The Muslim World League has been under investigation for years by the U.S. government based on suspicions that it knowingly or unknowingly provided funds to al Qaeda leader Osama bin Laden.

The case revealed that the Religious Section of the Saudi embassy, which paid Khouj and sought to control the Islamic Center, would frequently bring in radical Wahhabi Muslims to the United States. "They were invited to preach by Khouj, but he did so at the bidding of the Religious Section," a court paper in the embezzlement case stated. "When these radicals preached, it was a message of hate and discrimination against anyone who disagreed."

One radical whom Khouj invited to preach at the Center was Ali Al-Timimi. Darui opposed Timimi's Wahhabi message of hatred toward non-Muslims and non-Wahhabis, and refused to allow Timimi to return to the Center even though the Saudis sent messages to overrule that decision. In 2005, Timimi was convicted in Virginia federal court of ten counts relating to terrorism, and sentenced to life imprisonment.

Another case involved Osama Basnan. In the 1990s, Darui barred him from the Center despite an order to admit him from Prince Mohammed Bin-Faisal, the director of the Religious Section. Basnan was deported on November 17, 2002, for visa fraud, under suspicion of having terrorist ties. Bin-Faisal is now high up in Saudi Arabia's Ministry of Foreign Affairs, serving as director of the Department of European Union and Member States.

Darui ran afoul of the Saudis when he blew the whistle on a scheme to launder some $600,000 annually through Khouj's personal bank accounts, which Khouj used to pay the center's administrative costs as well as personal expenses, according to Darui's court filings. Darui believes this was part of an effort by the Saudi government to covertly control the Center; the Center rejected offers of major donations from other Muslim countries, including money for renovation of the façade. Because Darui tried to block Islamic radicals from the Center, the Saudis, via the Center, accused him of embezzlement.

Darui, who is independently wealthy, argued in court that he did not need to embezzle the money. He explained where the money really came from: Khouj. The imam, Darui said, was paying Darui back for years' worth of housing and feeding that Darui had provided for Khouj's additional "wives," or mistresses. During court testimony, Khouj was shown documents revealing that the checks he claimed Darui had embezzled were actually deposited into his personal account.

Prosecutors stated in court that they believed Darui changed the payee lines on the mosque's checks to state that they were payable to Zaal Inc. and Blue Line Travel Inc., his companies. But Darui claimed that he was innocent and that he never cashed any checks that were not approved by Khouj. The two-week trial ended in a mistrial in May 2008 as jurors were deadlocked.

The Saudi role in funding the Washington mosque is a microcosm of the Saudi regime's global campaign to build and fund thousands of Wahhabite centers that spread hatred and further the terrorists' violent anti-Western agenda.

Going Nuclear?

Even more troubling, there are indications that to counter Iran's nuclear arsenal, Saudi Arabia is secretly developing its own nuclear arsenal. As Sunni Muslims, the Saudis oppose the rise of Shias in Iran (as well as those emerging in Iraq).

U.S. intelligence officials confirmed European news reports that the United States is worried about a covert Saudi nuclear weapons program, although appeals to the kingdom for explanations and information have met with silence. The suspicion is that the Saudis are working to develop a nuclear weapon in their country or are working closely with Pakistan on a plan that would bring nuclear warheads to the kingdom for launch atop Saudi Arabia's Chinese-made intermediate-range ballistic missiles. The nuclear arms would be a strategic deterrent against Iran. The London *Guardian* newspaper reported in September 2003 that Riyadh embarked on a strategy review that included as one option the acquisition of a nuclear capability. Germany's *Cicero* newsmagazine reported in 2006 that Saudi Arabia was working on nuclear weapons secretly with Pakistan.

There is a precedent for this buildup. Despite its four decades of close cooperation with Washington, the Saudi government in the mid-1980s began secretly acquiring Chinese CSS-2 intermediate-range missiles, as satellite photos revealed. The 1,900-mile-range missiles are so inaccurate that any conventional explosive warhead would be useless: these were nuclear missiles. But the Saudis claimed that there were no plans to arm them with nuclear warheads. Contrary to that claim, reliable reports surfaced that Pakistan planned to secretly ship nuclear warheads to Saudi Arabia.

With its vast oil revenues, Saudi Arabia could easily buy both the infrastructure and the expertise to make nuclear bombs. And with its preexisting covert arms relationship with China, the world's most significant nuclear arms proliferator, Riyadh could easily become a nuclear power, despite its signing the Nuclear Non-Proliferation Treaty. That's the same treaty Iran signed and then repeatedly flouted.

India: "An Uncertain Friend"

India is another nation that the United States is courting as an ally but that continues to play a double game.

Sadanand Dhume, former correspondent for the *Far Eastern Economic Review,* notes that the Indian government has launched a public relations blitz in the United States designed to show its closeness to the country, in an aggressive attempt to move away from the antagonistic relationship with America that existed during the Cold War. But as Dhume observes, India continues to be a questionable ally.

India remains one of the poorest countries in the world, ranking 146th, between Syria and Georgia. Still, American foreign policy specialists ranging from Clinton defense official Ashton Carter to Nixon secretary of state Henry Kissinger favor an alliance with India, seeing India as a potential counterbalance to the emergence of China. The trouble is that the Delhi government, still influenced by the Communist Party of India, probably will not go along.

Consider, for example, that a U.S.-India nuclear deal that was announced in 2005 was supposed to help cement better ties between the two nations. But India's Communists scuttled the deal because the party opposed aligning India in any way with the United States—this even though the deal did not require Delhi to join the Nuclear Non-Proliferation Treaty. That part of the nuclear deal had been a significant concession on the part of the United States, pushed through by a bipartisan group of lawmakers including the late conservative Republican Henry Hyde to liberal Democrats like Senator Hillary Clinton and House Speaker Nancy Pelosi.

To allow the deal to go through, these politicians actually had to change U.S. rules that limit nuclear supplies to states that are not part of international controls. Henry Sokolski, director of the Nonproliferation Policy Education Center, pointed out what an extraordinary concession this was: "Article I of the Non-Proliferation Treaty (NPT) currently obliges the United States not to help a state's military nuclear efforts in any way if that state did not have a bomb before 1968. That's not Jim Crow, it's the rules. Violate them, as the United States is proposing to do by giving India access to foreign uranium, settle for the meager nonproliferation commitments India has offered so far, and the nuclear rules will only be weakened even further."

Despite all that U.S. politicians did to make the deal palatable to Delhi, the Communists in India nixed the arrangement.

While Indians remain among the most pro-American people in Asia, due in part to the fact that there are 2.5 million Indian-Americans, India's elite is dominated by America-haters, much like the U.S. intelligentsia. One example is prizewinning novelist Arundhati Roy, an anticapitalist who has jumped on the "antiglobalization" bandwagon, whose main feature is hatred of the United States and its power, economic or otherwise. Roy's 2004 collection of essays, *An Ordinary Person's Guide to Empire,* cautions India against cooperating with the United States in the war on terrorism, which she defines as "a superpower's self-destructive impulse toward supremacy, stranglehold, [and] global hegemony." When President Bush visited India in 2006, Roy and other leftists, along with communists and Muslims in India, were outspoken in their denunciations of the American leader. Another example is Vandana Shiva, a leading Indian scientist who has mounted protests against corporations that want to expand the retail sector in India. Somehow, it seems, this poses a threat to India's national identity.

The liberals in the U.S. intelligence community continue to link China and India as similar emerging states, but the fact is that China's buildup of power threatens to dwarf India's. And that could spell trouble for the alliance the United States is supposedly forging with India. Dhume writes, "Despite confident predictions that India will surpass the People's Republic, it is no less plausible that, twenty years from now, China's economic, military, and cultural heft will so dwarf India's that comparisons between the two countries will have become altogether meaningless. This, coupled with the demands of domestic politics, could cause India to slip back definitively into its historical comfort zone as an almost reflexively anti-Western power with an officially nonaligned policy—only this time calibrated to tiptoe around Beijing's sensitivities rather than Moscow's."

India's foreign policies continue the long Cold War tradition of bashing the United States. Delhi has, for instance, utterly failed to support U.S. policies aimed at pressuring Iran to denuclearize. The Indian government's public statements are equivocal and more often emphasize the terrorist state's right to have nuclear power than the threat of the Islamic bomb in Tehran. If India, as a leader in the developing world and as a country with some 151 million Muslims, had warned Iran to give up its arms, it would have gone a long way to countering Iran's efforts to frame the issue as a challenge between Muslims and the West. But India's government refused to do so, fearing accusations of supporting the United States. The failure is an indication that India is not a reliable international partner in America's efforts to prevent the spread of dangerous arms to rogue states.

As Dhume sums up the U.S.-India ties, rapprochement is a key benefit of the end of the Cold War, but "the jury remains out on the longer term."

Dhume continues, "Until India is able to view itself and its history dispassionately, reject the twin failures of socialism and nonalignment, modernize its Muslim citizens and bring their aspirations in line with those of the Hindu majority, it will likely remain an underachiever—and, for the U.S. and the West, an uncertain friend."

It is on the issue of radical Islam and the U.S.-led war on terrorism that India is like the enemy allies of Western Europe. The leftists in both India and Europe are banding together against the United States. In so doing, they are lending support to terrorists who are out to destroy Western and Eastern societies alike with radical tenets of a centuries-old religious dogma.

French Anti-Americanism . . . and a New Hope

European anti-Americanism is growing, led by France's patho-logical dislike of the United States. As the French writer Jean-François Revel put it in his book *Anti-Americanism,* the French dislike America because of a sense of envy and loss—envy of U.S. prosperity and loss of France's nineteenth-century role as a world leader. For the French, anti-Americanism is a stalking horse for antiglobalization, which is simply a new form of socialist anticapitalism. Revel noted how, when U.S. military forces moved into Afghanistan to go after al Qaeda bases a month after the 9/11 attacks, 113 leftist French intel-lectuals denounced the action as nothing more than an "imperial cru-sade." Additionally, the leftist Thierry Meyssan put forward the blood libel that the entire September 11 attack was a fraud carried out by U.S. intelligence services. For the deluded French, America created the al Qaeda attacks as merely an excuse to invade Afghanistan and then Iraq. Anti-Americanism became more vehement only as French antipathy toward George W. Bush intensified in response to the pres-ident's steadfast commitment to fighting Islamism, which led to the 2003 invasion of Iraq.

But then, in 2007, a turnaround began: Nicolas Sarkozy was elected president of France. Sarkozy moved quickly to replace the anti-Americanism of France with a more friendly posture toward the United States and better strategic dialogue. His book, *Testimony: France in the Twenty-first Century,* contains numerous pro-American references. In it he praised the American work ethic, the notion of giving a "second chance" to "those who try hard and deserve it," and the American "ca-pacity to recognize its own weaknesses" and to correct them "without useless nostalgia about the past."

Whereas French intellectuals portray the United States as a bastion of elitism and racism, Sarkozy said relations among U.S. minorities are "better managed . . . than in most European countries," and he stated that France will not attain true diversity "until it has a Colin Powell or

Condoleezza Rice as minister of foreign affairs" or "a John Abizaid as one of its top generals." The French president also pointed out that the U.S. Constitution has outlived fifteen French constitutions since 1791, and he praised U.S. political institutions as "among the most remarkable accomplishments in the history of human freedom."

Sarkozy still is not a conservative and opposes U.S. positions on climate change and the Kyoto environmental pact, but he has regretted the cool ties to the United States under his predecessor, Jacques Chirac, who was notable for his close ties to Saddam Hussein. France's bureaucracy, overwhelmingly anti-U.S., will ensure that the French make no major departures from the foreign policy that existed under Chirac. Still, Sarkozy, in his first major foreign policy address, was more combative in outlining the dangers from Iran and the growing authoritarianism in Russia than Chirac. He raised the prospect that France would take military action against Iran over its nuclear arms. He called an Iranian nuclear bomb "unacceptable," and proposed "increasing sanctions" while "opening up toward Iran" if it showed compliance. Sarkozy warned that this strategy remained the "only one" that would not lead to a "disastrous alternative: the Iranian bomb or the bombing of Iran." These remarks were in sharp contrast to Chirac's statement, in a 2006 speech, urging Tehran to "create a climate of trust," to encourage French-Iranian cooperation.

Sarkozy also criticized Russia for "asserting its return to the world scene by playing its trump cards—particularly oil and gas—with a certain brutality," a reference to Moscow's threats to cut off energy supplies from Ukraine and other neighbors.

Germany's New Rules for Fighting Terrorists

If the situation shows signs of improving in France, there is no such room for optimism with other European states. Germany is a prime example of the European opposition to the United States.

In early 2008, the Germans refused to send troops into battle against Taliban forces in southern Afghanistan, testing the resolve of NATO. Defense Secretary Robert Gates abandoned the rhetoric of his predecessor, Donald Rumsfeld, who shamed the Western Europeans by calling them Old Europe, in comparison with the vibrant pro-freedom democracies of Eastern Europe. Instead, Gates tried to foster a spirit of cooperation. He wrote a letter to his German counterpart, Defense Minister Franz Josef Jung, to urge the Germans to join a rapid reaction force in southern Afghanistan, where fighting against the Taliban had been tough. Germany had several thousand troops in the north, where there was no combat. The United States had sent an additional 3,200 Marines to fight the Taliban, and Gates wanted the Germans to pick up where the Marines left off when they finished their tour in the south.

Germany did not jump to support its NATO partner. In fact, the German newspaper *Der Spiegel* called Gates's eight-page letter to Jung an "outrage." The paper observed that German troops in Afghanistan were limited to civilian-military reconstruction. That was because the leftist-influenced German parliament had imposed restrictions forbidding soldiers from using deadly force "unless an attack is under way or imminent." The restrictions mean that if German troops find Taliban fighters, they can't fire at them unless fired on first. So Gates and other NATO allies wanted the Germans to go on the offensive, but the Germans refused. The German military, the Bundeswehr, stated on its Internet site that taking the fight to the Taliban was not their mission but that of the U.S.-led Operation Enduring Freedom. NATO's mission was "strictly separated" from the NATO international security force mission, the Germans insisted.

European Appeasement

Britain too remains in the appeasement mode. Despite Britain's reputation as a key supporter of U.S. policies and for backing the war on terrorism, British policies are weak and vacillating, and they contribute to a lack of support against the terrorist foe.

The British Left is growing in power and influence and is using claims of "Islamophobia" as part of its opposition to the U.S.-led war on terrorism. *The New Statesman,* the British Left's house organ, reported in December 2005 that "Islamophobia," or what it termed an irrational fear and or hatred of Islam, Muslims, and Islamic culture, was leading to the "next Holocaust," comparing the Nazi extermination of 6 million Jews in World War II to the coming treatment of European Muslims.

European Union bureaucrats have become even more craven than their American counterparts at lending support to organizations that monitor anti-Muslim prejudice. Most such organizations are simply leftist groups that have aligned themselves with radical Muslims or their supporters as a show of their anti-Americanism. In Britain, for instance, the Forum Against Islamophobia and Racism (FAIR) is being strongly backed by naïve and appeasement-oriented political leaders. France too has its pro-Islam group, the Collectif Contre l'Islamophobie en France (CCIF).

Britain's appeasement reached a new level in early 2008 when the British government let it be known that Muslims with multiple wives could be eligible for welfare benefits, even though polygamy is illegal in Britain. This was a breakthrough for Islamists seeking to carve out a separate culture in Europe and apply the tenets of Islamic law. Many specialists consider this to be a dangerous step toward allowing fundamentalists to act outside the Western tradition.

William Gawthrop, a former intelligence analyst and specialist on Muslim subversion, said one of the many ways Muslims seek to subvert non-Muslim societies is by quietly pressuring the society into gradually accepting Islamist ways. For example, by starting halal, or Islamically permissible, food stores, Muslim extremists can identify other Muslims in their communities and then begin to influence them into becoming fundamentalists. Extremists also use mosques and Muslim

religious schools for subversion, specifically the recruitment of terrorists for operations. "Assessing future allies by seeing who comes into
your food store is far less efficient than seeing who shows up for Friday
prayers," Gawthrop said. The ultimate result of such efforts is to create
a foundation for Islamists to institute Sharia law and take over the
society on behalf of the fundamentalist ideal.

To avoid offending supposedly pious Muslims, Europeans have
been taking absurd precautions. In England, a prison admonished
guards for wearing pins that featured the Cross of St. George. The
pins were a sign of support for a cancer charity, but that didn't matter
to the zealous defenders of "tolerance." The prison explained that the
banner of St. George could be "misinterpreted" as a racist symbol because it was worn by English soldiers during the Crusades in the elev-
enth century. Never mind that it is also the English national flag.

In another case in Britain, a Muslim customer at Burger King
complained that the graphics used on a cover of an ice cream dish appeared similar to the Arabic spelling for Allah and thus was supposedly blasphemous. The fast-food chain was forced to apologize. The
list goes on.

The British, in particular, have been guilty of appeasement. This is
a dangerous trend, since pro-Islamist groups have taken advantage of
the atmosphere created by such appeasement. Among those groups
are many supporters of the Muslim Brotherhood, an organization that
originated in Egypt and has proven to be one of the premier terrorist
organizations, even as the group has attempted to distance itself from
Islamist terror. The Muslim Brotherhood uses subversion as a key tool
to advance its goal of reestablishing a Muslim Caliphate and spread Islamism around the globe.

The Muslim Association of Britain (MAB) is an example. British
members of Parliament have described the MAB as the British wing of
the Muslim Brotherhood. The group promotes itself as a "moderate"
Muslim organization, and yet its ranks include the former military
commander of Hamas, which has carried out dozens of suicide bomb-

ings in Israel. Labour parliamentarian Louise Ellman told the *Daily Mail* in 2006 that the MAB is an extremist group. "They are an extremely dangerous organisation," she said. "Leading members of MAB have indicated their links with Hamas and their support for suicide bombings abroad."

In Britain, most mainstream Muslim organizations are openly anti-Semitic, blaming Israel for all the ills of the Middle East. And yet authorities continue to appease Muslim sensitivities and thus contribute to further Islamicization. When Israel went to war with the terrorist group Hezbollah in the summer of 2006, leftist British protesters took to the streets carrying signs that stated "We are all Hezbollah now."

Even British conservatives are turning pro-Muslim and anti-Israel. David Cameron, the leader of the opposition Conservative Party, said in a speech on September 11, 2006, that the problem of terrorism will continue as long as the "perception by many Muslims that Islam is under attack" endures, along with the "belief that the West deliberately fails to resolve issues of crucial concern to Muslims, like Palestine." He, like those on the Left, vowed to show greater "sensitivity" to Muslims.

Russia Goes Backwards

In 2001, President George W. Bush was asked at a press conference after a meeting with Russian president Vladimir Putin whether the West can trust Russia. "I looked the man in the eye," Bush said. "I found him to be very straightforward and trustworthy. We had a very good dialogue. I was able to get a sense of his soul; a man deeply committed to his country and the best interests of his country." The president said that he wanted the United States to have a new relationship "beyond the Cold War mentality," to now be "friends" with Russia because "friends don't destroy each other."

The ensuing years have proved that Russia was not seeking friendship with the United States. Instead it was working against America and America's interests in an effort to block the United States from helping to expand freedom and democracy.

Putin's Russia is the clearest example of wishful thinking on the part of American policymakers and bureaucrats who want to pretend that there is no threat. The truth is that Moscow's government is a regime stacked with unreformed KGB intelligence officials who still regard the United States as the main enemy to be defeated, or at the very least to be blocked and weakened.

After taking over as president in 2000, Putin, himself a former KGB officer, moved steadily to remake Russia into a Soviet-style system, albeit without the Communist institutions of power. The organs of power came firmly under his authoritarian control. Putin, who called the 1991 collapse of the Soviet Union a "catastrophe," gradually tightened the screws on Russia's post-Communist democratic system. Putin moved even more swiftly to consolidate power in the aftermath of the 2004 Chechen terrorist attack on a school in the Russian town of Beslan. The rescue attempt by Russian troops was botched, and more than 300 people died, most of them children.

Yevgeny Yasin, a key Russian economic reformer, called Putin's putsch beginning around 2002 as the "revenge of the bureaucracy." After decades of Soviet control over the economy, Russia in the first years after the collapse of the Soviet Union had finally moved to a system of private ownership and market institutions. But under Putin, the national government began to retake control of the economy, especially in the all-important gas and oil sector. The renationalization process began in 2004 with the government takeover of Yukos, the country's largest private company.

The new statist bureaucrats in charge quickly reverted to the policies of their Soviet counterparts. Many of them *had been* Soviet bureaucrats, in fact. Bear in mind that Soviet control of Russia's extensive oil and gas reserves was an utter disaster. As American Enterprise Institute scholar Leon Aron noted, oil production in the old U.S.S.R. "beautifully embodied the point of the old Soviet joke that, after seventy years of socialism in Africa, the Sahara would have run out of sand." Before Putin's renationalization, the privatized oil and gas firms were in the process of returning 88 percent of their profits, some $26 billion, back into developing Russia's natural resources. His power grab threatened to destroy the long-term health of the industry and therefore seriously damage the Russian economy.

And it *was* a power grab. Any Russians in the private sector who objected to the renationalization and even hinted at seeking political office were slapped down with imprisonment or exile.

Despite all these disturbing developments in Russia, the bureaucracy in Washington barely reacted. Evidence of aggressive Russian intelligence-gathering activities was ignored for years after Bush made the flattering comments about Putin, until November 2007, when a Russian military intelligence officer was caught attempting to illegally acquire U.S. military technology and was expelled from the country. Five months later a second Russian spy was ordered to leave the country for improper intelligence-gathering. Defense Secretary Robert Gates, representing the entrenched bureaucrats' mindset, dismissed Russia's retaliatory expulsions of two U.S. diplomats as "just the usual tit-for-tat." Gates declined to criticize the Russians for the aggressive spying or the growing antidemocratic dictatorship under Putin. "These things get into kind of a back and forth, and at some point everybody decides to stop," Gates said.

Meanwhile, Putin demonstrated the power of the state-run oil and gas industries when he handpicked as his successor Dmitry Medvedev, the chairman of the natural-gas monopoly Gazprom. Term limits kept Putin from running for president again in 2008, but Medvedev, his former chief of staff, who had never run for elective office, achieved a crushing victory in the March elections. Putin stayed on as prime minister and was also chosen to be the chairman of his political party, so there's no doubt that he will continue to wield extraordinary power in Russia.

No doubt President Bush's hope for friendship with Russia was inspired in part by the hope that America's addiction to foreign oil might be turned from the unstable Middle East to Russia. But the Putin regime made clear that Russia will be no friend of the United States. Instead, Russia looked east to China and developed a new anti-U.S. alliance, called the Shanghai Cooperation Organisation.

Putin rejected the pro-Western foreign policy of Mikhail Gorbachev and Boris Yeltsin in favor of a Russo-centric view of the world that dismisses concepts of democracy as weakness that led to the Soviet collapse. As Aron noted, "no longer is the integration of Russia into the family of Western capitalist democracy held to be a goal, even a distant one."

For the United States, the loss of Russia to the ranks of dictatorships is the result of the liberals and bureaucrats and will one day be examined by historians who will debate "who lost Russia."

How did the bureaucracy lose Russia? It was a combination of failures—the State Department's failure to produce a strong Russian policy and the intelligence agencies' failure to monitor and report the decline of democracy in Russia.

First, the State Department bureaucrats who sat at the center of foreign policy making and international relations failed to craft a coherent U.S. strategy to advance the nascent democratic reforms begun after the 1991 collapse. Again, the leadership of liberal Republicans like Secretary of State Colin Powell and Deputy Secretary of State Richard Armitage was lacking. Powell and Armitage miscalculated that Russia under Putin would continue on its own to follow the path of democracy and liberal economic reform. The same mistake was followed by Secretary of State Condoleezza Rice, who, like Powell and Armitage, neglected Russia policy, even though Rice considered herself a specialist on Russian affairs.

Despite all these failures, the liberal Nicholas Burns, undersecretary of state for political affairs, proclaimed in a February 2007 speech that on countering terrorism and arms proliferation, "Russia is one of our strongest partners worldwide." Only a month earlier, General Yuri

Baluyevsky, chief of Russia's general staff, had revealed the notion of U.S.-Russian partnership to be a delusion. General Baluyevsky said, "We [Russians] have no plans to attack anyone, but we consider it necessary for all our partners clearly to understand . . . that for the defense of the sovereignty and territorial integrity of Russia and its allies there will be resort to armed force also preventively, and also with recourse to nuclear weapons. Military power ought to be utilized to demonstrate the resolve of the country's leaders to assert its interests, and, as an extreme measure, in a concentrated manner when other measures prove ineffective." Reports of the statement in the state-controlled Russian press referred to Russia's right to use preemptive nuclear attacks to prevent what it regarded as massive aggression. This was a rare restatement of Soviet-era nuclear doctrine, but liberal U.S. bureaucrats did not take the threat to the United States seriously.

The career Foreign Service officer Daniel Fried, assistant secretary of state for European and Eurasian affairs, summed up the department's failed bureaucratic policy toward Russia: "U.S. policy . . . will remain consistent: we seek to cooperate with the government of Russia wherever our interests overlap, and we will do so in working with President Medvedev. And we will continue to stand by our principles and friends, dealing frankly with differences when these arise." There was no sense that Russia needed more than such policy platitudes; it simply needed to become more integrated into the global system.

Harvard Russian affairs specialist Richard Pipes stated in an article in *Commentary* magazine that unlike post-Nazi Germany, "post-Communist Russia has never made a clean break with its totalitarian past." Pipes wrote, "The relics of Soviet Communism are visible everywhere, so much so that according to a poll conducted earlier in this decade, fully 30 percent of Russian citizens are not even aware that the Soviet regime no longer exists."

The underlying cause of Russia's democratic decline, Pipes said, lay in the return to power of veterans of the KGB, like Putin, who adopted the Communist secret political police's ingrained anti-Western and particularly anti-American views. The KGB's mentality of "any means necessary" for preserving the state has led to the rise of the Putin dictatorship and the Soviet practice of assassinating regime opponents abroad. Pipes does not see a return to the Cold War but warns that the undemocratic Russia will produce a "constant state of tension" with the West.

The foreign policy and intelligence failure toward Russia could have been avoided if there had been more strategic vision and leadership and less reliance on the bureaucracy.

Russia's opposition to the United States has been visible in its arms sales and support to the world's terrorist regimes, including Syria and Iran, which both receive large amounts of Russian weaponry and related technology. Putin resumed arms sales to Iran that had been halted in 1995 at U.S. behest; among the weaponry the Russians have sent to Tehran's radical clerical regime are advanced warplanes, tanks, and air defense missiles. In 2008, Russia brazenly defied U.S.-led efforts to try to force Tehran to end its illegal uranium-enrichment program by beginning deliveries of fuel for Iran's Bushehr nuclear reactor, which cost $1 billion. Moscow quickly announced plans for another nuclear reactor, furthering its role as an irresponsible international player and complicating efforts to press Iran into ending its illegal nuclear program.

A U.S. intelligence report made public in 2008 underscored the threat posed by Moscow. It stated that Russia remained "a key supplier" of nuclear technology, chemical and biological weapons components, and advanced arms to a number of states. The report noted that nuclear technology and goods posed the greatest danger, because "the Russian assistance could be used in the recipient's nuclear weapons program directly—as in the case of China—or could be diverted to nuclear weapons programs." China was the greatest purchaser of Russian nuclear goods, along with Iran and India. Russian missile suppliers gave goods and know-how to China, Iran, India, and North Korea, and marketed Strelet surface-to-air missiles to Syria.

Russia has joined China in rejecting the concepts of liberty and democracy as fundamentals, favoring instead concepts of stability, which naturally were aimed at keeping regimes in power.

Internationally, Russia worked hand in hand with China in the early 2000s to block U.S. efforts at the United Nations to use diplomacy against North Korea for its nuclear test, and against Iran for its refusal to abide by international controls on its nuclear program.

Russia's most anti-U.S. position, however, has been toward U.S. plans to put a third long-range missile interceptor site in Eastern Europe as part of a global system to protect America and its allies from attacks by North Korea or Iran. The missile defense site will include ten interceptor missiles that are not capable of hitting the higher-speed Russian missiles but could intercept a future long-range Iranian missile. The site is to be operational by 2012, along with a radar tracking system located in the Czech Republic.

Despite clear understandings that the missile defense system had no offensive capabilities, Putin and his regime used the most inflammatory rhetoric against the United States and the governments of Poland and the Czech Republic, who were more than willing to host the interceptor and radar sites for the system.

Direct appeals from senior U.S. officials were ignored by Putin.

During a visit to Moscow in October 2007, Secretary of State Condoleezza Rice and Defense Secretary Robert Gates presented the Russians with an extraordinary plan to give the Russian military a role in controlling U.S. missile defenses. They offered to integrate Russian early warning radars at Armavir, in southern Russia, and at Gabala, Azerbaijan, into the central European missile defense interceptor sites, to be located in both Poland and the Czech Republic. They agreed to allow the Russians to station "liaison officers"—read "spies"—at the central European sites. And last they made the unusual offer to make the missile defenses operational only *after* Iran developed a capability to strike Europe or the United States. The concession sought to gain Moscow's approval, but failed to do so.

Gates told reporters in Moscow, "We put forward some thoughts about the presence of individuals from both sides at sites so that there was complete transparency perhaps at third sites, but also in the United States; and if there are radars and other facilities here in Russia, that there would be a presence there, too."

The proposal raised questions about whether such concessions would compromise U.S. defenses, both operating data and technology, and undermine U.S. sovereignty. Fortunately for the United States, the Russians rejected the written proposal that was ultimately presented in November 2007, claiming that it lacked the specific command-and-control and liaison presence that Gates and Rice first offered as a way to win Moscow's acquiescence.

Russian officials insist the missile defense site poses a grave threat to Russia. But Russian missile technicians know that the system technically is not capable of hitting the higher-speed Russian ICBMs. The only reason for the Russian opposition is that Moscow is running interference for its Iranian friends.

Bolstered by oil wealth, the Russian leader promised to launch a new arms race against the United States in response to the U.S. missile defense plan in Europe. "There is a new turn in the arms race. . . . Russia will always respond to this new challenge," Putin said. He also promised "new weapons that are qualitatively the same or better than those of other countries."

Where Is the U.S. Government?

As America's alleged foreign allies have ramped up their dangerous game, it has seemed that no one in the United States is standing up to these growing threats. Just what is the U.S. government doing to cope with these problems? Almost nothing, thanks to the Failure Factory's wholesale takeover of U.S. policies and its lack of interest in addressing these grave issues.

10

Political Surrender

Peace (and War) Through

Diversity, Multiculturalism, and

Political Correctness

In March 2006, an extraordinary memorandum came to light. The memo, written by Senate minority leader Harry Reid, offered a frightening look at the depths to which liberal Democratic politicians had sunk, and the extremes to which they would go for political gain—even if it meant seeing the military defeat of the United States.

Headlined "Real Security: Recess Events 3/18 to 3/26," Reid's memo revealed a liberal Democratic plan to politicize the war in Iraq in order to regain power in both the Congress and the White House. The Democrats had dropped all pretense in opposing the Iraq conflict. They wanted to see the United States and its military and civilian forces defeated in Iraq, as a way to attack and discredit the president of the United States.

The Senate Democrats' plan called on legislators to use their time off from Washington during the upcoming congressional recess to stage major political events with active-duty military personnel, veterans, and emergency responders, in which they would conduct political attacks focusing on President George W. Bush's national security policies. That such a campaign would be carried out in wartime is damaging and borders on treasonous.

231

The six-page memorandum, drawn up by Reid's staff, was distributed to Democratic senators during a closed-door meeting on March 16, 2006. Urging Democrats to hold town hall meetings on U.S. military bases, in weapons factories, at National Guard units, in firehouses, and at veterans' posts, the Reid attack plan instructed them to "draw attention to the security vulnerabilities caused by the Bush budget and explain how Democrats fought to restore programs that keep America safe."

The Democratic leader was careful to stage-manage the events for maximum political impact. One item instructed, "When selecting a location at the military installation for the event, make sure to select a space that allows easy press access and clearly conveys the message in the shot. Planes, vehicles, equipment and signage in the background enhance the pictures coming out of your event." Appearances would be important. The memo stated, "Ensure that you have the proper U.S. and state flags at the event, and consider finding someone to sing the national anthem and lead the group in the Pledge of Allegiance at the start of the event."

The activities that were actually held around the country violated Defense Department regulations that prohibit such political events on military bases. The rules stated that military commanders cannot allow "the use of installation facilities by any candidate for political campaign or election events, including public assemblies or town hall meetings." A Reid spokesman denied that the planned events were part of a political campaign, noting that they involved only incumbent Democratic senators. The spokesman, Jim Manley, said the activities were intended to highlight the need for increased funding for U.S. troops.

"It's an effort to paint the White House and the Republican Congress as having a failed effort on national security issues, which is a direct result of their misplaced priorities and mismanagement," Manley said.

But the memo urged vehement political attacks on the president for not spending enough money, and the events were clearly intended for political gain, with an eye toward the November elections.

Elements of the plan included:

- "Hold a town hall meeting with state officials and a local National Guard unit at their armory to discuss the security impact of long deployments. . . . Ask National Guard members to offer input on how security and disaster response at home is compromised by long deployments."
- "Hold a town hall meeting with troops at a local military installation."
- "Work with [veterans'] organizations . . . to find recently returned Iraq and Afghanistan veterans willing to discuss the mental effects they or their fellow veterans have experienced."
- "Tour a factory in your state that manufactures military equipment like Humvees or body armor and hold a press availability afterwards with Iraq and Afghanistan veterans on the importance of protective equipment."
- "Visit the home of a military family that has purchased body armor on their own for a family member serving in Iraq or Afghanistan and hold an open press 'conversion' on the issue. . . . Ask the family if they would be willing to hold the open press conversation/town hall meeting in their yard, on their front porch or in their home."

The Reid memo also called for senators to link up with groups critical of the president in their campaigning, such as the Iraq and Afghanistan Veterans of America (IAVA), which opposed the president on Iraq and whose political action committee had raised $100,000 for Iraq and Afghanistan war veterans running for Congress—all Democrats.

"When preparing for war in Iraq, the Bush administration greatly underestimated the threats our troops would face, and failed to plan for the post-war, leaving our forces to fend off a dangerous insurgency without needed body armor and armored vehicles on the grounds," the memo said. "Democrats believe in strengthening our military through investing in the best equipment and ensuring that military families receive the services they need while their family members are deployed."

The idea of the Democratic Party "strengthening" the U.S. military is laughable. Senate Democrats were suddenly posturing as the military's most ardent supporter solely for political purposes—namely, to regain control of Congress, and ultimately of the White House.

"Extraordinary Neglect"

Contrary to what Harry Reid's memo insisted, Democratic policies have repeatedly *weakened* the U.S. military. To understand how a future Democratic administration will handle the armed forces and U.S. national security, it's helpful to look at what the last Democratic administration did on these fronts.

From deep budget cuts during its eight years to the planned policy of allowing openly gay men and women to stay in the military, the Clinton administration's policies treated the military as a conservative institution to be gutted and replaced with feminist-oriented nonwarriors with a liberal political orientation.

The effects of those policies continue to be felt. One need only witness the likes of Admiral William J. Fallon, who in March 2008 quit as the commander of the U.S. Central Command, the leading combat command in Iraq and Afghanistan, at the height of the Iraq War over what he said were "perceived" differences over U.S. policy. Fallon cited a recently published magazine article that had portrayed his dovish views as conflicting with President Bush's policies. Despite being described as one of American's most important strategic thinkers by Defense Secretary Robert Gates, Fallon allowed himself to be used by the anti–Iraq War group Code Pink, which was noted for sending its members to disrupt congressional hearings and other public gatherings in order to spread its anti-American, antiwar message.

After Fallon resigned, the Pentagon announced that Fallon would not appear before the Senate the following month as part of the highly politicized debate on the Iraq War. To lobby for Fallon to testify, Code Pink stated in a section of its website headlined "Pressure Senate Foreign Relations Committee to Invite Admiral Fallon to Testify!" that "Fallon, who has graciously met with Codepink to discuss the Iraq War, was opposed to the surge in Iraq and urged President Bush to avoid war with Iran. He stated that he wouldn't let a war with Iran happen 'on his watch.'"

A Fallon spokesman said the admiral denied meeting with Code Pink but may have had a brief encounter with some of the antiwar activists after a public appearance. Sure enough, a photo showed the four-star admiral talking to some of the Code Pink members. Additionally, it seems the Central Command and Fallon made little or no effort to have the leftist group take the inaccurate claim off the website.

It wasn't just "Clinton generals" who caused serious harm to the U.S. military; during the Clinton years political appointees did as well. One of the key liberal Democrats responsible for the Clinton administration damage was Jamie Gorelick, who began the administration as a general counsel at the Pentagon and ended up at the Justice Department as deputy attorney general.

Gorelick, a likely attorney general candidate in the next Democrat administration, has become infamous for her tenure at Justice, where she put in place a number of anti-intelligence measures that contributed indirectly to the failures related to the September 11 attacks. Most notably, she was one of the key players in imposing the bureaucratic "wall" separating law-enforcement and intelligence agencies, ostensibly to protect prosecutions from taint, that prevented the detection of two of the 9/11 hijackers. The CIA had tracked the terrorists to the United States but then lost when the information was not handed off to the FBI. Gorelick then, astoundingly, was allowed to be part of the 9/11

Commission that examined the attacks and made sure the commission was never told about her conflict of interest, until it was raised by an outraged Attorney General John Ashcroft. The attorney general expressed disbelief that the commission had not been told about the restrictions put in place in adherence to a memorandum from Gorelick.

Gorelick's role in erecting this "wall of separation" has rightly drawn condemnation, but less noticed is the damage she did during her tenure at the Defense Department. From 1993 to 1994, Gorelick set up a special panel at the Pentagon to see how much defense money could legally be taken from the defense budget and turned over to spending on improving the environment. By the end of the administration, the Pentagon was diverting some $5 billion a year needed for weapons and training into what the Clintonistas euphemistically called "environmental security." Instead of focusing energy and money on preparing to fight and win any war the United States would be called to make, the Democrats ordered the military to ensure compliance with environmental laws and regulations on all military bases and "to reduce the use of hazardous materials, the generation or release of pollutants and the adverse affects on human health and the environment caused by DoD activities."

After the 1996 directive on "environmental security," it became Pentagon policy to adopt a management approach that "emphasizes pollution prevention," "incorporates pollution prevention at installations," and so on. The policy sought to turn the military into a conservation corps, further weakening the already stretched-thin armed forces, which were forced to make sharp cuts.

As one high-ranking conservative defense specialist put it, "We were wasting hundreds of millions of dollars to make the grass grow on military bases."

In a 2000 article in the journal *Foreign Affairs,* Condoleezza Rice, then a foreign policy adviser to Governor George W. Bush's presidential campaign, highlighted the Clinton administration's current neglect of the armed forces. These defense policies, she wrote, threatened the United States' "ability to maintain peace." Rice said the first Bush administration reduced defense spending somewhat after the Cold War in 1991. "But the Clinton administration witlessly accelerated and deepened these cuts. The results were devastating: military readiness declined, training suffered, military pay slipped 15 percent below civilian equivalents, morale plummeted, and the services cannibalized existing equipment to keep airplanes flying, ships afloat, and tanks moving."

And while the Clinton administration slashed defense spending (such spending reached its lowest point as a percentage of GDP since before the Pearl Harbor attacks), it "began deploying American forces abroad at a furious pace—an average of once every nine weeks," Rice pointed out. The administration deployed to some questionable places, such as Haiti, "but more than anything it was simply unwise to multiply missions in the face of a continuing budget reduction. Means and mission were not matched, and (predictably) the already thinly stretched armed forces came close to a breaking point."

The Clinton administration launched the military into a "death spiral"—what Rice described as "robbing procurement and research and development simply to operate the armed forces"—and did nothing to stop it. The Clinton Pentagon chose instead to "live off the fruits of Reagan's military buildup." This failure to act "constitutes an extraordinary neglect of the fiduciary responsibilities of the commander in chief," Rice said.

More of the Same

Of course, Rice herself would come under intense criticism after Bush was elected president and she became national security adviser and then secretary of state. The Bush administration, which had adopted as its mantra the new identifier "compassionate conservative," turned out to be neither. Its domestic, spending, and foreign policies mimicked and often exceeded those of the liberal Democrats. Its national security policies were based on the war against terrorism, which came to be dominated by Iraq.

The Iraq War would be the main item of criticism against Rice, and the Bush administration as a whole. Rice admitted in a March 2008 interview with the *Washington Times* that it was more difficult than expected. Asked about the 2003 invasion of Iraq and the subsequent insurgency, Rice said, "I thought it would be tough. I didn't think it would be this tough."

The war certainly proved to be more costly than expected. By 2008, the Pentagon was spending about $12 billion *a month* on funding the wars in Iraq and Afghanistan, costs that Democrats in Congress paid through annual and supplemental spending that severely taxed the U.S. treasury.

During the 2000 campaign, Rice and other supporters of candidate George W. Bush criticized the Clinton administration for its ill-fated attempts at "nation-building." By 2008, the United States under Bush and Rice was leading the way with building nations in both Iraq and Afghanistan, and Rice defended the shift. "Look," she said, "I think we always knew nation-building was important, but I think my view coming in was, look, this isn't something the 82nd Airborne should be doing." Rice suggested that the difference was that "we now know the real cost of failed states.

"We know the cost of Afghanistan as a failed state that became, then, a breeding ground for terrorism [and] became terrorism central," she said. "I don't think anybody wants to let that happen again. And we know the cost of Somalia as a failed state. But the question is who's going to . . . assist the people of those countries in building their own nation? I think if we say it's our responsibility to do nation-building, I would flip it and say it's our responsibility to help develop well-governed states. Because well-governed states can secure their borders, well-governed states can provide for their people, well-governed states can have intelligence and police and law enforcement that can deal with—whether it's terrorism or drug-running or trafficking in persons."

The Bush administration also continued on a course the Clinton administration had set with Communist China—that is, it took a soft line despite the growing dangers posed by Beijing. In early March 2008, the Chinese military conducted a massive crackdown on unarmed Tibetan Buddhist monks seeking religious freedom and independence from China. The military's brutal show of force triggered rioting and looting of Han Chinese businesses in the Tibetan capital of Lhasa and eventually other cities in Tibet. Secretary of State Rice told the *Washington Times* in the interview that she opposed a boycott of the 2008 Summer Olympics, hosted by Beijing, because she wanted to allow U.S. athletes to compete. The president agreed not to boycott the Beijing Olympics—which critics had dubbed the "bloody Olympics"—and he even refused to cancel his planned trip to attend the games. The strongest response the administration offered to the Chinese repression was to call for "restraint."

While Rice said she didn't want to punish American athletes, political considerations might have driven the decision not to boycott the Olympics. Bush's father, former president George H. W. Bush, had been named honorary president of the American delegation to the Olympic Games. It was a move no doubt calculated by pro-China U.S. officials to prevent any disruption in Beijing's Olympics.

An Obama Future

As this book documents, at almost every turn the Bush administration's strong conservative policies were undermined and even defeated entirely. But the Democratic contenders for the presidency in 2008 clearly would weaken national security even more, in no small part because as president they would further empower the liberal bureaucrats and politicians who control the Failure Factory.

All the candidates used carefully scripted language that was tailored to avoid being pinned down on national security issues—except for the Iraq War, which the Democrats wanted ended.

Barack Hussein Obama presented his "Plan for America," and one of its few clear statements of policy involved his call for ending the war in Iraq. Of course, his plan for ending the war considers it irrelevant that terrorists or Iranian Islamists will almost certainly take over Iraq and turn it into a new haven for spreading hatred against the West. It made clear that he had long advocated the cut-and-run strategy: "In 2006, he called for a timetable to remove our troops, a political solution within Iraq, and aggressive diplomacy with all of Iraq's neighbors."

"Obama will immediately begin to remove our troops from Iraq," the plan stated. "He will remove one to two combat brigades each month, and have all of our combat brigades out of Iraq within 16 months. Obama will make it clear that we will not build any permanent bases in Iraq. He will keep some troops in Iraq to protect our embassy and diplomats; if al Qaeda attempts to build a base within Iraq, he will keep troops in Iraq or elsewhere in the region to carry out targeted strikes on al Qaeda." Obama's announced solution was a prescription for disaster, built on appeasement and surrender. Then again, Obama later equivocated on his plan for an "immediate" withdrawal, saying in early July that he would "refine" his timeline to ensure the security of the troops. But then he switched back to his sixteen-month timeline, perhaps because he drew fierce criticism for what seemed like a political gambit to attract centrist, pro-military voters.

Obama's regional diplomacy plan involves what he calls "the most aggressive diplomatic effort in recent American history to reach a new compact on the stability of Iraq and the Middle East," as if negotiation will resolve the problems of the war-torn ethnic and tribally unstable region that provides more than half of all the world's oil.

For Iran, Obama "believes we have not exhausted our non-military options in confronting this threat; in many ways, we have yet to try them." The Obama approach of "non-military options" will center on the rigid adherence to failed arms-control agreements and feckless diplomacy—precisely the approach favored by the liberal career bureaucrats who dominate the government. As we will see, this sort of approach has been a root cause of the security problems facing the United States today.

Obama's solution to all the world's ills is diplomacy. Yet it is the liberal bureaucrats in the diplomatic corps who have led us to the current situation. The diplomacy-at-all-costs approach has made the world more dangerous and will never resolve the problems of the Middle East, which respects no diplomacy and knows only the tenets of raw geopolitical power.

Obama also wants to engage Iran in diplomacy, even though this radical clerical regime has never explained its act of war in seizing American hostages in 1979 and has only become more dangerous as various diplomatic stratagems have failed to mollify the threatening revolutionary Shiite Islam of the country. But Obama wants to "offer the Iranian regime a choice," according to his plan. "If Iran abandons its nuclear program and support for terrorism, we will offer incentives like membership in the World Trade Organization, economic investments, and a move toward normal diplomatic relations."

The Islamist mullahs in Iran have made clear that their nuclear program, carried out in violation of Iran's agreement with the International Atomic Energy Agency that it would use imported nuclear technology and equipment only for peaceful purposes, is nonnegotiable. Yet Obama thinks somehow the bureaucrats in government who have failed and made the Iranian nuclear threat worse will be able to resolve the problem of the terrorist-backed regime in Tehran.

On Asia, Obama has no initiatives to deal with the growing power of an increasingly hostile Communist China. His plan called for a vague search for "new partnerships" and said he would "work to ensure that China plays by international rules." A key adviser to Obama is former Clinton administration national security adviser Anthony Lake. In 1997, Lake was nominated to be CIA director but withdrew after Senate critics challenged his handling of the National Security Council, which included the appointment of questionable political cronies to an intelligence review board, personal financial questions, and allegations that he ignored serious FBI reports that China's government was covertly seeking to influence the presidential reelection campaign in 1996.

The failed Clinton administration has provided other Obama advisers as well: State Department bureaucrat Susan Rice was a key player in the disastrous 1994 Agreed Framework with North Korea. Then there is State Department Policy Planning official Gregory Craig, whose outlook on foreign policy can be seen in the fact that in 2000, he represented the Cuban father of Elián González, the Cuban immigrant boy who floated to freedom in Florida and whose mother died on the way, only to be forcibly returned back to Communist Cuba by the Clinton administration, in one of the administration's most immoral foreign policy acts.

Indeed, most of Obama's key strategists are Clintonistas, who once in power will be easy prey for the likes of Osama bin Laden and Kim Jong-il. One prominent Clinton adviser who joined Obama's national security team is former secretary of state Madeleine Albright. Albright will be famously remembered for being the first secretary of state to lend prestige and credibility to one of the worst dictators of the modern era, Kim Jong-il. Albright, following the credo of Diplomacy Over All, allowed herself to be used in numerous propaganda appearances by a dictator who is responsible for the deaths of millions of North Koreans through famine and political repression.

Other Obama advisers include longtime liberal Democrat Daniel Shapiro, a former aide to liberal House Foreign Relations Committee chairman Lee Hamilton, and Dennis McDonough, a liberal policy adviser to Tom Daschle, who was Senate majority leader in the early 2000s.

A key Obama defense adviser is retired Air Force major general Jonathan Scott Gration, who signed on early to the campaign and would be a senior official in his administration if elected. Gration was a combat pilot who fought in the 1991 Persian Gulf War whose career path gives no clue as to why he chose to sign on with the liberal Obama. He was raised in Africa and once served as a White House fellow during the administration of President Ronald Reagan. Gration worked as a deputy to Air Force chief of staff General Merrill McPeak in the early 1990s. McPeak would become a key supporter of Obama and was disliked by many Air Force airmen because of his redesign of the U.S. Air Force uniform, turning a distinguished traditional uniform into what many called an "airline pilots" uniform. It was McPeak who made the astounding claim that President George W. Bush had turned Iran into an enemy.

This kind of muddleheaded thinking by liberal military officers who failed to see the reality of the threats facing the country and were blinded by their disdain for George Bush has left the country deeply divided. They would be certain to follow misguided policies under a President Obama.

Obama's outlook for nuclear weapons is alarming. The Illinois senator, who has no foreign policy or defense experience, stated that his plan as president would be "to set a goal of a world without nuclear weapons, and pursue it." While recognizing that nuclear weapons are needed as a "strong deterrent" as long as nuclear weapons exist, he advocates abandoning the Bush administration's plan for a Reliable Replacement Warhead, an important program that would modernize and actually shrink the U.S. nuclear arsenal by making weapons more efficient and safer. Instead Obama plans to "stop the development of new nuclear weapons." He also would seek "dramatic reductions in U.S. and Russian stockpiles of nuclear weapons and material," ignoring the fact that China's nuclear arsenal is being built up in utmost secrecy and without any good intelligence as to the scope and nature of it.

Obama also promises to give troops new equipment, armor, and training, and claims that he will "make the investments" needed to allow the U.S. military to meet twenty-first-century threats. But given that the track record of many of his key advisers—Clinton veterans who badly damaged U.S. military capabilities—the focus will likely be on humanitarian work and nonmilitary functions for the U.S. military around the world, as was done during the Clinton administration.

On intelligence, Obama vows to take politics out of the process by giving the director of national intelligence a fixed term. His plan also calls for creating a National Declassification Center to make the release of secrets "secure but routine." During the Clinton administration, rampant declassification led to the inadvertent release of nuclear weapons secrets, requiring the unprecedented "reclassification" of defense nuclear data.

Perhaps no other Obama adviser has better signaled the direction of the Illinois senator's national security policies than John Holum, the former director of the U.S. Arms Control and Disarmament Agency and later undersecretary of state for arms control. Holum is a liberal arms-control advocate who worked in the disastrous administration of President Jimmy Carter and served as an aide to liberal senator George McGovern before moving on to the senior arms-control posts under President Bill Clinton. His arms-control policies are at the far left of the political spectrum and have in the past bolstered the weapons programs of China and Iran.

In 1998, I exposed Holum's classified proposal for a space cooperation agreement with China. The proposal was to be signed in the summer of 1998 by NASA officials and representatives of the State Science and Technology Commission of China (SSTCC), a key developer of weapons-related technology that in 1990 had concluded a ten-year agreement with Iran to share military technology. "Under this agreement, American space technology would pass automatically to the Iranian missile program," a Republican Senate aide said at the time. But for Holum, the loss of missile technology did not seem to matter. Fortunately, the deal was never signed. It was scuttled because of opposition from members of Congress and also because of federal investigation into two U.S. high-technology companies, Hughes Electronics Corp. and Loral Space & Communications Ltd., which improperly shared with China missile data that significantly boosted Chinese strategic missiles.

Holum also stated in a classified memorandum to the Pentagon in late 1994 that testing plans for the Theater High-Altitude Area Defense (THAAD) should be limited to avoid upsetting contentious talks with Moscow on regional defenses against short-range missiles. "The key near-term objectives, in my view, are achieving a needed negotiating breakthrough on Anti-Ballistic Missile/Theater Missile Defense demarcation and protecting effective TMD program development," Holum stated in the memo (marked "Secret") to Deputy Secretary of Defense John Deutch. The memo—and the entire arms-control negotiation with Russia—represented yet another example of the liberal arms controllers' reverence for the 1972 Anti-Ballistic Missile Treaty. Holum and other liberals regarded it as the centerpiece of U.S.-Russian strategic relations, and therefore limited missile defenses against short-range missiles such as the Iraqi Scud, which had caused the single largest number of casualties during the Persian Gulf War.

When, years later, President George W. Bush finally withdrew from the ABM Treaty, liberals like Holum protested that the decision would trigger a war. In reality, it is the defeatists like Holum who are leading the country to war by promoting national security policies that weaken the United States and strengthen America's enemies.

And such defeatists have rallied to Barack Obama's cause. Indeed, Holum told a meeting of the Arms Control Association in June 2008 that Obama's promise to unconditionally talk to world dictators in North Korea, Iran, and Cuba "cemented" his commitment to the Democratic candidate.

Holum stated that Obama will revert to the arms-control-agreement approach of the past. Obama, he said, believes that "the strong global regimes we need to fight proliferation depend upon progress in arms control." He dismissed the conservative approach to arms control as a "fringe philosophy."

Holum also defended Obama's opposition to modernizing the

U.S. nuclear weapons arsenal, even though this opposition would mean the United States would not develop lower-yield tactical weapons and the much-needed earth-penetrating bomb that can get at deeply hardened underground nuclear facilities known to exist in both Iran and North Korea. "To Senator Obama," Holum said, "a nuclear-weapon-free world is not merely a dream on a far horizon, but an objective we should be working hard through tangible steps to achieve." Of course, the reality of the world today is that such ideas would leave the United States defenseless against the rapidly increasing Chinese nuclear forces, Russia's nuclear weapons modernization, and North Korea's nuclear arsenal.

Holum even said Obama's ruling out using nuclear weapons to go after Osama bin Laden if he was found in Afghanistan or Pakistan was a sign that Obama was willing to "challenge conventional wisdom and to depart from time-worn talking points." In other words, Obama is more committed to liberal policies that deny the use of military force in almost all circumstances in favor of the failed diplomatic and arms-control approach favored by Holum.

Beyond his formal advisers, Obama's links to other individuals raise serious concerns as well. Obama was, of course, widely criticized for his association with his pastor, the radical Reverend Jeremiah Wright, whose sermons attacked America as the source of the world's evils. The Democrat at first said he would not disavow the minister, but eventually did. Less attention was paid to Obama's relationship with radical Bill Ayers, a professor of education at the University of Illinois at Chicago who, during the 1960s, helped found the violent radical leftist group the Weathermen, also known as the Weather Underground, which was responsible for several bombings. The Weathermen claimed credit for multiple bombings in the United States, but Ayers told the *Chicago Tribune* that "we weren't terrorists. . . . The reason we weren't terrorists is because we did not commit random acts of terror against people. Terrorism was what was being practiced in the countryside of Vietnam by the United States." In fact, on the morning of September 11, 2001, the *New York Times* ran a profile of the unrepentant Ayers with the headline NO REGRETS FOR A LOVE OF EXPLOSIVES, which quoted him as saying, "I don't regret setting bombs. I feel we didn't do enough."

Obama dismissed criticism of his friendship with Ayers by stating that Ayers had engaged in "detestable acts" when Obama was eight years old. But as conservative commentator Cliff Kincaid pointed out, that statement does not deflect the whole problem for Obama. "The real issue," Kincaid wrote, "is whether Obama shares Ayers' communist views. Obama admitted to exchanging ideas with Ayers on an irregular basis but did not say what those ideas were. But we know that Ayers, rather than just being a 1960s 'radical,' was a member of a Marxist-Leninist communist group."

This is not a matter to be taken lightly. The views of Obama, an inexperienced one-term senator, have not been fully explored by anyone in the press or revealed by the candidate himself. And Ayers, whose defenders—including the Obama campaign—often dismiss his terrorist past by saying he has become a "respected" member of the political "mainstream," has as recently as November 2007 called America a place of "great stress and oppression and authoritarianism" and denounced "a kind of rising incipient American form of fascism."

Apparently these are the sorts of views that pass as "mainstream" in today's Democratic Party.

The Burglar

Barack Obama's plan for less secrecy and more declassification in intelligence would likely be welcome news to one of Hillary Clinton's unofficial presidential campaign advisers: the former national security adviser in her husband's administration, Samuel R. "Sandy"

Berger, whose story typifies the scandal-plagued administration of her husband. It's a remarkable statement about the state of the Democratic Party that Berger could be counted as a trusted (if unofficial) aide to a top presidential candidate—one who, had Hillary won the presidency, could well have been appointed to a high-level national security position.

At about six P.M. on October 2, 2003, an event took place that was unique in the annals of American politics. Berger, the most senior White House national security official in the Clinton administration, walked out of the majestic white marble building of the National Archives in Washington, D.C., carrying stolen highly classified documents. He walked up the street to a construction site. After looking both ways, he carefully removed several pages of notes from his pocket, shaped them into a V, and then placed a small stack of the stolen records inside them and underneath a trailer at the construction site on the 900 block of Pennsylvania Avenue.

Berger had been designated by former president Clinton to research documents and provide testimony to the 9/11 Commission, which was looking into the failures related to the attacks on the World Trade Center and the Pentagon. He left the classified documents at the construction site overnight and then recovered them later, or so he stated.

Archives officials had noticed Berger acting suspiciously during three earlier visits to view classified documents and e-mails in a secure office. They suspected Berger was stealing secret documents and placing the documents in his socks, pants, and coat. Among the documents were reports classified at the "Top Secret codeword" level and included one that outlined the Clinton administration's response to a 2000 terrorist plan. It was titled the Millennium Alert After Action Review and had been written by liberal NSC aide Richard Clarke.

One Archives inspector general investigator described one of the document thefts this way: "Mr. Berger took the first opportunity when [Senior Official 1] was out of her office to remove the document. He most likely put it in his jacket pocket, after folding it." A second official stated in an e-mail about Berger's stealing documents, "Okay, I know this is odd. He walked out the door in front of me and into the hallway. The door closes. Shortly after it closed, I proceeded to go get him a Diet Coke. When I opened the door and started down the hall, he was stooped over right outside the doorway. He was fiddling with something white which looked to be a piece of paper or multiple pieces of paper. It appeared to be rolled around his ankle and underneath his pant leg, with a portion of the paper sticking out underneath."

After enough suspicions were raised, the Archives inspector general was called in; after an unexplained delay, the Justice Department was alerted; and after further delay, an investigation was launched.

What made the event extraordinary was that the Justice Department never informed the 9/11 Commission about their investigation into Berger's theft of classified documents. On March 22, 2004, months after the theft occurred, the two lead Justice investigators— John Dion, chief of the espionage section, and Bruce Swartz, deputy assistant attorney general for the criminal division—told Archives inspector general Paul Brachfeld that the Justice Department did not plan to alert the 9/11 Commission about their Berger investigation. It was an astounding revelation: Berger had deliberately interfered with the most important U.S. government investigation since the investigation into the assassination of President John F. Kennedy. The commission was going to hear testimony from him without knowing that he had stolen documents—including, probably, materials that were germane to the commission's inquiry, and that the commission therefore would not have seen.

But we will never know for sure about all the documents Berger took, because, amazingly, the Justice Department and FBI never investigated two of Berger's four visits to the Archives.

Just as amazingly, even after the 9/11 commissioners were finally informed about Berger's theft of classified documents around the time of his testimony, they still were not told that during those visits Berger viewed original National Security Council documents and could have removed them, for whatever reason.

Ultimately, on April 1, 2005, Berger pleaded guilty to one misdemeanor count of unauthorized removal and retention of classified documents as part of a plea agreement. On September 8, 2005, Berger was sentenced to two years' probation, 100 hours of community service, and a $50,000 fine. But most significant, his security clearance was revoked for just three years. After that time, the former national security adviser would be again given access to classified information. The Justice Department bureaucrats had done their best to protect a liberal Democrat, one of their own. In fact, Justice had not recommended even that high a fine; Magistrate Judge Deborah A. Robinson took it upon herself to impose a stiffer fine, stating that "the court finds the fine [recommended by Justice] is inadequate because it doesn't reflect the seriousness of the offense."

Compare Berger's treatment to that of I. Lewis "Scooter" Libby, the conservative aide to Vice President Dick Cheney who was accused and convicted of perjury and obstruction of justice. Libby was sentenced to thirty months in prison and a $250,000 fine, although his jail time was commuted by President George W. Bush. He had claimed he didn't remember conversations with reporters about the case of the unauthorized disclosure of Valerie Plame's identity as a CIA officer—even though prosecutors at the very earliest stages of their investigation knew that the source of the leak to newspaper columnist Robert Novak had been liberal Republican Richard Armitage, the deputy secretary of state.

It was a classic case of liberal government bureaucrats siding with liberal Democrats.

The reason Berger's clearance was only revoked for three years became clear in October 2007, when word got out that Hillary Clinton's presidential campaign had retained the convicted classified-document thief Berger as an adviser. By then, Berger had become known in Washington political circles as "Sandy Burglar." He had also been an adviser to Democratic presidential candidate John Kerry in 2004 but had been forced to quit after the Archives scandal broke. Because of the controversy over the theft, Senator Clinton publicly distanced herself from the discredited former national security adviser by insisting that he was an "unofficial" adviser, with no formal role in the campaign.

Aside from the theft controversy, Berger was closely linked to the Clinton administration's 1996 Chinese fundraising scandal, in which Chinese individuals linked to the Beijing government funneled money into Bill Clinton's reelection coffers. Other notables linked to the Chinese influence-buying operation also came back to Hillary Clinton's campaign, and another notorious official was brought in: Maggie Williams.

Williams was a longtime aide to Mrs. Clinton in the White House and was hired for the campaign after Hillary was accused of racial insensitivity; in February 2008, she became Clinton's campaign manager. Williams, who is black, was never prosecuted on federal charges related to the 1996 Justice Department investigation into illegal campaign contributions from China, even though she accepted a $50,000 check made out to the Democratic National Committee from Chinese agent Johnny Chung in 1995. Chung told Justice investigators that he was the main conduit to the 1996 Bill Clinton reelection campaign for money supplied by the Chinese government through Lieutenant Colonel Liu Chaoying. He also told investigators that he took his direction from a Chinese general in charge of running Beijing's spies. Williams would later become campaign manager for Clinton and appeared to be part of the campaign's reassembly of the scandal-plagued Clinton administration, something that fueled Republican critics.

The outrage of Hillary Clinton's campaign was that she actually sought to run on the record of her husband, whose national security scandals far overshadowed his personal peccadilloes.

The Clinton record need not be repeated. It is a record of disaster for U.S. national security and includes the Clinton administration's siding with government bureaucrats in refusing to prevent the spread of dangerous nuclear, chemical, and biological weapons to rogue states like Pakistan and North Korea. There also was the failure to take action against Osama bin Laden and al Qaeda until it was too late, and the refusal numerous times to take military or intelligence action against bin Laden. In addition, the administration emboldened terrorists by not taking action against them despite their attacks on embassies and military facilities and warships. The Clinton administration also concluded a fraudulent agreement with North Korea that made the danger worse for the Bush administration, which has not been able to resolve the problem despite years of feckless diplomacy. Moreover, Bill Clinton helped create the growing threat from China, a threat that has become worse in the intervening years. And the list goes on.

The Republican Side

It is not only the Democrats who have been supported by the liberal government bureaucracy. The Republican presidential hopeful too is expected to rally the liberal bureaucrats to his side with his "maverick" Republican policies, which will further erode national security. John McCain, the Republican nominee in 2008, ran in the primaries on a record that appeared to many conservatives to make him more attuned to Democrats and liberal Republicans than to conservatives.

In particular, he drew the ire of radio talk-show maestro Rush Limbaugh, who led the conservative political charge against McCain. Limbaugh acknowledged that McCain was a hero who had survived years as a prisoner of war in Vietnam, and that the Arizona senator had supported the troop surge that turned the tide in Iraq and neutralized a lot of Democratic opposition to the war. But the talk radio host demanded that McCain tell voters his true views on a variety of other issues where he had seemed to side with liberals.

Limbaugh focused mainly on domestic issues, but even on foreign policy McCain raised concerns for conservatives. In March 2008, the Arizona Republican gave a major foreign policy speech in which he declared himself to be a "realistic idealist," which had echoes of George W. Bush's 2000 campaign device "compassionate conservatism." McCain was combining the concept of foreign policy "realism," the school of foreign policy identified with the likes of Henry Kissinger that takes few moral stands with the liberal notion of idealism in world affairs.

McCain began his speech by stating that he detested war, calling it the worst thing to befall human beings. He was speaking as a Vietnam War veteran who had lost friends in combat. He lamented the "million tragedies" that ensue when nations seek to resolve differences by force of arms. "Not the valor with which it is fought nor the nobility of the cause it serves can glorify war," he said.

True, war is a horror of civilization, but sometimes war is necessary and sometimes it has to be fought despite the great sacrifice in blood and treasure it requires. To denounce war and hate it is to fail to understand the existential threats to the United States, which can't be wished away.

McCain called for continuing American leadership but also for strengthening global alliances and creating a "league of democracies" that together will advance shared values and interests.

But McCain said that terrorists captured in the current war must not be treated inhumanely, and he called for closing down the terrorist prison at Guantánamo Bay, Cuba. The position showed that McCain has bought into the liberal argument that terrorists should not be interrogated harshly and that when they are, American values are undermined. The protect-the-terrorists'-rights movement is one of the most nefarious of the liberal government bureaucrats' claims; sadly, it has been adopted by some of the most senior military and intelligence leaders.

McCain showed by his design to close Guantánamo that he does not understand the nature of the enemy and the need to use extraordinary measures to prevent the terrorists from carrying out even more deadly attacks than those of September 11.

Crossroads

The presidential election of 2008 will be remembered as a crossroads in American history. The simple reason is that both candidates for president have shown through their speeches and campaigns that they do not fully understand the dangers facing the country.

America's political leadership is divided, projecting a strategic posture to the world of weakness and vacillation at a time when it is facing new mortal dangers. There is open aggression by terrorists who have vowed to acquire and use nuclear, chemical, biological, or other weapons in even greater mass-casualty attacks than those of 2001. Russia is moving toward greater authoritarianism and adopting threatening and anti-democratic policies, while building up its nuclear forces and aligning itself with another dangerous force: a Communist China that is intent on increasing its national power while covertly seeking to weaken that of the United States.

Weakness and vacillation by the United States are compounded by a government system of bureaucracy that has been hijacked by liberal bureaucrats and is effectively operating outside of effective political control. Important political policies and programs that are the bedrock of the current system of U.S. democracy and liberty are under assault. Never before in history has the need for leadership, true American-centered leadership, been more urgently needed.

With the United States divided and threats growing, the danger that the United States will be embroiled in a major conflict is real and growing. As one high-ranking former White House national security official put it, "America appears to be in a kind of time-out period for its leadership because the important issues of war and peace are not being properly addressed." John McCain has focused on the threat of terrorism and has offered some practical solutions for Iraq but has not outlined a strategic vision to produce a more stable and peaceful world the way Ronald Reagan did when he stressed that to preserve peace, we must prepare for war. Obama, by contrast, has said he will revert to the failed national security policies of past Democratic administrations that gave us American hostages, and terrorist attacks against Americans and allies abroad as well as at home.

As states such as China, Russia, and Iran watch the United States sink into an energy crisis with soaring gas prices, those seeking America's destruction are studying carefully. It is in such an environment that a major war could begin through an adversary miscalculating that the United States could be knocked out with a strategic attack. If that were to happen, the question is, Will the political candidates now running for commander in chief be capable of rallying the country and responding to such a life-and-death scenario?

And because of sharp cutbacks in military spending on the necessary weapons systems and forces needed to address those dangers—cuts that have largely escaped the public's attention—the reality is that when the next president needs to pull the lever in a major war, there may not be enough power for the country's forces to prevail.

The current phase of world history is analogous to the 1930s, when world leaders had no idea that a great and devastating world war was only years away.

The next president must prepare for a coming conflict, which most likely could start with a miscalculation by a nation such as China that resents the United States. Beijing's leaders believe the United States has deliberately kept the world's most populous state weak and underdeveloped. China's Communist Party–ruled military leaders also have demonstrated in recent history that their concept of deterrence includes sudden, unannounced military attacks, such as those in Korea, India, Vietnam, and along the border with the former Soviet Union. With a new xenophobic nationalism on the rise in China, with anti-Americanism as one of its most important features, a war with China cannot be ruled out in the next ten to fifteen years.

John Bolton, the staunch conservative former United Nations ambassador and senior State Department official who knows better than most how vicious and petty the liberal bureaucracy is, would throw his support behind McCain. "McCain's long involvement in national security issues means he has a firm grasp of what the big-picture issues are, and how he feels about some of the specific issues," Bolton told me. "He has been consistently for a victory over terrorism in the wake of Saddam Hussein's fall in Iraq, for a strong line against the Iranian nuclear weapons program, and far more skeptical of North Korean commitments to end its nuclear program than the Bush administration. In addition, McCain knows the national security bureaucracy. He knows where the bodies are buried, what skeletons are in what closets, and where the worst bureaucratic obstacles are."

Bolton warned that Obama's inexperience is troubling. "By contrast, at best Obama is a tabula rasa on foreign policy," he said. "More likely, unfortunately, is that his foreign agenda will mirror the limousine liberal domestic agenda he has pursued, more like a European social democratic salon dweller than a U.S. Scoop Jackson Democrat. No wonder polls show him the winner over McCain in many European countries."

The candidates for president must address the serious problems exposed in this book—an intelligence community politicized to influence policymakers against using force, and a State Department intent on controlling policies that more often hurt rather than help American security, such as the appeasement of Iran over its illegal nuclear program. The other national security bureaucracies also are saddled with weak leadership that does not fully understand America's global responsibility as the last best hope for mankind and instead adheres to false notions that history has ended and thus responsibilities can be forgotten.

Whether the next president is Barack Obama or John McCain, there remains the desperate need to address the problems outlined in this book and reform the Failure Factory into a government that works.

CONCLUSION

ENDING THE FAILURES

Reforming the federal government bureaucracy must be the highest priority of the president of the United States. Unless the out-of-control system of bureaucrats and their liberal supporters is changed, the country will remain ill-equipped to confront dangers. Whether the challenge is waging war against Islamist extremism in Iraq, Afghanistan, and elsewhere, or the growing threat from Communist China, America's government needs to function effectively and without the anti-Americanism of the liberal policymakers, intelligence officials, and other government bureaucrats throughout the White House, State Department, Pentagon, Department of Homeland Security, Justice Department, and elsewhere. Taking on entrenched bureaucrats and their liberal supporters will not be easy. But the challenge must be addressed if the nation is to survive and the well-being of our younger generation is to be assured.

The following recommendations are a guide for future leaders to use in reshaping the government national security bureaucracy:

Create a National Net Assessment Council. The first and most important step is for the president to create this special group to counteract the widespread undermining of U.S. policy and politicization of intelligence, as seen in efforts like the December 2007 National Intelligence

Estimate (NIE). Congress should mandate in law—by amending the 1947 National Security Act—that the executive branch produce annual Net Assessments, which would in essence be the policy equivalents of NIEs. They would integrate all foreign affairs and national security issues into a single document that would be used to assist the president and his top advisers in policy formulation. The document would assess the challenges posed by foreign states such as China, Russia, North Korea, and Iran and issues such as arms proliferation and foreign spying. Net Assessments would require input from defense, military, national security, foreign policy, economic, diplomatic, and intelligence officials to help identify and define critical national security needs and interests.

In addition to clearly defining enemies and potential adversaries, the Net Assessment Council, chosen by the president and his closest advisers, would gauge foreign nations' level of support or opposition to U.S. interests. Nations that are working against American security interests should not be treated in the same category as those that support the fundamental values of liberty and democratic rule. Proposed diplomatic, economic, intelligence, and military options should be included in Net Assessments to support a national strategy of promoting the spread of democratic forms of government, including basic freedoms and liberties, as well as other U.S. objectives.

The Net Assessments would help solve the current problem of divergent U.S. government policies toward nations like Saudi Arabia, a strategic energy source but also a covert supporter of Islamist extremism, and China, where U.S. business interests have produced one national policy and national security worries have produced a second.

A model for the national Net Assessment Council would be the Pentagon's current Office of Net Assessment.

Require Senate confirmation of National Intelligence officers. To reduce the problem of politicized National Intelligence Estimates, all National Intelligence officers should be nominated by the president and confirmed by a majority of the Senate. This reform will prevent intelligence bureaucrats from using these flagship products of the National Intelligence Council, the analysis arm of the Director of National Intelligence, to improperly force policymakers to adopt policies that conform to their often skewed intelligence analyses. Additionally, the president should require that all presidential appointee positions within the CIA and other intelligence agencies be filled with noncareer intelligence personnel. Those with intelligence experience, of course, should not be blocked from these appointee positions, but those appointed to the posts should not come from within the bureaucracy.

Remove all intelligence agencies from the career Civil Service system. To ease the hiring of experienced, mid-career specialists, all intelligence agencies should be removed from the current requirement that all employees be part of the Civil Service. This reform would make it easier for intelligence leaders to hire and promote people with specialized skills and would produce a more robust intelligence workforce. Currently, hiring non–civil service employees requires a waiver from agency directors. This reform would help create the much desired "outside-the-box" thinking and action within intelligence agencies. The "box" currently constraining intelligence agencies is mainly due to the limitations on the people who are hired and promoted under the Civil Service system. The result is that younger, inexperienced bureaucrats get favored treatment over mid-career hires.

Limit the use of executive branch officials as congressional staff. Except in extraordinary and rare circumstances, no executive branch employees should be detailed to the House of Representatives or the Senate as support staff. The use of such detailees has expanded rapidly to the point that hundreds of executive branch officials now work in the legislative branch of government.

This practice raises serious constitutional questions about whether the use of such detailees by Congress violates the separation of powers.

The system has also created conflicts of interest. For example, many staffers of the current House and Senate intelligence oversight committee are detailed officials from within the intelligence agencies. As a result, these staffers are often used by intelligence agencies to block aggressive oversight efforts and have severely limited the effectiveness of the oversight panels. Additionally, the use of executive branch detailees has led Congress to cut back on hiring and training its own qualified congressional staff. Congressional staff must remain separate from the executive branch in order for the effective functioning of checks and balances in government.

Reform the mission of the State Department. Currently, the culture and mission of the State Department is directed at a main overriding goal: diplomacy. As preparations for the war in Iraq revealed, the U.S. government has no institution that can take charge of restructuring nations—a growing fact of life for the government in the current global environment. If the U.S. government is going to be called on to help reshape the world toward American-inspired principles of liberty and democracy in Asia, Africa, Latin America, the Middle East, and elsewhere, it will need a better system. The Pentagon and the military are not well suited for such tasks, since their mission is essentially to fight and win wars, or as military warriors like to say, "to break things and kill people." The State Department has been given the mission by default but is not equipped to rebuild nations. Its main activity, in simplified terms, is to accommodate and negotiate with foreign nations; these are useful functions but they are severely limited, covering only a fraction of the needs of the United States, which has global interests to protect. The State Department and the Foreign Service should be reformed and restructured to meet the challenges and missions we face in the twenty-first century. The president should appoint a blue-ribbon panel of experts to study and recommend such reforms.

Additionally, greater presidential control needs to be asserted. The president should require all offices and bureaus in the State Department, as well as in other national security and foreign affairs agencies, to be headed by appointees selected by the president and confirmed by the Senate. Career officials should not be permitted to hold positions as secretaries, deputy secretaries, undersecretaries, and assistant secretaries, except in the rarest and most extraordinary circumstances. This reform would help place clear lines between those ultimately in charge of making policy—representatives of elected officials—and those with a supporting role.

Create a Presidential Appointee Training Center. One of the most serious problems facing all incoming presidents is a lack of qualified and trained people who are prepared and can quickly move into presidential appointee positions. This is a particular problem because presidential candidates so often win the Oval Office by cultivating an image as "outsiders," disdainful of the normal ways of Washington. But presidents' failure to appreciate the fundamental need to appoint people who understand how to execute their policies has led to disaster. The country needs a central institution that can provide training for presidential appointees who could be called to government service— or perhaps two institutions, with one run by each political party. The training center (or centers) would be a vitally needed reform that would vastly improve the functioning of government and reduce the problems encountered during transitions between presidential administrations. The center would provide both management and policy training for future political appointees, what in baseball terms would be called a farm team for presidential administrations. Presidents would not be mandated to fill slots exclusively from these resources, but having a "bench" would greatly enhance a president's ability to swiftly and efficiently begin governing.

Restructure U.S. intelligence agencies. Post-9/11 intelligence reforms have failed to make urgently needed fixes to intelligence collection, analysis, covert action, and other intelligence functions. The creation of an intelligence czar, the director of National Intelligence, has resulted in more—not less—stifling bureaucracy within a system that was already overly bureaucratic. The president and Congress must work together and start over, if need be, to reshape intelligence for the twenty-first century that is free from the bureaucratic constraints and biases of the past several decades.

One of the fundamental biases within the current intelligence system is resistance to any function or activity that is labor-intensive, in fitting with the overall government culture that labor should be reduced or replaced by machines and technology. However, the craft of spying is labor-intensive, and at its core is a one-on-one function; to steal secrets requires recruiting people, and that must be done by other people. There is no technology solution to such human spying. The CIA and other intelligence agencies, despite hiring thousands more people, have not recovered from the devastating loss of human intelligence-gathering specialists during the 1960s and 1970s, when human intelligence-gathering forces were five times larger than they are today. A policy decision was made then to shift away from always difficult human spying to technical spying, with disastrous results. Additionally, the current workforce of recruits is dominated by inexperienced younger people who are eager and committed but who lack international experience.

As part of needed analytical reform, Congress should take action to require more and better competitive intelligence analysis to counteract widespread "groupthink" that remains a problem today. Congress also must pass laws that will end the U.S. intelligence agencies' funding and otherwise supporting large numbers of left-liberal academics by calling on them for intelligence analysis, and their refusal to provide political diversity and conservative specialists in their analysis support activities.

Reform the White House personnel system. Some of the most significant failures of the past two presidential administrations can be traced to a

White House system that is broken. To fix the problem, the first step in reform must be to require all White House and National Security Council staff to be appointed by the president after his election. More important, all staff held over from earlier administrations, whether of the same party or not, must leave office. This reform will prevent opposition political staff from subverting an elected president's policies, as occurred with National Security Council aide Richard Clarke, and will help ensure that presidential policy is carried out by those who were selected by the president.

Place Defense Department policy representatives with U.S. combatant commands. Currently, the U.S. combatant commands, those charged with waging war, have at least one State Department and one CIA adviser posted permanently to the command headquarters, but no representative from the Office of the Secretary of Defense or another Department of Defense policymaking office. CIA and State agencies often use their representatives to subvert Defense Department policies. To counteract this negative influence, the president should require that at least one representative from the Office of the Undersecretary of Defense for Policy be deployed to the major U.S. combatant commands to work as an adviser to military commanders on policy issues. This would, for example, balance the influence of pro-China State Department political advisers at the U.S. Pacific Command, who have come to dominate the commander's nonwarfighting responsibilities, which are extensive, and include such duties as visits to foreign countries and exchanges with foreign militaries. Similarly, according to senior defense officials, CIA bureaucrats used agency advisers at the U.S. Central Command to undermine Pentagon intelligence directives for the command prior to the 2003 Iraq invasion.

Develop a strategic critique and comprehensive counterproposal to Islamist extremism. The Pentagon and other national security agencies currently are undermining the U.S. war on terrorism by engaging in public relations and community outreach programs with groups sympathetic to Islamist extremists. These programs are being run by liberal bureaucrats who do not understand the need for a strategic war of ideas against Islamist extremism. Such programs must be halted or at least modified so that Islamist groups, and others sympathetic to the main enemy in the current war on terrorism, are not permitted to be involved. As the case of Pentagon analyst Stephen Coughlin shows, the U.S. government desperately needs to develop a strategic critique and counterproposal to Islamist extremism as one of its highest national security priorities. The program will identify clearly the root causes of the Islamist terror threat and then develop ways to carry out global programs of countering Islamist ideology.

Adopt a new code of conduct for former government and military officials. The revolving door between government and the private sector must be reformed and the relationship clarified formally by regulation or law. Former government officials must be stopped from using their influence as advisers or consultants to foreign governments and from making money at the expense of U.S. national security or American commercial interests.

Create a new government entity to identify and publicize the true activities of foreign governments working against the United States. The mission of this urgently needed agency will be similar to the role played by an element of the now-disbanded U.S. Information Agency during the Cold War, but will use twenty-first-century technology and techniques to counter the lies and deception of foreign governments, terrorists, and others. The model for this agency will be the highly effective Active Measures Working Group within USIA that was formed to counteract the Soviet Union's use of strategic disinformation against the United States and its allies. The most salient feature of the international political environment today is the use of disinformation and deception by foreign governments and other enemies. The new agency will become in effect a "truth squad" to counter disinformation and deception in world affairs. This agency will provide what in government is called counterdenial and counterdeception efforts by scrupulously adhering to the highest standards of factual and accurate information analysis and dissemination. A key target of this agency must be China, which has engaged in a dangerous double game of appearing to be friendly and supportive toward the United States while covertly working abroad to undermine American interests.

These reforms are urgently needed to fix the problems plaguing what has clearly become a Failure Factory. As much as the liberal bureaucrats and their political allies—in *both* parties—want to ignore the threats to America, these dangers are not going away. In fact, they are growing. And they are growing largely because the entrenched government powers have blocked the United States from standing up to existential threats.

Amazingly, these powers have flourished even under eight years of a supposedly conservative administration. The most frightening aspect of this crisis is that very soon the United States likely will not have even the small check on the Failure Factory that existed for most of this decade.

The only way to protect America's national security is to dismantle the Failure Factory.

//////////////////////////////

THE FAILURE FACTORY

The following pages provide a snapshot of the crisis plaguing the U.S. government today, and the devastating consequences that have resulted. The documents shown here reveal that the vast network of bureaucrats extends across the State Department, the CIA, the FBI, the Pentagon, and many other agencies. They also demonstrate the extent to which the unelected powers work with the political class to undermine America's national security.

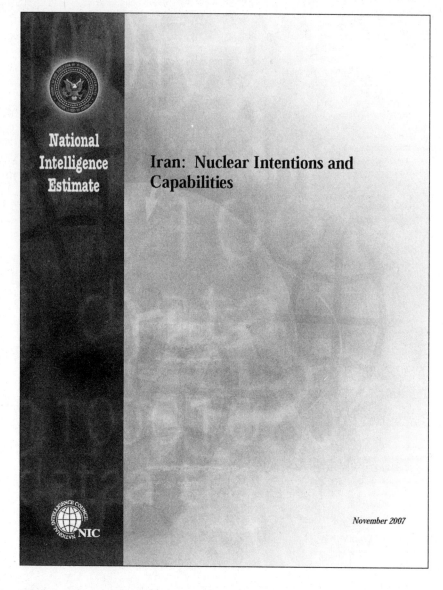

National
Intelligence
Estimate

Iran: Nuclear Intentions and
Capabilities

NIC

November 2007

The controversial 2007 National Intelligence Estimate (NIE) on Iran features the "key judgment" that "in fall 2003, Tehran halted its nuclear weapons program." A close investigation indicates that politically motivated intelligence analysts used the NIE to undercut U.S. policy toward Iran's radical Islamist regime. *(pp. 268–269)*

Key Judgments

A. We judge with high confidence that in fall 2003, Tehran halted its nuclear weapons program[1]; we also assess with moderate-to-high confidence that Tehran at a minimum is keeping open the option to develop nuclear weapons. We judge with high confidence that the halt, and Tehran's announcement of its decision to suspend its declared uranium enrichment program and sign an Additional Protocol to its Nuclear Non-Proliferation Treaty Safeguards Agreement, was directed primarily in response to increasing international scrutiny and pressure resulting from exposure of Iran's previously undeclared nuclear work.

- We assess with high confidence that until fall 2003, Iranian military entities were working under government direction to develop nuclear weapons.

- We judge with high confidence that the halt lasted at least several years. (Because of intelligence gaps discussed elsewhere in this Estimate, however, DOE and the NIC assess with only moderate confidence that the halt to those activities represents a halt to Iran's entire nuclear weapons program.)

- We assess with moderate confidence Tehran had not restarted its nuclear weapons program as of mid-2007, but we do not know whether it currently intends to develop nuclear weapons.

- We continue to assess with moderate-to-high confidence that Iran does not currently have a nuclear weapon.

- Tehran's decision to halt its nuclear weapons program suggests it is less determined to develop nuclear weapons than we have been judging since 2005. Our assessment that the program probably was halted primarily in response to international pressure suggests Iran may be more vulnerable to influence on the issue than we judged previously.

B. We continue to assess with low confidence that Iran probably has imported at least some weapons-usable fissile material, but still judge with moderate-to-high confidence it has not obtained enough for a nuclear weapon. We cannot rule out that Iran has acquired from abroad—or will acquire in the future—a nuclear weapon or enough fissile material for a weapon. Barring such acquisitions, if Iran wants to have nuclear weapons it would need to produce sufficient amounts of fissile material indigenously—which we judge with high confidence it has not yet done.

C. We assess centrifuge enrichment is how Iran probably could first produce enough fissile material for a weapon, if it decides to do so. Iran resumed its declared centrifuge

---

[1] For the purposes of this Estimate, by "nuclear weapons program" we mean Iran's nuclear weapon design and weaponization work and covert uranium conversion-related and uranium enrichment-related work; we do not mean Iran's declared civil work related to uranium conversion and enrichment.

PERMANENT SELECT COMMITTEE ON INTELLIGENCE

U.S. HOUSE OF REPRESENTATIVES

PETER HOEKSTRA
CHAIRMAN

May 18, 2006

The Honorable George W. Bush
President
The White House
Washington, D.C. 20500

Dear Mr. President:

Mr. President, I write to address three issues of great
importance to me, and, for that matter, to our collective
efforts to improve intelligence. I wish to address the nominees
for leading the CIA, very briefly discuss concerns about
intelligence reform in general, and, finally, the oversight of
intelligence activities of the U.S. Government.

First, I am concerned that the nominations for Director
and Deputy Director of the Central Intelligence Agency signal a
retreat from needed reforms of the Agency. I have respectfully
shared my strong concerns regarding these nominees, and I think
it would be an understatement to say that I am disappointed that
Congress was never consulted on either of these choices. I have
clearly stated my objections for the Director's position based
on what I perceive to be a very real need to have a civilian
lead this fundamentally and essentially civilian organization.
My position here is purely principled and substantive. However,
the choice for Deputy Director, Steve Kappes, is more troubling,
both on a substantive and personal level. Allow me to explain.

I have taken great pride in the work that we have been
able to accomplish, together with the Administration, to reform,
improve, and empower our intelligence capabilities to protect
the Nation. Regrettably, the appointment of Mr. Kappes sends a

In this 2006 letter, the chairman of the House Permanent Select Committee on Intelligence warns the president about politicization at the CIA—about "a strong and well-positioned group within the Agency" that "intentionally undermined the Administration and its policies." *(pp. 270–271)*

The Honorable George W. Bush
May 18, 2006
Page Two

clear signal that the days of collaborative reform between the
White House and this committee may be over. I am concerned that
the strong objections - not just about this personnel selection
- are being dismissed completely, perhaps sending us back to a
past, less cooperative relationship, at a time when so much more
needs to be done. Individuals both within and outside the
Administration have let me and others know of their strong
opposition to this choice for Deputy Director. Yet, in my
conversations with General Hayden it is clear that the decision
on Mr. Kappes is final. Collaboration is what got us successful
intelligence reform. Why would we want to eschew such a
relationship and process that proved so successful?
Unfortunately, it is beginning to appear that we have evolved,
on several levels, to a different philosophical direction for
intelligence reform. I'm disappointed by this because there was
such hope for progress after 9/11 and the successful passage of
the reform bill in December of 2004.

    I understand that Mr. Kappes is a capable, well-qualified,
and well-liked former Directorate of Operations (DO) case
officer. I am heartened by the professional qualities he would
bring to the job, but am concerned by what could be the
political problems that he could bring back to the agency.
There has been much public and private speculation about the
politicization of the Agency. I am convinced that this
politicization was underway well before Porter Goss became the
Director. In fact, I have been long concerned that a strong and
well-positioned group within the Agency intentionally undermined
the Administration and its policies. This argument is supported
by the Ambassador Wilson/Valerie Plame events, as well as by the
string of unauthorized disclosures from an organization that
prides itself with being able to keep secrets. I have come to
the belief that, despite his service to the DO, Mr. Kappes may
have been part of this group. I must take note when my
Democratic colleagues - those who so vehemently denounced and
publicly attacked the strong choice of Porter Goss as Director -
now publicly support Mr. Kappes's return.

TRADOC DCSINT Handbook No. 1

A Military Guide to

Terrorism

in the Twenty-First Century

US Army Training and Doctrine Command
Deputy Chief of Staff for Intelligence
Assistant Deputy Chief of Staff for Intelligence - Threats
Fort Leavenworth, Kansas
15 August 2005

DISTRIBUTION RESTRICTION: Approved for public release; distribution unlimited.

This report from the U.S. Army Training and Doctrine Command highlights how political correctness has hindered crucial ideological efforts against terrorism. Rather than confronting the threat of Islamist extremism, the report downplays it, politely noting that "all of the major world religions have extremists that have taken up violence to further their perceived religious goals." *(pp. 272–273)* small groups who have no particular dedication to any ideology, and are looking for a convenient philosophy to justify their actions.

Religious

Religiously inspired terrorism is on the rise, with a forty-three percent increase of total international terror groups espousing religious motivation between 1980 and 1995.[134] While Islamic terrorists and organizations have been the most active, and the greatest recent threat to the United States, all of the major world religions have extremists that have taken up violence to further their perceived religious goals. Religiously motivated terrorists see their objectives as holy writ, and therefore infallible and non-negotiable.

Religious motivations can also be tied to ethnic and nationalist identities, such as Kashmiri separatists combining their desire to break away from India with the religious conflict between Islam and Hinduism. The conflict in Northern Ireland also provides an example of the mingling of religious identity with nationalist motivations. There are frequently instances where groups with the same general goal, such as Kashmiri independence, will engage in conflict over the nature of that goal (religious or secular government).

Christian, Jewish, Sikh, Hindu and a host of lesser known denominations have either seen activists commit terrorism in their name, or spawned cults professing adherence to the larger religion while following unique interpretations of that particular religion's dogma. Cults that adopt terrorism are often apocalyptic in their worldview, and are highly dangerous and unpredictable. It is interesting to note that religiously motivated terrorists are among the most energetic developers of Weapons of Mass Destruction (WMD) for terrorist use. Also, religiously inspired cults executed the first confirmed uses of biological and chemical nerve agents by terrorists.

Social

Often particular social policies or issues will be so contentious that they will incite extremist behavior and terrorism. Frequently this is referred to as "single issue" or "special interest" terrorism. Some issues that have produced terrorist activities in the United States and other countries are:

- Animal rights

- Abortion

- Ecology/environment

- Minority rights

> **"The overall threat posed by special interest extremism appears to be increasing."**
>
> From "Terrorism in the United States, 1999" FBI Publication #0308, Federal Bureau of Investigation

---

[134] Bruce Hoffman, *Inside Terrorism* (New York: Columbia University Press, 1998), 90.

Embassy of the United States of America
Baghdad, Iraq

MEMORANDUM

To: Ambassador Crocker
From   Manuel Miranda, Office of Legislative Statecraft
CC: ALCON
Date: February 5, 2008
Re: **Departure Assessment of Embassy Baghdad**

Introduction

As I prepare to sign out after a year with the State Department, I feel it my last duty to offer you my assessment of what I observed. Please accept this assessment in that spirit. The presence of so many Section 3161 temporary direct hires in various areas of expertise in the Embassy is a unique opportunity for the evaluation and oversight of the Foreign Service and the State Department's bureaucracy and competence, whether it is a Service at War or Peace.

We all have opinions. If there is any doubt of the sincerity of mine, I am ready to share to list the names of those scores of other 3161's who share it, each from the vantage point of their areas of expertise and particular experience in the Embassy.

I have kept my observations to the areas that I have most directly observed as Senior Advisor for Legislative Framework in the Iraq Reconstruction Management Office and the Embassy's Rule of Law community, and as Director of the Office for Legislative Statecraft in the Political Section. I apply to this assessment my background as a former counsel to the Senate Majority Leader and as a student of legal institutions, and, as importantly, as a lawyer with 12 years experience in sovereign government negotiations, comparative and international law, and the legal framework and conditions needed for foreign direct investment in energy infrastructure and domestic economic progress and stability in developing democracies.

Nothing in this assessment is intended to be critical of General Petraeus, his leadership, his staff, the efforts of the Coalition forces in Iraq, or the success of the security component of the "Surge" initiative, now one year old. Nothing in this assessment is intended to cast doubt on the diplomatic strengths of the Foreign Service in Iraq. Nothing in this assessment should be read as critical of the hundreds of civilian men and women, of all ages and backgrounds, who work in Iraq tirelessly and at great personal sacrifice of their careers and family lives, and the many at lower levels of internal management who support us. Although my assessment is limited to certain areas of expertise, it is applicable Embassy-wide.

A scathing assessment of the State Department bureaucracy from a worker at the U.S. embassy in Baghdad. The ten-page document, portions of which are shown here, bluntly states that "the State Department and the Foreign Service is not competent to do the job that they have undertaken in Iraq." *(pp. 274–276)*

-- 2 --

I should point out that I support America's mission in Iraq, while fully recognizing our many errors over time. I support the President's policy that ignores the historic stereotypes of the Middle East and offers the region a culture of liberty protected by responsible government and the rule of law. I support a long-term American military presence in Iraqi bases, welcomed by the overwhelming majority of Iraqis and a democratically-elected government, as a means of bringing peace and stability to the region, as we did in Europe and the Far East. History may recognize this end as singularly worthy of the sacrifice that America's sons and daughters have made. I believe, however, that the potential for this peace requires the progress of Iraqi society and the confidence of the Iraqi people in their government.

That civilian progress, and the *Pax Americana*, will not be achieved with the Foreign Service and the State Department's bureaucracy at the helm of America's number one policy consideration. You are simply not up to the task, and many of you will readily and honestly admit it. I believe that a better job can be done. It is simply that we have brought to Iraq the worst of America – our bureaucrats – and failed to apply, as President Roosevelt once did, the high-caliber leadership class and intellectual talent, whose rallying has defined all of America's finest hours.

Summary

America's success in Iraq requires pacifying the country and assisting its government to inspire the confidence of Iraq's people. America can be confident that the former task is in good hands, but the latter effort will fail if we continue to rely on the State Department and the Foreign Service to lead or manage our civilian support efforts. As we did with the military Surge, America and Iraq would be well served by retaining our diplomats to do the work of diplomacy, but putting the effort to stand up the GOI in more competent hands. This is especially true in the areas of legislative reform and the rule of law. But it is also true in other areas.

At stake, as a whole, is not only the success of the mission, the lives of Americans and the future of a country for which we must now bear some responsibility, but also hundreds of millions of taxpayer dollars being wasted and poorly managed.

GENERAL ASSESSMENT

After a year at the Embassy, it is my general assessment that the State Department and the Foreign Service is not competent to do the job that they have undertaken in Iraq. It is not that the men and women of the Foreign Service and other State Department bureaus are not intelligent and hard-working, it is simply that they are not equipped to handle the job that the State Department has undertaken. Apart from the remarkable achievements of Coalition forces in the pacification of Iraq, the few civilian accomplishments that we are presently lauding,

-- 10 --

to sign on for more than a year.   Recruitment is not your problem.   Your system of staffing is.

The State Department would do the nation a service if it admits that it is not equipped to the job you have undertaken. Our Congress has an obligation to give you the oversight our national sacrifice demands. We are now living our latest error.

As a graduate of Georgetown's School of Foreign Service, I was proud last year when I swore in at the State Department. By the middle of 2007 that changed. I was ashamed for my country. I repeat, however, that my observations are not that you all are anything but wonderful Americans, it is that you are doing a job for which you are not prepared as a bureaucracy or as leaders.

The American and Iraqi people deserve better.

(continued from page 274)

/5

UNITED STATES DISTRICT COURT
EASTERN DISTRICT OF MICHIGAN
SOUTHERN DIVISION

FILED

NOV 13 2007

CLERK'S OFFICE
U.S. DISTRICT COURT
EASTERN MICHIGAN

UNITED STATES OF AMERICA,

　　　　　　Plaintiff,

v.

D-1 NADA NADIM PROUTY,
　　　a/k/a Nada Nadim Alley,
　　　a/k/a Nada Nadim Deladurantaye,
　　　a/k/a Nada Nadim Al Aouar,

　　　　　　Defendant.
_____/

CRIMINAL NO. 07-20156

HON. AVERN COHN

VIO. 18 U.S.C. § 371
　　　　18 U.S.C. § 1030
　　　　18 U.S.C. § 1425

SECOND SUPERSEDING INFORMATION

THE UNITED STATES ATTORNEY CHARGES:

General Allegations

1. On June 24, 1989, NADA NADIM PROUTY, also known as "Nada Nadim Alley," also known as "Nada Nadim Deladurantaye," also known as "Nada Nadim Al Aouar," defendant herein, first entered the United States from Lebanon on a one year non-immigrant student visa.

2. After defendant's visa expired on June 11, 1990, she remained in the country residing in Taylor, Michigan with her sister, Elfat El Aouar, not named as a defendant herein, and Samar Khalil Nabbouh, also known as "Samar Khalil Spinelli," not named as a defendant herein.

Portions of the indictment against former FBI and CIA agent Nadim Prouty, whom U.S. counterintelligence officials believe was a spy for the Iranian-backed terrorist group Hezbollah. Such officials were outraged by what they considered the government's weak plea deal with Prouty and the even weaker sentencing against her. *(pp. 277–278)*

COUNT TWO
(Unauthorized Computer Access – 18 U.S.C. § 1030)

D-1 NADA NADIM PROUTY

The general allegations set forth above are hereby incorporated by reference as if fully set forth herein.

On or about June 4, 2003, within the Eastern District of Michigan, Southern Division, and elsewhere, NADA NADIM PROUTY, defendant herein, while employed as a Special Agent of the Federal Bureau of Investigation (FBI), an agency of the United States, intentionally accessed the FBI's Automated Case Support (ACS) computer system and obtained information from case file number DE-74791, Serial 489, a national security investigation conducted by the FBI's Detroit Field Office concerning the designated foreign terrorist organization, Hizballah; defendant did so without authorization and in excess of her authorized access within the ACS system; all in violation of Title 18, United States Code, Section 1030(a)(2)(B).

COUNT THREE
(Naturalization Fraud – 18 U.S.C. § 1425)

D-1 NADA NADIM PROUTY

The general allegations set forth above are hereby incorporated by reference as if fully set forth herein.

On or about August 5, 1994, within the Eastern District of Michigan, Southern Division, and elsewhere, NADA NADIM PROUTY, defendant herein, knowingly procured, and attempted to procure, contrary to law, her own naturalization as a

13

(continued from page 277)

REAL SECURITY
Recess Events – 3/18 to 3/26

HOMELAND SECURITY

From uninspected cargo making its way across the country by truck and train to nuclear power plants where access is loosely controlled, homeland security is an issue that extends beyond just the major cities. Local police and firefighters are the first responders in a hazardous situation and a security threat can easily move across state lines by air, road or rail. Unfortunately, the Bush budget significantly cuts programs that are key to improving local security and Congressional Republicans have repeatedly voted against proposals that would improve America's safety.

During the upcoming recess, make use of the following event ideas to draw attention to the security vulnerabilities caused by the Bush budget and explain how Democrats fought to restore programs that keep America safe:

- **Hold a press conference on cargo security vulnerability at an airport, train station or port in your state that handles commercial cargo.** While attention has been focused recently on ports, keep in mind that uninspected port cargo often finds its way onto trains and trucks traveling across the country. In addition, airline cargo faces similar vulnerabilities and is not subject to a 100% inspection policy either. The Bush Administration's continued inaction on this issue has resulted in failing grades from the 9/11 Commission when it comes to securing our ports and air cargo.
  - Make sure that there is a plane, ship, train or related signage in the background at the press conference so that it is clear in the footage where the event is taking place.
  - Visit the event site ahead of time to look for any noise or lighting issues that could make it difficult for press to film, photograph or record your event.

- **Ask local police officers to provide a tour of security equipment purchased through Federal grants targeted for elimination by Republicans.** The Bush budget aimed to eliminate the Law Enforcement Terrorism Protection Program this year which provides grants to local law enforcement to purchase needed equipment – a clear indication of Republican's misplaced priorities when it comes to security. In the past, these grants have allowed local government to buy SWAT equipment, bomb detecting robots, crime scene vans and emergency medical equipment for schools.
  - Work with your legislative staff and state staff to find a police department or school in your state that has benefited from the program.
  - Ask police officers to appear at the open press tour in uniform and to demonstrate equipment if possible.

- **Conduct a "First Responder Forum" with police officers, firefighters EMTs and state and local emergency managers on how underfunding of programs**

This memorandum from the office of Senator Harry Reid reveals the extent to which Democrats have consciously politicized the war in Iraq in order to make gains at the ballot box. *(pp. 279–282)* affects their ability to respond in a crisis. Hurricane Katrina demonstrated the importance of adequate funding for police, firefighters and emergency managers when it comes to managing a disaster. From earthquakes to tornados to major storms or terrorist attacks, providing first responders with the resources they need in case of disaster makes a difference. Unfortunately, the President does not share this view and aimed to cut funding for the COPS program, local fire departments and Emergency Management Performance Grants this year.

- o Consider conducting this panel discussion event at a fire station (a "Fire Hall Meeting") or a police training school. Arrange for an on-camera tour of the location post-panel discussion.
- o Invite firefighters, police officers and EMTs to attend in uniform.
- o Work with state and local government contacts to find an emergency manager that can speak first hand about preparing for disasters.
- o Focus on training, equipment, and cutting-edge technology that they need, yet has been denied to them.

- **Hold a town hall meeting with state officials and a local National Guard unit at their armory to discuss the security impact of long deployments.** In addition to creating a hardship for families, the extended absence of National Guardsmen can also impact the security situation in a state. From restoring order to responding to disasters, National Guardsmen play an important role when comes to keeping our communities safe and secure. These extended deployments lead to both a loss of equipment and a limited number of Guardsmen in states when disaster strikes.
  - o Meet with the State Adjutant General and express your commitment to fully fund the National Guard at its authorized level of 350K troops.
  - o Invite a Democratic Governor from your state or a neighboring state to the event discuss how security and disaster response is being shortchanged at home.
  - o Bring together a group of Democratic mayors from across the state to share their local security concerns at the event.
  - o Ask National Guard members to offer input on how security and disaster response at home is compromised by long deployments.

Contacts:

The office of the Adjutants General of each state can put you in touch with National Guard units in your state. You can find first responders in your area by contacting the following national representatives:

National Association of Police Officers
Andrea Mournighan
(202) 842-4420
amournighan@napo.org

International Association of Firefighters
Kevin O'Connor

(continued from page 279)

United Spinal Association can be a resource for activities and events related to body armor, armored humvees and veterans benefits. They can help Senators find individuals and families in their respective States who are willing to participate in roundtable discussions, dialogues, etc.

TROOPS & MILITARY FAMILIES

When preparing for war in Iraq, the Bush Administration greatly underestimated the threats our troops would face and failed to plan for the post-war, leaving our forces to fend off a dangerous insurgency without the needed body armor and armored vehicles on the ground. While our troops cope with these shortages, their families face their own challenges at home. Long deployments can lead to drops in income, job loss, significant stress and, for National Guard and reservist families in particular, a loss of health insurance. Democrats believe in strengthening our military through investing in the best equipment and ensuring that military families receive the services they need while their family members are deployed.

Make use of the following event ideas over recess to demonstrate Democrat's commitment to strengthening our military and caring for military families while their family members are away:

- **Visit the home of a military family that has purchased body armor on their own for a family member serving in Iraq of Afghanistan and hold an open press "conversation" on the issue.** The Washington Post reported in January that a secret Pentagon study found that as many as 80 percent of the Marines who have been killed in Iraq from wounds to the upper body could have survived if they had had extra body armor. It took the Pentagon so long to provide the armor that many military families took the matter into their own hands and purchased the armor themselves. They are just now being reimbursed for the costs.
    - Ask the family if they would be willing to hold the open press conversation/town hall meeting in their yard, on their front porch or in their home.
    - If possible, bring body armor similar to what the family purchased to the event and demonstrate how it provides important protection for our troops.

- **Hold a town-hall meeting with troops at a local military installation.** Explore the issues of concern to active or reserve forces in your area. Inquire about stresses related to back-to-back deployments, problems with pay and medical benefits, training and education. Visit with the warfighters, the support troops, officer and enlisted corps. Also consider visiting the base medical clinic and family support center, and express your support for the valuable quality of life programs that are critical to morale and welfare.
    - When selecting a location at the military installation for the event, make sure to select a space that allows easy press access and clearly conveys the message in the shot. Planes, vehicles, equipment and signage in the background greatly enhance the pictures coming out of your event.

(continued from page 279)

- o Package the town hall meeting with at least one of the visits suggested above, so that TV crews have b-roll footage to accompany the substantive discussion that takes place at your event.
- o Hold an interview post-event with the base newspaper.

- **Tour a factory in your state that manufactures military equipment like humvees or body armor and hold a press availability afterwards with Iraq and Afghanistan veterans on the importance of protective equipment.** The Pentagon has continued to fail to provide a sufficient number of armored humvees for our troops, leaving them vulnerable to roadside bombs. Secretary of Defense Rumsfeld has argued that production can not keep up with demand, but many manufacturers' offers to increase production have been ignored by the Pentagon. In the meantime, troops continue to jerry-rig unarmored humvees with sandbags and scrap metal in hopes of improving their safety.
  - o Look for military equipment manufacturer in your state that can provide an open press tour of their production facilities for your Senator.
  - o Encourage veterans participating in the post-tour press availability to wear any attire that indicates their veteran status.

- **Convene a panel discussion with National Guard and Reservist family members to discuss the impact of unexpectedly long deployments on their families.** Originally limited to six-month deployments, National Guardsmen can now be deployed for up to 24 months in a six year period. Since they do not live on military bases, Guard families often lack the health care, counseling and child care support services necessary to survive long deployments and face a potential drop in income. Because of the Administration's poor planning in Iraq, Guardsmen are being asked to go above and beyond their normal duties – and their families are paying the price. The same stresses apply to reservists and their families as well.
  - o Have visuals created that demonstrate the financial costs of an extended deployment for an average National Guard or Reservist family.
  - o Provide individual tabletop microphones for each participant to keep the dialogue moving.

Contacts:

Iraq and Afghanistan Veterans of America (IAVA)
Vanessa Williamson – Field Director
212-982-9699

United Spinal Association
Len Selfon – Veterans Service Representative
301-495-4460
Dan Anderson – Assistant Director of Legislation
718-803-3782 x294

(continued from page 279)

ACKNOWLEDGMENTS

I n the newspaper business, the saying goes that a reporter is only as good as his sources. Developing, working with, and protecting news sources is at the heart of all good news reporting. Events in early 2008 demonstrated to me that freedom of the press, as guaranteed by the Constitution of the United States, is not cost-free. Those I have worked with over many years as news sources are extremely dedicated people who believe earnestly that liberty and democracy are not self-sustaining and must be preserved and defended. In April 2008, a federal court in Santa Ana, California, took the unusual step of issuing a subpoena to me, demanding that I appear at a hearing about a story I had written for the *Washington Times* nearly two years earlier on the Chinese spy case involving Chi Mak, a defense contractor who was convicted of supplying embargoed defense-related technology to China. The subpoena was a wake-up call for me that freedom of the press is under assault.

The press has often been considered the fourth branch of government. In reality, journalists like me have no real power. We do not have military forces or law-enforcement power. We have neither lawmaking authority nor power of the courts.

What news reporters do have is the power to shed light on the workings of government. In more than twenty-five years of writing and reporting on government, I have become convinced that aggressive and responsible news reporting plays a vital role in protecting the nation's fundamental freedoms and ultimately the national security of the United States. As one colleague at the *Washington Times* likes to say, the role of newspaper reporters is to "comfort the afflicted, and afflict the comfortable." No place is more comfortable and more in need of independent, nongovernment oversight than government itself.

While writing this book I became embroiled in a government effort to identify sources for my news reporting and books. I am currently in the process of resisting what I regard ultimately as a serious threat to press freedom. Without First Amendment protection, news reporting in the United States is in danger of coming under the control of the government. What is really going on behind the scenes is a sub-rosa effort by government bureaucrats to control what is reported in the press, claiming falsely that press disclosures have harmed U.S. national security and that press freedoms must be curtailed.

The case in point was the disclosure in the *New York Times* about the electronic surveillance program against terrorists. Without passing judgment on whether the terrorist surveillance program was damaged by public disclosure, the simple question is: who had access to the information? Reporters do not have security clearances. It is wrong for government bureaucrats to basically undermine the First Amendment press freedoms that are so vital to our democratic system by compelling reporters to reveal their news sources, either through imprisonment or through financially ruinous fines.

At its core, the legal process the government initiated against me reflects the problems and concerns highlighted in this book about an out-of-control government bureaucracy. At press time, the legal matter is ongoing and I am constrained from providing details on the case. But it is my hope that it will be a lesson in protecting and preserving one of the most important freedoms enshrined in the Constitution.

I want to acknowledge and thank the many people who assisted me in writing this book by providing interviews and background information or sharing their experiences in government. The information presented here is what I believe to be accurate and true.

Those deserving of special praise include my editors and other co-workers at my employer, the *Washington Times*. The *Times* was founded in 1982 by the Reverend and Mrs. Sun Myung Moon and is widely acknowledged as a leading authoritative source for political and national security news, both in the nation's capital and worldwide.

Special thanks also go to my editor at Crown Forum, Jed Donahue, who provided great help and assistance. Joseph Brendan Vallely, my agent, was helpful in providing valuable insights as well.

Last, thanks to my wife, Debra, who provided wonderful support for this project.

About the Author

BILL GERTZ is the defense and national security reporter for the *Washington Times* and the author of the *New York Times* bestsellers *Enemies, Treachery, Breakdown,* and *Betrayal.* An analyst for Fox News Channel, he has been interviewed on many television and radio programs, including *This Week, John McLaughlin's One on One, Hannity & Colmes, The O'Reilly Factor,* and *The Rush Limbaugh Show.* He has lectured at the FBI Academy and the National Defense University. Gertz lives with his family near Washington, D.C.